Homosexuality and the Politics of Truth

This book is a beacon of light to anyone struggling to emerge from homosexuality or struggling with the homosexual debate. In clear, eloquent prose, Dr. Satinover demonstrates that homosexuality, though not a "choice" and deeply embedded, is neither innate nor unchangeable. . . . With so many lives at risk and with so many young people confused about love, family, and sexuality, his point of view desperately needs to be heard. *Homosexuality and the Politics of Truth* is a definitive handbook that should be read by every concerned parent, teacher, counselor, minister, priest, and rabbi—as well as by the many people who struggle with homosexual feelings and behaviors, and who, for purely political reasons, have been misled into thinking that there is no way out.

Rabbi Daniel Lapin, president,
Toward Tradition

Homosexuality and the Politics of Truth

Jeffrey Satinover

A Hamewith Book

BakerBooks

A Division of Baker Book House Co
Grand Rapids, Michigan 49516

© 1996 by Jeffrey Satinover

Published by Hamewith Books
an imprint of Baker Book House Company
P.O. Box 6287, Grand Rapids, MI 49516-6287

Seventh printing, August 1999

Printed in the United States of America

Library of Congress Cataloging-in-Publication Data

Satinover, Jeffrey Burke, 1947–
   Homosexuality and the politics of truth / Jeffrey Burke Satinover.
      p.   cm.
   Includes bibliographical references and index.
   ISBN 0-8010-5625-X (pbk.)
    1. Homosexuality—United States. 2. AIDS (Disease)—United States. 3. Homosexuality—United States—Religious aspects.
   I. Title.
HQ76.3.U5S35   1996
306.76'6—dc20   95-35839

For current information about all releases from Baker Book House, visit our web site:
http://www.bakerbooks.com

To my wife, Julie (M.E.)

Contents

Introduction

Homosexuality didn't start out as a major focus of my professional life, but the day it came home to me is one I will never forget. It was 1981. I had just returned home from the medical center in New York City where I worked. Physicians in inner-city hospitals spend week after 70- to 80-hour week witnessing, battling, and—occasionally—salvaging people from the most horrendous savagery done to their bodies by illnesses and fellow human beings. After awhile, most doctors develop a battle-hardening that allows us to escape the horror in order to do our jobs effectively.

Still in the early years of my training, my armor had nonetheless begun to grow. But however thick it becomes, that armor is never completely effective. Some "cases" always get under one's skin—mostly involving young people.

That day was particularly difficult. I had been called in for a neurological assessment of a young man suffering from multiple problems, some of which had begun to affect his nervous system and mind. Perhaps the difficulty arose merely because I had restored personhood to the "case": I was young myself and therefore identified with him; I'm inclined to think, however, that it went beyond that.

Somewhere under the surface lies the belief that for all the grief and sense of loss that attends sickness and death, when old people get sick and die (and the vast majority of ill people in a hospital are old) there is something expected and even proper about it. But when someone young dies something rises up within us and shouts at heaven, "No! This is wrong! You can't do this!" As that silent cry of protest and rage breaks through the armor, the true horror comes flooding in, if only briefly.

In order to assess my patient, I had to don another kind of armor as well—the full complement of sterile isolation precautions: latex gloves, a full-length gown, a surgical cap, and paper booties. As I had spent many years as a psychotherapist and psychoanalyst before returning for medical and psychiatric training, I was especially aware of how isolating my appearance would seem to this poor man. Had he grown accustomed to it? Foolishly, I hoped so.

Something about this garb inevitably suggested to me that I was protecting myself from him because he was infectious and I was not. (The illness ravaging his nervous system had been diagnosed as an "unusual fungal infection.") This thought recurs no matter how many times one goes through the routine. So this time, too, I reminded myself that I was *not* protecting myself from him; I was protecting him from me—from the untold trillions of germs that surrounded me like a cloud and followed me everywhere I went, clinging with tenacity to each exposed surface of my body. Under normal circumstances, the bacteria and viruses that were now ravaging his body were part of the microscopic fauna and flora that form a benign background to our everyday lives. But because this young man was in a state of severe suppression of his immune system, many of these normally innocent fellow travelers had turned viciously destructive to him.

I braced myself for the encounter, trying to squeeze every bit of empathy I could into my eyes, the only part of my body left open to his view. The young man lay stretched out on the hospital bed, his eyes closed. I saw from the clipboard that he was in his thirties. His disheveled, straw-colored hair framed a face so pale that all the blood seemed to have drained out of it, like someone already dead. A tangle of intravenous lines entered both his arms and chest; the pumps that fed these and the various electronic monitors that surrounded and clung to him whirred in a constant high-tech din. The medications being administered through these lines were the most potent available to modern medicine, so potent, in fact, that most of them carried grave risks of their own. As with cancer chemotherapy, such drugs are used only when "treatment" consists of a race to see which the chemical agents will kill first: the illness or the patient.

Though terribly gaunt, the man at one time had obviously been strikingly handsome. I introduced myself warmly, trying to sound less the doctor and more the human being, but in response I got a barely audible, unintelligible gurgle. He opened his eyes and rolled them vacantly around the room, responding to my greeting as to a vaguely perceived stimulus of some sort. I knew immediately that a formal examination of his mental status would be fruitless. As I anticipated, the neurological exam revealed multiple severe abnormalities.

Subjectively, most striking in the exam were the angry purple welts that covered most of both arms and wrapped around his sides toward his back. These, I knew, were Kaposi's sarcoma, a virulent, ugly cancer once so rare that a single incident instantly made the medical literature. Now suddenly it was popping up in clusters of two, three, ten at a time at major medical centers across the country, especially in San Francisco and here, in New York.

By the time my visit ended, it was apparent that the entire consultation was more important to me—from an educational perspective—than to him. He would surely not survive the week.

The story of this young man, of his all-too-brief life and painful, wasting death, soon appeared in a landmark report in one of the world's premier medical journals along with the nearly identical stories of seven others. AIDS had appeared on the scene, the deadly modern disease that has stalked our lives, headlines, and imaginations like a medieval plague. It was known to us then simply as GRID, "gay-related immune disorder." This name reflected the fact that in Europe, America, and Asia, AIDS was then—as it remains today—dramatically disproportionate among male homosexuals.

Alone, Terrifyingly Alone

Tired and empty when I arrived home, I poured myself a glass of orange juice and stood in my cramped New York kitchenette, distractedly flipping through that Sunday's *New York Times*. Without serious interest, but nonetheless being curious, I came to the obituaries and idly perused them as I usually did. Suddenly my attention was arrested by the name of someone I knew, a man who though only thirty-nine was reported to have died of "viral pneumonia." I was stunned, realizing that he, too, had died of this new "gay-related immune disorder." I hadn't thought of him in some time and so had never put it together. The syndrome had not yet been discovered when I knew him, but now all the pieces fell into place.

A few years before, Paul (not his real name[1]) had come to me for psychotherapy. His chief complaint was a chronic sense of listlessness and fatigue associated with a vague feeling of depression. His internist was a well-known and well-respected professor at a major medical center who had been unable to help him; thinking that his problems might be psychosomatic, Paul came to me. The internist made it clear that although he himself had no idea what was wrong with his patient, he was skeptical that it was anything psychotherapy could fix. My treatment, too, was probably a waste of his patient's time and money—just as had been his earlier pilgrimage to a specialist in Alabama who diagnosed him (and everyone else he saw) as suffering from "systemic yeast infection." There, too, the treatment had been fruitless and expensive.

Paul was in his mid-thirties, from the South, scion of a pillar-of-the-community father whose long and distinguished military career Paul had never been interested in emulating. Indeed, Paul felt he was rather a disappointment to his father, who found it hard to relate to his son's unusually sensitive nature, his compact, unathletic stature, his keen aesthetic sensibility and intelligence, and his love not of matters martial but of the arts. Paul was happy to leave his home and what he perceived as the stiflingly conservative atmosphere of his hometown to attend an Ivy League school in the more cosmopolitan Northeast. There he had shone brilliantly and in his chosen field had enjoyed a meteoric rise to success and acclaim. Even before he had completed college, his name was on the lips of everyone knowledgeable in his field; within a few years it was a household word in any home with even a smattering of culture. He was already in demand internationally.

But Paul was lonely, and his growing fame offered him little solace. He longed for an intimate, permanent relationship and wondered whether his growing sense of fatigue and ever more frequent colds might be related to this loneliness. And there was something else, though he mentioned it almost as an after-thought: Every night, no matter how tired he was, this eminent, accomplished, exquisitely sensitive, brilliant man of culture set out on a desperate search for the "partner of his dreams." Yet what he invariably found instead—indeed what he was intelligent enough to know that he could not help but find, given where he searched—was night after night of anonymous sex, always with different men, sometimes ten or fifteen in a night. He was almost invariably the "passive" or "receptive" partner in these encoun-ters, hungrily inviting men to possess him rectally.

Paul wanted to know if I could help him. Perhaps, he suggested, he could stop if he could only find someone to love. But he didn't really want to stop the nightly cruising. And in fact he couldn't stop, though on this point he waffled. "If only I had someone to love, then I wouldn't need to. . . ." But I was familiar with this pat-tern of compulsion. Linked to the denial that says "I can always stop—if I want to," compulsion is a routine dimension of all addictions.

I wondered what was going on under the surface, beneath the denial, and asked him if he had had any dreams lately. In fact, he had had a dream very recently that quite disturbed him. This dream had solidified his resolve to seek counsel beyond a med-ical solution to his fatigue. He had dreamt:

> I am a skater in an Olympic figure-skating competition. I am being swung around in a circle by my feet, my head a fraction of an inch from the ice in a brilliant display of technique. I look up toward my partner, but in shock I see that there is no one there at all. I awake in horror.

The dream spoke eloquently of his behavior and more impor-tantly of his psychological state. Though his field was not sports, he had achieved in his own way the status of an Olympic star. The picture was especially fitting given his lack of athleticism as a youngster and the wounding he suffered because of it. And yet in spite of all his brilliance, he was terrifyingly alone, seeking help from an absent partner in an environment as harsh and cold as ice, his life seemingly suspended above death by a hair. In spite of all he had accomplished, at the core his life was empty.

Yet there was more to this dream. For it contained a chilling prophesy, a prophesy that could not possibly have been foreseen then in 1978—before AIDS had been identified but when its dread, invisible fingers had already begun to clasp so many young men in its icy grip, Paul included.

Over a decade later, as I began this book, the terror of the absent partner in the center had become a reality in many parts of the gay world, especially in the world of figure skating. Within three years of Paul's dream, he himself would be dead of "gay-related immune disorder," and within fifteen years so too would over forty of the top Canadian and U.S. male championship figure skaters. As we now know only too well, having followed the celebrity stories of such sport superstars as Greg Louganis and such world-famous intellectuals as Michel Foucault, innumerable others would be HIV-positive and far too many would die.

Free Sex, Free Sickness

AIDS was certainly unexpected and more horrifying than anyone could have imagined. And yet to an extent, it should not have been unexpected. For in the ten years or so before the bright young men began turning up in major medical centers with alarming purple splotches and rare infections, the scientific literature showed a startling increase in gay-related conditions: hepatitis B causing sometimes fatal liver collapse; bowel parasites causing systemic infections rare outside the homosexual community; immune dysfunction less severe than AIDS would prove to be, but serious nonetheless. The medical community understood that as the influence of the 1960s' counterculture had lifted all constraint on human sexuality—not just the homosexual variety—so too had it lifted the constraints on every imaginable form of sexually related illness.

Whereas one generation earlier syphilis had been all but eradicated, an epidemic now raged among teens. Where infertility had been rare, permanent loss of childbearing capacity was now a common result of a massive increase in gonorrhea-related pelvic inflammatory disease (PID). Those frequenting the bars and "meat markets," gay or straight, spoke of herpes as the terrible nuisance and stigma it was. But few considered the blindness and death it caused to children born of actively infected mothers.

In 1981 as GRID began to spread, the condition began proving itself inevitably fatal with a frighteningly long incubation time. One thing seemed obvious: Medical sanity would soon have to prevail over our clearly catastrophic, two-decades-long experiment in sexual liberation. It also seemed obvious that GRID would continue to be grouped with the other unequivocally gay-related conditions, such as "Gay-Related Bowel Syndrome." Not that these conditions were exclusive to gays, but gays were far more prone to them because of the practices typical of the gay life, anal intercourse in particular.

Many anticipated that homosexual men would react swiftly and decisively to the now clear and growing danger to health and survival engendered by their way of life. The fledgling "gay liberation" movement would likely be dealt a severe setback—not for political or moral reasons, but for medical ones. Many more gays, it was expected, would likely seek ways out of "the lifestyle."

In fact, the reaction in the gay community was indeed swift, but startlingly unexpected. Not only did the gay community mobilize to attack GRID, they worked to ensure that GRID would not be perceived—by either the medical profession or the public—as in any way related directly to their sexual way of life. Homosexuals indeed needed protection from illness, but that became only a third priority. The second priority was to keep gays from straight disapproval and hatred, and the first priority was to *protect homosexuality itself as a perfectly acceptable, normal, and safe way of life*. Massive interventions were designed and funded to a greater extent than with any other illness, but none were allowed to target the number-one risk factor itself, homo-sexuality. Even treatment to help those homosexuals who fervently wished to change came under fierce attack, regardless of the dramatic—indeed, potentially life-saving—benefit afforded by even modest success.

So the first move in the early eighties was to eliminate the earlier name of the condition. Because under the right circumstances the virus was transmissible to anyone, pressure was swiftly generated to rename "gay-related immune disorder" to AIDS: "Acquired Immune Deficiency Syndrome." Though the connection to homosexuality is universally understood to be valid and medical literature still speaks of homosexuality as the major risk factor for AIDS, the fact that gay male anal intercourse and promiscuity created the American reservoir for HIV (the pathogen that causes AIDS)—and continues to preserve it[2]—quickly became an unspeakable truth. A publication of the American Psychiatric Association reported, "We've 'homosexualized' AIDS and 'AIDS-ified' homosexuality,"[3] just as though "we" did it, and that the connection were not a self-evident feature of the condition itself. In short, the response to AIDS was politicized from the start.

Has the politicized campaign against AIDS been successful in halting the spread of this disease? In Europe, Asia, and the United States, AIDS has not exploded into the population at large as many feared it would, as it has in parts of Africa. Perhaps this is due to the success of "safe-"—later renamed "safer-"—sex campaigns that started in homosexual communities.

But a recently published, widely respected survey on the sexual practices of Americans, *Sex in America*,[4] shows otherwise. On the one hand, the researchers point out that AIDS is likely to remain contained within certain groups and is *not* likely to spread to the population at large. This containment, they discovered, is rooted in the traditionalism, fidelity, caution, and restraint observed by the great majority of Americans when it comes to sex.

On the other hand, the politicized form of intervention has not been nearly successful enough among homosexuals. Indeed, *the homosexual community has paid the highest price.* Fifteen years into the epidemic the American Psychiatric Association Press reports that "30 percent of all 20-year-old gay men will be HIV positive or dead of AIDS by the time they are age 30"[5] because they are resuming "unsafe sex" anyway.

A Striking Cultural Indicator

Homosexuality is one of the most crucial issues we all must consider. At the personal level most of us know at least one of our friends, colleagues, or fellow-Americans who is dying the terrible death of AIDS. At the cultural level one of the most revealing indexes of a civilization is the way it orders human sexuality.

When left to itself, human sexuality appears unconstrained and to the innocent mind shockingly polymorphous. But the hallmark of a society in which all sexual constraints have been set aside is that finally it sanctions homosexuality as well. This point is hotly disputed today, but is reflected in the wisdom of the ages. Plutarch, the first-century Greek moralist, saw libertinism to be the third and next-to-last stage in the life-cycle of a free republic before its final descent into tyranny. Edward Gibbon in eighteenth-century England understood this principle with respect to ancient Rome, but from a historian's perspective. Sigmund Freud emphasized the same principle with respect to many cultures in the West— although from a radically secular psychoanalytic perspective. For him, universal sexual repression was the price of civilization. Without constraints civilization would lose its discipline and vitality. And, of course, the Bible repeatedly shows the effects of unconstrained sexuality, such as its stories of the rise and fall of Sodom, Gomorrah, and indeed Israel itself.

Dennis Prager, a reform Jewish cultural commentator, writes:

> Man's nature, undisciplined by values, will allow sex to dominate his life and the life of society. . . . It is not overstated to say that the Torah's prohibition of non-marital sex made the creation of Western civilization possible. Societies that did not place boundaries around sexuality were stymied in their development. The subsequent dominance of the Western world can, to a significant extent,

be attributed to the sexual revolution, initiated by Judaism and later carried forward by Christianity.[6]

In sum, it is a simple and sobering fact that no society that has sanctioned unconstrained sexuality has long survived.

Case and Countercase

No book on homosexuality and AIDS today can be both honest and easy to write or read. On the personal level, the topics are bound to be harrowing. On the scientific level, they are complicated, and on the political they are controversial. But as we have seen, the issue is vital today. It raises key questions in at least three sectors of society: politics, education, and religious communities.

The impact of homosexuality on politics is obvious. Gay activists, working closely with mental health professionals for the past twenty years, have successfully shaped and promoted a new consensus on homosexuality that is a potent political force. This consensus is composed of three key propositions that fit the so-called "bio-psycho-social" model of mental functioning that is now in vogue. As the propositions have slowly spread throughout society, people use them to demand that all sectors of society—including religious institutions morally opposed to homosexual practice—treat practicing homosexuals in exactly the same way as active heterosexuals.

The three propositions follow:

- First, as a matter of biology, homosexuality is an innate, genetically determined aspect of the human body.
- Second, as a matter of psychology, homosexuality is irreversible. Indeed, the attempt to reverse it requires so profound a denial of self—akin to Jewish anti-Semitism or black "passing" (pale blacks trying to pass as whites)—that it is said to cause the widely acknowledged, higher-than-average mental problems among homosexuals, such as depression, suicide, and alcohol and drug abuse.

- Third, as a matter of sociology, homosexuality is normal, akin to such other social categories as sex and race. This point does more than repeat the first, because something may be inborn without it being normal—as in the case of genetic illnesses.

When combined, these three propositions are used to form a powerful argument in favor of normalizing homosexuality. It runs as follows:

The historical condemnation of homosexuality by the Jewish and Christian faiths, while well-intentioned, has been based on ignorance of the recently discovered medical facts. As neuroscience research proceeds, scientific discovery has advanced almost uniformly in one direction: toward an ever-greater appreciation of the strength of nature, that is innate biology, in determining human characteristics. Traditional religion's condemnation of homosexuality, based on ignorance, has unwittingly involved it in the unjust persecution of an innocent minority.

The reevaluation of homosexuality in the light of modern science can therefore contribute to a genuine expansion of religious toleration. Churches and synagogues should embrace a formerly despised and rejected limb of their own bodies.

Furthermore, the conservative point of view within churches and synagogues that urges homosexuals to remain celibate actually lends support to the belief that homosexuality cannot be changed. This belief is more consistent with homosexuality being innate than with its being a development of some sort. Indeed, the new Roman Catholic catechism not only calls for celibacy among homosexuals but notes that homosexuality cannot be easily altered. When even the call to priestly celibacy is under attack from many directions, it seems especially cruel to urge it on those who feel no such call and are incapable of changing their sexuality.

In opposition to this argument traditionalists agree that homosexuals should not be treated cruelly, but reject all three propositions on which proponents argue for the normalization of homosexuality. Nonetheless, traditionalists acknowledge the claim that these three propositions stake out a critical framework for determining the moral and political status of homosexuality.

Traditionalists therefore present an argument that is precisely the opposite of the activists' contention at each point. Their argument follows.

- First, as a matter of biology, homosexuality is not innate, but a choice.
- Second, as a matter of psychology, homosexuality is reversible.
- Third, as a matter of sociology, homosexuality is not normal, but an illness or a perversion of nature.

As the book develops we will examine these contrasting claims from two distinct angles: First, to what degree are the claims true? Second, what bearing does their truth or falseness have on the "normalization" and moral status of homosexuality? If, for example, research shows that homosexuality is not changeable, would not the activists' hand be greatly strengthened? Perhaps stable, monogamous homosexual couples should enjoy the same special privileges and incentives to family formation that conventional, heterosexual couples enjoy: marriage, adoption rights, estate-planning, inheritance exemptions, and so on. And shouldn't such individuals also be eligible without prejudice for positions of leadership and spiritual authority within churches, synagogues, public schools, and other institutions where moral leadership and influence are exerted? On the other hand, if research shows that this is not the case, should our conclusions be completely different? The answers are not so obvious as they may at first seem.

The Politics Are Not the People

My reaction to the gay activism that has spawned this massive debate—and here I find I am far from alone—is entirely different from my reaction to people who happen to be homosexual. Gay politics arouses in me an exasperated, somewhat stifled, outrage, exasperated and stifled because of the tangle of conflicting emotions that arise when "political power" is joined to "victim" status; outrage because gay activism distorts the truth and harms not only society but homosexuals themselves, especially young people.

To the extent that homosexuals have been victimized, we can only reach out in compassion for the suffering, struggling soul. How can our hearts not go out to the young, prehomosexual boy or girl who is already shy, lonely, sensitive, and who surely suffers taunting rejection and maybe even beatings by the very peers he or she envies and most longs to be with? Can we really blind ourselves to the presence of that still-suffering child within the adult, however bristling and exotic an exterior with which he protects himself? And finally, just how different is "the homosexual" from ourselves? We so easily see—and then look down on—the self-protective maneuvering in others, which is far less painful than to admit it in ourselves.

But the organized, political side of the picture is entirely different. Here we too often see on violent display the brute aspect of human nature in all its crudity, stupidity, vanity, selfishness, disregard for others, and disregard for the truth. Like so many of its predecessors, too often gay activism follows the dictum that desired ends justify all means.

Here then is the conundrum we face now that gay activism has burst onto the national scene. On the one hand we must decide how best to counter the tactics of intimidation and refute the false claims of a group that operates in the hostile mode of raw, power politics. On the other hand we must retain the profound compassion and fellow-feeling toward individual homosexuals that we ourselves need and yearn for from others. We must respect as fellows the very individuals whom we may reject as claimants in the public square.

Gay activists, by contrast, deliberately seek to confuse these two dimensions. They insist that respect for a person is identical with accepting his or her political claims for equality in all areas of life. Even principled opposition is therefore tantamount to bigotry, "homophobia," and the equivalent of race-hatred.

But by deliberately confusing these two sides—the political and the personal—gay activism has created a dangerous mon-

ster. The lesser danger is that our very sympathy for the perse-
cuted will blind us to the social danger. In the name of a murky,
confused "inclusiveness" we will thereby sell our cultural birthright for a mess of political pottage. The greater danger, by far, is
that our justifiable protest will stifle and eventually kill our understanding that "homosexuals" are, as we will see, simply us. Should
this occur, we lose not only our birthright, but our souls.

Lives versus Lifestyle

A second arena where gay activism raises key questions is education. In some ways this is the most crucial of all because it
affects the attitudes and habits of the rising generation. There is
no question that the failed AIDS education policies of the last
decade and a half have had an effect—we now have a generation
of twenty-year-old gay men with a certain mortality of 30 percent. We can only wonder how many twenty-year-olds (who were
five when AIDS first appeared in America) might have been
spared had activists made it their number-one priority to protect individual lives rather than the gay lifestyle. For as the recent
survey *The Social Organization of Sexuality* makes clear, the vast
majority of youngsters who at some point adopt homosexual
practices later give them up.[7]

These young people, however, are the very ones told by educators to treat homosexuality as equally good—and safe—as heterosexuality. In one typical incident in the Northeast, a generally
liberal, nonreligious mother of a nine-year-old boy reported her
son's return home in tears from public elementary school. He
hung his head in embarrassment and shame and finally told his
outraged mother how the teacher had explained to the class how
to perform anal intercourse "safely."

These courses are careful to avoid presenting anal intercourse
as the predominantly homosexual practice that it is. (Data confirming this will be presented later.) Students are taught to accept
homosexual behavior fully without being instructed as to its typical features and typical consequences. But this subtle distortion of reality is minor compared to the major one that becomes

common and lethal—*that anal intercourse is safe so long as a condom is used.*

The word *lethal* is deliberate. Even before we have examined the evidence, I cannot stress too strongly that anal intercourse is not safe for anyone, under any circumstances. As the evidence makes abundantly clear, anal intercourse is a terribly dangerous practice whose dangers mount with the frequency and multiplicity of partners, conditions that predominate among male homosexuals. Gay activism is critical in the arena of education. Teachers of youth should surely consider carefully before advising a course of action that in thousands of cases has led to preventable death.

A Tale of Three Conferences

The third arena where gay activism raises key questions is in the communities of faith. Here is where the battles over homosexuality will ultimately be lost or won—because, along with the family, communities of faith are the decisive shapers of beliefs and morals. The narrow questions of homosexuality—What is it? Is it normal? Is it good?—have become heated because they point toward the central questions of human nature and morality: How do we understand life and humanness? By what authority do we decide between right and wrong? What do we consider "the good life" and "the good society"? Is it truly possible for homosexuals to change? Thus, especially as gay activists demand full standing in the hierarchies of religious leadership, they are forcing all of us in communities of faith to come to terms with what we really believe and how we really mean to live our lives.

Ultimate questions of right and wrong can always be found where the political intersects with the personal. For a relatively small percentage of Americans such questions of right and wrong are determined solely in the privacy of their own reflections, but the great majority of Americans still work out their answers in the context of their relationship to God, and thus in the context of a particular community of faith. This is why *social law* has always been *moral law.* And this is why our religious institutions' response to the issues of homosexuality will powerfully affect the future of our society.

This point came alive for me when I was invited to take part in three conferences that touched on homosexuality, two of which were held in religious settings. The first occasion was when I was invited to be a plenary speaker at a conference on AIDS in Connecticut. The conference brought together professionals from three formerly unrelated disciplines: hospice workers, substance-abuse counselors, and AIDS professionals.

A new class of patients was emerging that drew these disparate professional groups together and taxed them severely: young, racially mixed, male intravenous drug abusers, maybe homosexual, maybe not, who were quickly dying of AIDS. They were accompanied by a growing number of their wives and girlfriends who had also become infected—usually by them.

I chose to speak on the spiritual dimension of the AIDS crisis. If the word "cure" could mean anything beyond a bitter joke to these sad young people whose desperate lives were swiftly being closed off, it would not be offered by the secular professions. At heart, they needed God.

I spoke directly of sin, guilt, and reconciliation with others and with God. And I showed them how these matters affect the immune system. The talk was well-received, not because they heard much that was new, but because hearing a *psychiatrist* (instead of a minister or rabbi or priest) boldly speak of God validated their deep longing for him. Today a minister is just a minister, but a psychiatrist is the new tribal high priest whose words come wrapped in the aura of the new high canon: science. Overall I was heartened. The communities of faith could play a constructive role.

Because of this first speech, I was invited to address a New England conference on AIDS sponsored by the Episcopal Church. Over three hundred people attended. About half were clergy, male and female; the other half were predominantly HIV-positive homosexual men, a small number of HIV-positive men with a history of IV-drug use, and a small number of heterosexual women who were HIV-positive because of previous relationships with homosexual, bisexual, or drug-using men.

The program included numerous healing services and all the speakers spoke of "spirituality." But apart from me, none mentioned the word "sin" (of any sort, not just sexual), for in the name of not being "judgmental" it had been made taboo. Problematic and dangerous aspects of the gay life were never discussed, nor was the tragedy of the women addressed from the point of view of ethics in sexual relationships. The clergy who ran the conference belonged to ACT-UP—the "AIDS Coalition to Unleash Power," a militant activist group. Following communion they distributed "solidarity" pins to the conference attendees—condoms encrusted with glue and glitter.

The denial at this conference was so dense that self-examination was entirely precluded. How could healing possibly take place without an honest facing up to the realities of the situation? I returned from the experience saddened by the depth of suffering I had seen but angered as well. Churches and synagogues were influential in the politics and pastoral care of those caught in homosexuality and AIDS, but their influence could be destructive as well as constructive.

Shortly after that I watched a similar situation play itself out in my hometown. In the space of six months, a local minister altered the liturgy to make it more "inclusive" and "married" the music minister to his male lover. With that, a core group of members left.

The minister was a friend, so I spoke to him of my concerns. He immediately adduced as support for his position the recent research that demonstrated, as he had heard, that "homosexuality is genetic." Perhaps the seed of this book was conceived at that moment when I heard "science" being cited to justify an alteration in morality. For I understood well the distorted science behind these claims—as well as the minister's philosophical confusion. But I also knew that the scientific issues surrounding all matters of "behavioral genetics" are difficult and complex, far more complex than I could explain in a brief meeting, even had the minister been open. What was plain was that churches could be constructive, destructive—or confused.

The last experience that germinated and nourished the seed of this book was my discovery of the work of Leanne Payne and her colleagues in Pastoral Care Ministries. Over the years I had slowly come to realize that much of what I—like so many of my generation—had taken for true spirituality was a mirage or worse. When I first encountered the books of C. S. Lewis, reading him from my Jewish background, I had the distinct impression that here was Truth—with a capital "T." I realized that depth-psychology could be advanced by taking Lewis's insights and formalizing them in psychological terms. Much to my surprise, Mrs. Payne had done just that—without losing Lewis's vibrant spirit. Indeed, she added her own distinct spirit. After striking up a correspondence I decided to attend one of her conferences.

The conference was to be held in Wichita, Kansas. As a Jewish psychiatrist, educated at MIT, Harvard, and Yale and living in a cosmopolitan East Coast suburb, I felt that Wichita was a rather unlikely place for me. Nonetheless I went, not knowing what I would find.

What I found was that about two hundred of the three hundred people in attendance were homosexuals, male and female, struggling to emerge out of their homosexuality. And among the conference leadership a large number were *former homosexuals*, some now married and with children, all devoted to helping others out of the gay lifestyle. They were remarkable, tender human beings, enviable in their humanity and humility and in their longing for and connectedness to God. From out of the cosmopolitan desert that offers itself as the best that life has to offer, I had stepped directly into an oasis with a rushing torrent—not just a well—of living water.

Nothing in my experience prepared me for this third conference. The professional and personal circles within which I normally move are oblivious to such phenomena. If they note their existence at all, it is as a hazy blob at the periphery of mainstream, "enlightened" vision or as the butt of media jokes. With rare exceptions, *I had never once heard from others within my own profession any mention at all of such people as these healed homosexuals*. Clearly, communities of faith could be not only constructive and caring but healing.

God and Gay Science

One further point needs to be made in this introduction. Conflicts over homosexuality have settled into a relentless trench warfare in the broader strategies of America's culture wars. But the battles are fraught with unrecognized confusion because they rest on concepts and findings from a new and extremely complex branch of science—the genetics of behavior. The overarching goal of behavioral genetics is to clarify the relationship between nurture and nature in human life. This, however, has been an area of concern for philosophers and theologians since time immemorial. Therefore we should not be surprised that a science that encompasses such complicated questions is hard to grasp and easy to distort. Behind gay politics is gay science, which we also must assess.

In today's relentless barrage of words, images, slogans, and ideas that assault us from all sides, many of us have become dependent on sound bites—short, simple, predigested, emotion-laden, one-stop conclusions. We have neither the time nor the ability to sort through the primary information for ourselves in order to arrive at our own considered conclusions. As a result, the deep complexity of the scientific research into homosexuality is easy for people to misinterpret and easier still to misuse.

To disentangle this confusion and form solid principles by which to reach responsible conclusions requires effort. But readers who persist and grasp the basic truths about the science of human behavior will gain an invaluable insight into the debate over homosexuality. And these readers, whether politicians, educators, clergy, mental health professionals, or concerned citizens, will also understand how limited are science's answers to questions of right and wrong. We will find too that when we reach the proper limits of science, we have to leave science behind to proceed further.

In part one, then, we examine science and in part two we turn to a consideration of the deeper sources of human motivation—to psychology, to the human will, and to considerations of faith. As we make this transition from genetic science to psychology to religion, the language will change accordingly: from the neutral, rigorous, statistics-based tenor of modern research methodology to the more general, often impressionistic, but still neutral concepts and case reports of philosophy and psychology; and finally to the deepest aspects of human character revealed in the profound disclosures of the Hebrew and Christian Scriptures. Only the latter deal with such utterly unscientific but profound realities as moral law, sin, guilt, atoning sacrifice, and divine forgiveness.

In the end the debate over homosexual behavior and its implications for public policy can only be decided conclusively on moral grounds, and moral grounds will ultimately mean religious grounds. As the generally liberal Brookings Institution noted in a 1986 report, a representative government such as ours "depends for its health on values that over the not-so-long run must come from religion. . . . Human rights are rooted in the moral worth with which a loving creator has endowed each human soul, and social authority is legitimized by making it answerable to a transcendent moral law."[8]

We must make a choice: Shall we determine good and evil for ourselves—viewing the ancient serpent either as an irrelevant fable from the childhood of our race or as the great messenger of consciousness-raising—or shall we stand on a word outside ourselves, a word from the one between whose first word of creation and last word of judgment we live our fleeting lives?

PART 1

Gay Science

In this age, in this country, public sentiment is everything. With it, nothing can fail; against it, nothing can succeed. Whoever molds public sentiment goes deeper than he who enacts statutes, or pronounces judicial decisions.

—Abraham Lincoln

1

Neither Scientific
nor Democratic

O ur society is dominated by experts, few more influential
than psychiatrists. This influence does not derive, however, from our superior ethics or goodness nor from any
widespread consensus that we are especially admirable. Indeed,
the extent to which we are castigated represents the all-too-accu-
rate skewering of our fundamental professional claim: the pre-
tense that because we know something about *what* makes people
tick, we are therefore uniquely qualified to tell them *how* to lead
their lives. Nonetheless, because Americans have become a
nation dependent on experts, the same psychiatrist is at once
lampooned and consulted for direction. For better or for worse,
mental health professionals exert influence that greatly exceeds
the actual wisdom we demonstrate.

In the early years of "gay liberation," this reality was used for
the fledgling gay activists' advantage. They anticipated that if the
influential American Psychiatric Association (APA) could be convinced to redefine homosexuality, the other guilds would follow
shortly thereafter and then so would the rest of society. Their plan
was implemented with swift and near-total success.

Consider the rapid change. In 1963 the New York Academy of Medicine charged its Committee on Public Health to report on the subject of homosexuality, prompted by concern that homosexual behavior seemed to be increasing. The Committee reported that:

> homosexuality is indeed an illness. The homosexual is an emotionally disturbed individual who has not acquired the normal capacity to develop satisfying heterosexual relations.[1]

It also noted that:

> some homosexuals have gone beyond the plane of defensiveness and now argue that deviancy is a "desirable, noble, preferable way of life."[2]

Just ten years later—with no significant new scientific evidence—the homosexual activists' argument became the new standard within psychiatry. For in 1973 the American Psychiatric Association voted to strike homosexuality from the officially approved list of psychiatric illnesses. How did this occur? Normally a scientific consensus is reached over the course of many years, resulting from the accumulated weight of many properly designed studies. But in the case of homosexuality, scientific research has only now just begun, years *after* the question was decided.

A Change of Status

The APA vote to normalize homosexuality was driven by politics, not science. Even sympathizers acknowledged this. Ronald Bayer was then a Fellow at the Hastings Institute in New York. He reported how in 1970 the leadership of a homosexual faction within the APA planned a "systematic effort to disrupt the annual meetings of the American Psychiatric Association."[3] They defended this method of "influence" on the grounds that the APA represented "psychiatry as a social institution" rather than a scientific body or professional guild.

At the 1970 meetings, Irving Bieber, an eminent psychoanalyst and psychiatrist, was presenting a paper on "homosexuality and transsexualism." He was abruptly challenged:

[Bieber's] efforts to explain his position . . . were met with derisive laughter. . . . [One] protester to call him a _____. "I've read your book, Dr. Bieber, and if that book talked about black people the way it talks about homosexuals, you'd be drawn and quartered and you'd deserve it."[4]

The tactics worked. Acceding to pressure, the organizers of the following APA conference in 1971 agreed to sponsor a special panel—not *on* homosexuality, but *by* homosexuals. If the panel was not approved, the program chairman had been warned, "They're [the homosexual activists] not going to break up just one section."[5]

But the panel was not enough. Bayer continues:

Despite the agreement to allow homosexuals to conduct their own panel discussion at the 1971 convention, gay activists in Washington felt that they had to provide yet another jolt to the psychiatric profession. . . . Too smooth a transition . . . would have deprived the movement of its most important weapon—the threat of disorder. . . . [They] turned to a Gay Liberation Front collective in Washington to plan the May 1971 demonstration. Together with the collective [they] developed a detailed strategy for disruption, paying attention to the most intricate logistical details.[6]

On May 3, 1971, the protesting psychiatrists broke into a meeting of distinguished members of the profession. They grabbed the microphone and turned it over to an outside activist, who declared:

Psychiatry is the enemy incarnate. Psychiatry has waged a relentless war of extermination against us. You may take this as a declaration of war against you. . . . We're rejecting you all as our owners.[7]

No one raised an objection. The activists then secured an appearance before the APA's Committee on Nomenclature. Its chairman allowed that perhaps homosexual behavior was not a sign of psychiatric disorder, and that the Diagnostic and Statistical Manual (DSM) should probably therefore reflect this new understanding.

When the committee met formally to consider the issue in 1973 the outcome had already been arranged behind closed doors. No new data was introduced, and objectors were given only fifteen minutes to present a rebuttal that summarized seventy years of psychiatric and psychoanalytic opinion. When the committee voted as planned, a few voices formally appealed to the membership at large, which can overrule committee decisions even on "scientific" matters.

The activists responded swiftly and effectively. They drafted a letter and sent it to the over thirty thousand members of the APA, urging them "to vote to retain the nomenclature change."[8] How could the activists afford such a mailing? *They purchased the APA membership mailing list* after the National Gay Task Force (NGTF) sent out a fund-raising appeal to *their* membership.

Bayer comments:

> Though the NGTF played a central role in this effort, a decision was made not to indicate on the letter that it was written, at least in part, by the Gay Task Force, nor to reveal that its distribution was funded by contributions the Task Force had raised. Indeed, the letter gave every indication of having been conceived and mailed by those [psychiatrists] who [originally] signed it. . . . Though each signer publicly denied any role in the dissimulation, at least one signer had warned privately that to acknowledge the organizational role of the gay community would have been the "kiss of death."
>
> There is no question however about the extent to which the officers of the APA were aware of both the letter's origins and the mechanics of its distribution. They, as well as the National Gay Task Force, understood the letter as performing a vital role in the effort to turn back the challenge.[9]

Because a majority of the APA members who responded voted to support the change in the classification of homosexuality, the decision of the Board of Trustees was allowed to stand. But in fact only one-third of the membership did respond. (Four years later the journal *Medical Aspects of Human Sexuality* reported on a survey it conducted. The survey showed that 69 percent of psychiatrists disagreed with the vote and still considered homosexuality a disorder.) Bayer remarks:

> The result was not a conclusion based upon an approximation of the scientific truth as dictated by reason, but was instead an action demanded by the ideological temper of the times.[10]

Two years later the American *Psychological* Association—the professional psychology guild that is three times larger than the APA—voted to follow suit.

How much the 1973 APA decision was motivated by politics is only becoming clear even now. While attending a conference in England in 1994, I met a man who told me an account that he had told no one else. He had been in the gay life for years but had left the lifestyle. He recounted how after the 1973 APA decision he and his lover, along with a certain very highly placed officer of the APA Board of Trustees and his lover, all sat around the officer's apartment celebrating their victory. For among the gay activists placed high in the APA who maneuvered to ensure a victory was this man—suborning from the top what was presented to both the membership and the public as a disinterested search for truth.

Twenty Years Later

The scientific process continues to be affected by political pressure today. In 1994 the Board of Trustees of the APA decided to consider altering the code of ethics. The proposed change (presented by a man who is a prominent and vocal gay-activist psychiatrist and chairman of the APA's Committee on the Abuse and Misuse of Psychiatry) would make it a violation of professional conduct for a psychiatrist to help a homosexual patient become heterosexual *even at the patient's request.* This is in spite of the fact that one of the association's own professional standards holds that psychiatrists need to accept a patient's own goals in treatment so as to "foster maximum self-determination on the part of clients." The final version read, "The APA does not endorse any psychiatric treatment which is based either upon a psychiatrist's assumption that homosexuality is a mental disorder or a psychiatrist's intent to change a person's sexual orientation." The Board approved the statement and sent it to the APA Assembly—its legislative body—for final approval.

A swift and fierce battle ensued. Enough Assembly members spoke against the resolution, because of its chilling effect on practice, to defeat it prior to a vote. According to APA members closely involved, even the threat of a first-amendment controversy would not deter the activists. But the turning point came when therapists who help homosexuals change—*and a large number of ex-homosexuals*—made it clear that if the resolution passed, they would file a lawsuit against the APA and reopen the original basis on which homosexuality was excluded from the list of diagnoses. With that the activists retreated. Had the change been approved, it would have opened the door to malpractice suits and ethics charges against psychiatrists who help homosexuals change—in accord with their patient's own wishes. Indeed, the chairman of the APA Gay and Lesbian Task Force made it clear that the activists had in their sights not only psychiatrists who undertook reparative therapy, but eventually psychologists, social workers, and even pastoral counselors and ministers.

The APA is not the only guild affected by political pressure. The National Association of Social Workers, which accredits the largest body of mental health practitioners in the country, also continues to be influenced by gay activists. The NASW Committee on Lesbian and Gay Issues has lobbied the NASW to declare that the use of reparative therapies is a violation of the NASW Code of Ethics. The committee issued a paper in 1992 stating that:

> Efforts to "convert" people through irresponsible therapies . . .
> can be more accurately called brainwashing, shaming or coer-
> cion. . . . The assumptions and directions of reparative thera-
> pies are theoretically and morally wrong.[11]

Of the three major mental health guilds, the NASW is farthest
along in the attempt to politicize clinical questions regarding
homosexuality.

All of these changes in the definition and classification of
homosexuality have occurred in a scientific vacuum. Nonetheless, the small amount of hard-science research that has been
conducted has complex yet predictable implications, which
are consistent with findings from other areas of behavioral
genetics. These studies suggest that a composite of mutually
interacting factors influence almost all aspects of human
behavior, thoroughly confounding the notion that someone
could simply answer the questions "Whence arises homosexuality?" and "What is it?" with the responses "nature" or "nurture," "normal" or "abnormal." And these studies neither explain nor even address the role of choice in human behavior.
Indeed, they do not because, as we will discuss in greater detail,
they cannot.

The Public's Perception

Recent articles in the media create the mistaken impression
that scientific closure on the subject of homosexuality has been
or soon will be reached. Such actions as the APA's 1973 decision
and its recent deliberations further reinforce unjustified conclusions in the public mind. Few understand the complexities of
good biological research; most would be amazed at the extent
that politics has corrupted the scientific process. They depend
on the accuracy of the accounts in the popular press.

But the purported scientific consensus that the press touts is
a fiction. A good example is Chandler Burr's article in the March
1993 issue of the *Atlantic Monthly*.[12] He states baldly: "Five
decades of psychiatric evidence demonstrates that homosexuality is immutable, and non-pathological, and a growing

body of more recent evidence implicates biology in the development of sexual orientation." In a later *New York Times* opinion piece he states even more flatly that science has long since proven that homosexuality is biological and unchangeable, and that *there is simply no disagreement on this among scientists.*

But *these claims are absolutely not true,* except for the meaningless statement that "biology is implicated in the development of homosexuality." Biology is, of course, "implicated" in everything human. In conducting his research for the *Atlantic Monthly,* Burr interviewed a number of scientists and clinicians who expressed the view that homosexuality is neither genetic nor immutable. He simply did not cite them.

We will see later the falsity of activists' repeated assertions that homosexuality is immutable. They seek to create the impression that *science* has settled these questions, but it most certainly has not. Instead, the changes that have occurred in both public and professional opinion have resulted from politics, pressure, and public relations.

For in response to the explicit efforts of the activists, a mass change of opinion in accepting homosexuality as normal *has* occurred. But it remains unsupported by the very sources the activists manipulate for their own ends. Such "disinformation" seems to arise partly from a deliberate campaign, especially given the willingness of some to use "any means necessary" to convert public opinion. "Any means necessary" is no exaggeration. Eric Pollard formerly belonged to the prominent homosexual organization ACT-UP and founded its Washington, D.C., chapter. In an interview with *The Washington Blade,* a major homosexual newspaper, he stated that he and other group members learned to apply "subversive tactics, drawn largely from the voluminous *Mein Kampf,* which some of us studied as a working model."[13]

In contrast to the widely promoted claims, many eminent scientists disagree with the media's conclusions about the "biology of homosexuality."[14] A scientist who leads one of the nation's largest behavioral genetics laboratories commented that the latest genetics research only means that some tentative, indirect, partial genetic relationship *might* exist, so perhaps it is worth looking into.[15] *Scientific American*'s cover read "The dubious link between genes and behavior." But what is remembered by the general public is the catchy, inaccurate headline in a major newsweekly: "The Gay Gene."

An Uncontrolled Factor

The sociological—not medical or scientific—transformation of the opinion of mental health professionals regarding homosexuality has greatly influenced the current research. Unfortunately, many of those now researching homosexuality explicitly aim at a particular outcome. For instance, Simon LeVay, the San Francisco neuroanatomist who published a widely cited study on the brains of homosexual men, left his position as a neuroanatomist at the Salk Institute in San Diego to found the Institute of Gay and Lesbian Education. Richard Pillard, coauthor of two major twin studies on homosexuality, admits in the very text of one these papers that his research was designed "to counter the prevalent belief that sexual orientation is largely the product of family interactions and the social environment."[16]

A series of critical studies started in the 1960s demonstrates that researcher bias in favor of a specific outcome is one of the most important and most commonly uncontrolled factors that distorts any scientific study.[17]

Charles Socarides, a psychoanalyst and expert in the field of homosexual treatment, notes that the 1973 APA decision

> remains a chilling reminder that if scientific principles are not fought for, they can be lost—a disillusioning warning that unless we make no exceptions to science, we are subject to the snares of political factionalism and the propagation of untruths to an unsuspecting and uninformed public, to the rest of the medical profession and to the behavioral sciences.[18]

Still in its infancy, psychiatry remains a far from coherent composite of medicine, art, hard science, amateur philosophy, and secularized spiritual direction. This lack of scientific rigor—not surprising given the subtlety and complexity of its object of study—may have opened psychiatry to be the first among the professions to political manipulation. But now, over two decades since the APA decision in 1973, numerous "scholarly" treatises seek to "prove" that *all* of science is a racist, sexist, age-ist, Eurocentric, class-based, homophobic endeavor whose primary purpose is to maintain class dominance. The effect of politics continues.

2

Who Says? And Why?

Ironically, it is doubtful that homosexuality really is an "*illness*"—according to any scientifically rigorous meaning of the word. It is as doubtful as psychiatry's characterization of many other conditions as "illnesses."

A number of serious mental conditions arise from physical diseases of the brain. Some are acquired before birth, some after; some are inherited, some acquired; most result from a variety of causes. Many of these conditions are partially reversible by treatments that target the chemistry and physiology of the brain. Likewise, many conditions once thought to be purely psychological are now understood to have significant genetic components (for example, many cases of depression or Obsessive Compulsive Disorder). But most of what has been termed "neurosis" can be considered "illness" only if "illness" is used poetically, as in T. S. Eliot's felicitous phrase, "our only health is the disease. . . ."[1]

Homosexuality thus was considered an "illness" in the same way that early psychoanalysis defined *all* forms of human suffering associated with unconscious internal conflict as "illness." Thus the man who both hates and loves his mother and does not "know" it enacts his hidden ambivalence in his relations with women and so is "neurotic." We consider him "ill," however, in a sense altogether different from when he contracts cancer. Likewise the man who "can't" love women.

In all such cases of "neurosis," nothing is wrong with the brain and its nerves. It is rather that the healthy brain is being used in a way that we deem to be socially, morally, or practically wrong or merely inefficient. And so like all conditions characterized solely by mental and behavioral traits, it took little for "science" to "prove" that homosexuality was not an illness.

The Politics of Definition

What, then, is illness? Is it "abnormality?" Only one essential but obvious point needs to be underlined here: By definition illnesses are *undesirable* conditions or states of the organism. Many biological states—say, unusual strength—may be "abnormal" but are not illnesses because they are not undesirable. In fact, in this example of strength, the condition is not just neutral but positively desirable and is therefore likely to be considered a *gift*.[2]

Now bring into the discussion the distinction between psychological and biological conditions. We can say that all undesirable *physical* conditions are categorized as illnesses, even if the boundary between illness and health is difficult to define. But when we consider *psychological* or *behavioral* traits, the definition of illness becomes more difficult. This is especially true of those traits associated with no identifiable underlying physical factors. In fact, if we were to consider such conditions—say, nastiness—as illnesses at all, then the definition of illness is reduced to mere desirability. Such a definition expands the meaning of illness to the point of meaninglessness.

But this is precisely the error into which psychology has been trapped for nearly a century now. A large number—if not the majority—of conditions that the mental health professionals treat as "illnesses" or "disorders" are simply undesirable character traits. When the APA excluded homosexuality from its list of psychiatric disorders, it did nothing more than shift it from the column headed "undesirable" to the column headed "not undesirable." This shift exposes the key questions: "Not undesirable to whom?" "Not undesirable by what criteria?"

Although psychiatrists and other mental health professionals may know how a given trait comes about or how it may be altered, *they have no expertise in determining whether a trait is desirable.* Individual professionals and the organized professional guilds are no more capable of deciding whether *any* trait—including homosexuality—is *consensually desirable or undesirable* to society than are any other citizens or groups. If people agree to consider homosexuality to be undesirable, then it is consensually undesirable. This does not necessarily make it an illness, for to be an illness it would also need to be associated with identifiable abnormalities. But neither does its not being an illness inevitably make it desirable.

Going Round in Circles

This question of homosexuality's desirability or undesirability is a hotly debated, central issue in the controversy. On one side gay activists claim that homosexuality is in no way undesirable. On the other side many people do *not* wish to be homosexual, in spite of behaving or feeling compelled to behave in that way. For them homosexuality is undesirable.

Gay activists explain this contradiction through their concept of "internalized homophobia," which is inherently circular. Homosexuals who wish to change, they claim, have swallowed ("internalized") the "homophobic" argument that being gay is undesirable; therefore they have adopted a position of hatred toward themselves that is based on an illusion. Their own genuine feeling—of which they are themselves unaware— is that being gay is fine and acceptable. We, and they, cannot therefore accept their own perceived position that homosexuality is undesirable, even for themselves.

The circularity of this concept is striking. The evidence for "internalized homophobia" is the fact that such people do not wish to be homosexual; and the reason they do not wish to be homosexual is "internalized homophobia."

This sort of circular thinking is now common in "politically correct" literature:

> . . . membership of [sic] a stigmatized minority sexuality may exacerbate causes of sexual dysfunction. The effects of discordant lifestyle and identity, homosexual identity formation, dysphoria and internalized homophobia on sexual functioning are three examples of these factors of specific relevance to being homosexual in this culture. The effects of AIDS, difficulties arising from the mechanics of safer sex and the psychosexual effects of oppression on healthy sexual functioning all indicate how factors important to (but not caused by) minority sexual status may influence sexuality functioning.[3]

The self-serving explanation for homosexual distress, however, is undermined by the terrible effects of childhood trauma on the emotional well-being of adults. Many studies demonstrate a sadly disproportionate amount of sexual abuse in the childhoods of homosexual men, suggesting that both homosexual unhappiness and homosexuality itself derive from common causes, and therefore that unhappiness is an inherent accompaniment of homosexuality:

> 1,001 adult homosexual and bisexual men attending sexually transmitted disease clinics were interviewed regarding potentially abusive sexual contacts during childhood and adolescence. Thirty-seven percent of participants reported they had been encouraged or forced to have sexual contact before age 19 with an older or more powerful partner; 94 percent occurred with men. Median age of the participant at first contact was 10; median age difference between partners was 11 years. Fifty-one percent involved use of force; 33 percent involved anal sex.[4]

In spite of its superficial plausibility and the activists' repeated claims, no studies support the hypothesis that the social disapproval of homosexuality causes any of the high levels of internal distress in homosexuals—even long before AIDS.

Such studies as the one cited above suggest that both the high levels of emotional distress as well as homosexuality itself have at least one common root in painful childhood experiences. The distortions that have crept into psychiatric diagnosis is nicely put into perspective in a recent issue of *Science* by one scientist's assessment of the latest edition of the DSM:

> . . . the fourth edition in this constantly evolving series . . . [reflects] the latest accumulation of knowledge, plus a fair dose of habit and prejudice. The potential for disrupting research is "obvious."[5]

Psychoanalysts and Homosexuality

When psychiatrists used to characterize homosexuality as an illness, they were perhaps mistaken on scientific grounds. But because illnesses are morally neutral, they could discuss homosexuality without stigmatizing it as though it were a simple *choice*. And they could discuss the suffering specific to homosexual behavior without condemnation while identifying this suffering as arising largely from within the individual. Psychiatrists could thereby suggest to those suffering that, through their own actions, they might one day be free from their affliction.

But not only was the definition of homosexuality as a medical illness flawed, the earliest methods that medical psychiatry offered to "cure" this illness often failed, effective only in the hands of a small number of gifted specialists. As a whole the *psychoanalytic* profession—the branch of mental health that focuses on unconscious emotional conflict as a source of "neurosis"—more or less turned away from homosexuality as too difficult a problem to deal with consistently. A parallel phenomenon occurred with respect to problems of so-called "narcissists"—a related condition, in fact—about which it was commonly quipped that "the most difficult patient to treat was a successful narcissist."

Perhaps because there are so many heterosexual narcissists (and so few homosexuals), over time many psychoanalytic resources were allocated to its treatment. After forty years of consistent effort, effective methods for the treatment of narcissism were developed.[6] But the treatment of homosexuality remained a quiet, "minority" pursuit. Therefore the continued labeling of it as an illness began to seem cruel, and was increasingly protested by activists as being cruel, in light of the subjectivity involved in all psychological "illnesses."

As with the change in status of homosexuality within organized psychiatry, this emerging change within organized psychoanalysis has nothing to do with hard, new scientific evidence or even new clinical data. Rather, the activists claim, the previous rejection of homosexuality by classical Freudian psychoanalysis was entirely due to a bias caused by flawed reasoning.

Indeed it *was* caused by flawed reasoning. Psychoanalysis has no firm category for morality, so behaviors that were considered undesirable had to be reconceptualized as illnesses. In critical circumstances—as in the case of the admittance of avowed homosexuals into the profession—these behaviors were evaluated just as though they were moral defects. But in time the "illness" model came to be viewed as mere metaphor. And by then the moral evaluation had faded away entirely anyway.

The first of these quasi-moral categories to fall was "narcissism."[7] Narcissists were once deemed untreatable and unsuitable as analysts; now entire institutes of narcissists treat and train other narcissists. The next major exclusionary "diagnosis" to fall, unsurprisingly, was homosexuality.

The Jungian psychoanalytic institutes have followed a somewhat similar path even though C. G. Jung's theory of homosexual development differed considerably from Freud's. Jung and his followers generally saw male homosexuals as having an unusually strong identification with the feminine part of the psyche (the "anima"), female homosexuals with the masculine part (the "animus"). This identification could skew sexual relations, but did not necessarily have to do so. And they saw it bringing certain positive values as well.

A Jungian analysis of homosexuality therefore aimed to remove the negative, opposite-sex identification from the realm of sexuality while preserving its positive value in creative, relational, and even "spiritual" domains. The Jungians met with some success using this rather more compassionate approach. But those who were not in this way "cured" of their homosexuality faced a difficult battle gaining acceptance as Jungian analysts, although not as tough as among the Freudians. In fact many were rejected.

In theory both schools shared the basic belief that homosexuals who could not work through their homosexual *behavior* were unsuitable for the clinical practice of analysis—as would be any candidates whose training had not succeeded in curing them of their major arena of "acting out." Both schools shared the idea of the "wounded healer," especially in their early years. And both adhered to the Galenic dictum, "physician, heal thyself," believing that the best physician was one who had done so. The Jungians were not more tolerant than the Freudians, simply more optimistic.

But recently a sea change has occurred among the Jungians that parallels the change among the Freudians. An actively homosexual way of life now no longer bars one from becoming an analyst. In fact, a few recently published articles by Jungian theorists have even "supernormalized" homosexuality as an especially creative, enlightened, and individuated variant of normal development.[8]

Both schools now also share, if somewhat reluctantly, the activists' insistence that homosexuals suffer mainly because of the discrimination, rejection, and hostility they face from a "homophobic" culture. Many analysts increasingly adopt this posture in public. But in private most analysts I know—of whatever school—maintain a fairly skeptical stance about the now commonly accepted normality and benefits of homosexuality.

In sum, conventional psychiatry's and psychoanalysis' frequent failures to treat homosexuality successfully lend credence to the claim that homosexuality is *not* an illness and that nothing is wrong with it. The sufferings associated with homosexuality must therefore be rooted in the social rejection it stimulates among the unenlightened. In other words, if we can't fix it, it must not be a problem.

A better way to determine the desirability or undesirability of homosexuality is to leave behind the circular thinking and the self-serving rhetoric and instead examine the medical facts. As we will see in the next chapter, much detailed and sophisticated research shows that homosexuality is unequivocally associated with a large number of severe *medical* problems—even apart from AIDS.

3

Is Homosexuality Desirable?
Brute Facts

What would you think if a relative, friend, or colleague had a condition that is routinely, even if not always, associated with the following problems:

- A significantly decreased likelihood of establishing or preserving a successful marriage
- A five- to ten-year decrease in life expectancy
- Chronic, potentially fatal, liver disease—hepatitis
- Inevitably fatal esophageal cancer
- Pneumonia
- Internal bleeding
- Serious mental disabilities, many of which are irreversible
- A much higher than usual incidence of suicide
- A very low likelihood that its adverse effects can be eliminated unless the condition itself is eliminated
- An only 30 percent likelihood of being eliminated through lengthy, often costly, and very time-consuming treatment in an otherwise unselected population of sufferers (although

a very high success rate among highly motivated, carefully selected sufferers)

We can add four qualifications to this unnamed condition. First, even though its origins are influenced by genetics, the condition is, strictly speaking, rooted in behavior. Second, individuals who have this condition continue the behavior in spite of the destructive consequences of doing so. Third, although some people with this condition perceive it as a problem and wish they could rid themselves of it, many others deny they have any problem at all and violently resist all attempts to "help" them. And fourth, these people who resist help tend to socialize with one another, sometimes exclusively, and form a kind of "subculture."

No doubt you would care deeply for someone close to you who had such a condition. And whether or not society considered it undesirable or even an illness, you would want to help. Undoubtedly, you would also consider it worth "treating," that is, you would seek to help your relative, friend, or colleague by eliminating the condition entirely.

The condition we are speaking of is alcoholism. Alcoholism is clearly undesirable precisely because of all the adverse conditions directly associated with it, although not every alcoholic develops all the problems associated with it.

Alcoholism is a form of compulsive or addictive behavior that has volitional, family, psychological, social, and genetic "causes." Whether it can be considered an "illness" in the strict sense makes for an interesting philosophical discussion but a useless practical one—as is true for all addictions. Nonetheless, and in spite of the relatively modest "cure" rate, it is still well worth treating, and treating as though it *were* an illness (as does organized psychiatry, which lists it as a disorder), because of the enormously serious personal and social consequences of not doing so.

Putting Two and Two Together

And now imagine another friend or colleague who had a condition associated with a similar list of problems:

- A significantly decreased likelihood of establishing or preserving a successful marriage
- A *twenty-five to thirty*-year decrease in life expectancy
- Chronic, potentially fatal, liver disease—infectious hepatitis, which increases the risk of liver cancer
- Inevitably fatal immune disease including associated cancers
- Frequently fatal rectal cancer
- Multiple bowel and other infectious diseases
- A much higher than usual incidence of suicide
- A very low likelihood that its adverse effects can be eliminated unless the condition itself is
- An at least 50 percent likelihood of being eliminated through lengthy, often costly, and very time-consuming treatment in an otherwise unselected group of sufferers (although a very high success rate, in some instances nearing 100 percent, for groups of highly motivated, carefully selected individuals)

As with alcoholism: First, even though its origins may be influenced by genetics, the condition is, strictly speaking, a pattern of behavior; second, individuals who have this condition continue in the behavior in spite of the destructive consequences of doing so; third, although some people with this condition perceive it as a problem and wish they could rid themselves of it, many others deny they have any problem at all and violently resist all attempts to "help" them; and fourth, some of the people with this condition—especially those who deny it is a problem—tend to socialize almost exclusively with one another and form a "subculture."

This condition is homosexuality. Yet despite the parallels between the two conditions, what is striking today are the sharply different responses to them. We will address some of the above points in detail in other sections of this book. But for now, we will turn to the brute facts about the adverse consequences of homosexuality.

In doing so, we will look at a number of recent studies that discuss the problems typically found among male homosexuals.

These studies generally examine the medical problems that are attendant to typical homosexual *behavior,* an important point to emphasize because homosexual *desire* is no more intrinsically problematic than any other desire. We should underscore that these studies focus on *male* homosexuals for two main reasons: Lesbian sexual practices are less risky than gay male practices; and lesbians are not nearly so promiscuous as gay men.

Most of these studies are aimed—as are all medical studies, ultimately—at alleviating distress and suffering. But they leave unexamined whether homosexual behavior itself is the source of the problem. In any event, they presume that homosexual behavior is unchangeable. Therefore they concentrate on changing the "high risk" behaviors found among homosexuals so as to lower the risk. In other words: Because changing homosexuality to heterosexuality is both taboo and impossible, they claim, one should alter the behaviors associated with homosexuality so as to make it safe, or at least safer.

Different Lifestyles, Different Life Spans

Gay activists deliberately paint a picture of homosexual life, especially among men, that is the counterpart of heterosexual life. Their purpose is to avoid alienating support from sympathetic heterosexuals who constitute the vast majority of people. For example, one activist handbook advises: "In any campaign to win over the public, gays must be portrayed as victims. . . . Persons featured in the media campaign should be . . . indistinguishable from the straights we'd like to reach."[1] Another cautions: "The masses must not be repulsed by premature exposure to homosexual behavior itself."[2]

In spite of clear evidence that homosexual standards are strikingly different from the heterosexual norm, the general public impression has been created that gays are little different from straights. The above quotations show the keen awareness of some gay activists for the need for deceptive cover. But in many cases it seems as though many gays have bought this artificially constructed picture in all hopefulness.

The following comparison between heterosexuals and homosexuals is presented to show *why* homosexuals are at risk for the conditions that will be discussed in the next section. Once again, I must emphasize that a so-called "homosexual orientation" or "homosexual identity" does not itself cause medical problems; only typically homosexual behaviors can. Similarly, the desire for alcohol is not itself harmful; only real drinking is.

In the chart that follows, the data on heterosexual practices are drawn from two sources. One source is *The Social Organization of Sexuality: Sexual Practices in the United States,* the most scientifically rigorous survey to date on the sexual habits of Americans. (*Sex in America* condenses the same research for a more general audience.) The other source is composite data on homosexual practices from a series of studies in homosexual behavior and behavior change, mostly aimed at studying gay-related medical conditions and at reducing the risk of AIDS.

It would be preferable if the data on both homosexuals and heterosexuals were drawn exclusively from the same sample set and study. But as the authors of *Sex in America* point out, because of sampling techniques ensuring that the study would be an accurate cross section of the American populace, "there were few homosexuals in our survey"[3]—too few to study independently.

More specifically, the authors found a nationwide incidence of male homosexuality of only 2.8 percent and of female homosexuality of only 1.4 percent. Of the 3,432 respondents only 192 of the men and 96 of the women were homosexual, so there was not a large enough sample from which to draw meaningful conclusions for some of the most important questions.

The following table clearly shows that the *typical* homosexual lifestyle—especially among males—differs dramatically from American averages. This difference means little by itself, but the fact that *these same differences are all critical risk factors for multiple medical illnesses* is highly significant. And because, as the authors of *Sex in America* note, people tend to have sex predominantly with people who share their lifestyles and preferences, the risks associated with homosexuality tend to be shared with other homosexuals. This is an obvious point, but it has important consequences when we consider disease.

Table 1 Key Parameters of Homosexual versus Heterosexual Behavior			
Parameter	Homosexual	Heterosexual	Ratio: Homo-sexual to Heterosexual
Total percent of population, males	2.8 percent	97.2 percent	1:35
Total percent of population, females	1.4 percent	98.6 percent	1:70
Average number of lifetime partners	50	4	12:1
Monogamous*	<2 percent	83 percent	41:1
Average number of partners last 12 months	8	1.2	7:1
Anal intercourse during last 12 months	65 percent (men)	9.5 percent (women)	13:1

*Defined here as 100 percent faithful to one's spouse or partner. Twenty-six percent of heterosexuals have only one lifetime partner (recall that approximately 50 percent of all marriages end in divorce, and someone who is remarried would not be included in this 26 percent, but would be in the 83 percent).

Therefore the risk of any single factor—say, anal intercourse—is amplified by the fact that it tends to be associated with other risk factors; the entire cluster of factors remaining typical of one group of people but not another. For this reason the authors of *Sex in America* also concluded that, although AIDS can be transmitted to anyone, in America it will likely remain a predominantly homosexual, IV-drug-abusing, and transfusion-related syndrome—with the female partners and their unborn children at risk as well. Heterosexuals *who do not abuse drugs* remain at relatively low risk because on average they are far less promiscuous and in general tend to have sex with people who are also far less promiscuous.

Risky Business

Two major risk factors listed in the table contribute to the disproportionately greater incidence of non-AIDS illnesses among (male) homosexuals: anal intercourse and the number of different partners. In other words, the sexual profile of the typical gay male is precisely the most dangerous one. The typical homosexual (needless to say there are exceptions) is a man who has frequent episodes of anal intercourse with other men, often with many different men. These episodes are 13 times more frequent than heterosexuals' acts of anal intercourse, with 12 times as many different partners as heterosexuals.

These statistics, it should be added, are quite conservative. The most rigorous single study—the Multicenter AIDS Cohort Study—recruited nearly five thousand homosexual men and found that:

> A significant majority of these men . . . (69–83 percent) reported having 50 or more lifetime sexual partners, and over 80 percent had engaged in receptive anal intercourse with at least some of their partners in the previous two years.[4]

One of the most carefully researched studies of the most stable homosexual pairs, *The Male Couple,* was researched and written by two authors who are themselves a homosexual couple—a psychiatrist and a psychologist. Its investigators found that of the 156 couples studied, only seven had maintained sexual fidelity; of the hundred couples that had been together for more than five years, none had been able to maintain sexual fidelity. The authors noted that "The expectation for outside sexual activity was the rule for male couples and the exception for heterosexuals."[5]

A 1981 study revealed that only 2 percent of homosexuals were monogamous or semi-monogamous—generously defined as ten or fewer lifetime partners.[6] And a 1978 study found that 43 percent of male homosexuals estimated having sex with five hundred or more different partners and 28 percent with a thousand or more different partners. Seventy-nine percent said that more than half of these partners were strangers and 70 percent said that more than half were men with whom they had sex only once.[7]

By contrast, the authors of *Sex in America* found that 90 percent of heterosexual women and more than 75 percent of heterosexual men have never engaged in extramarital sex.

With respect to AIDS, however, as well as to other semen-related conditions, we must introduce another factor that affects the amount of risk, namely condom use.

Table 2 Condom Use		
Parameter	Homosexual— Anal Intercourse	Heterosexual— All Types of Intercourse
Used a condom in past year	60 percent	35 percent

Not surprisingly, heterosexuals generally use condoms less frequently than do homosexuals. But among heterosexuals the risk of AIDS associated with the lack of condom use, while not entirely negligible, is so much lower than among homosexuals that the risk of not using a condom in heterosexual sex is vastly smaller than in homosexual sex. (Please note that this comment pertains *only* to AIDS, not to other sexually transmitted diseases.) This difference reflects the other factors discussed above: Most heterosexuals are in relatively monogamous relationships and engage in anal intercourse infrequently; many homosexuals are in relatively polygamous relationships and engage in anal intercourse frequently.

A most important further consideration is that, in spite of both the extraordinary risks of not using a condom and the decade-long education programs, approximately 40 percent of male homosexuals still never use condoms during anal intercourse. Many of the public pronouncements concerning these education programs trumpet their "success" in increasing the rate of condom use from near zero to 60 percent. But when dealing with an epidemic illness that is 100 percent fatal, anything shy of a near 100 percent success rate is a terrible failure from the perspective of public-health policy. The resistance to change of high-risk behavior is so great that a major study recently published in *Science* cautions that even a vaccine against AIDS is unlikely to eliminate the AIDS virus; indeed, it might actually increase its prevalence.[8]

Even apart from the risk of AIDS, failure to use a condom during male homosexual sex opens one to a marked suppression of the immune system by a cause unrelated to AIDS, probably related to sperm antibodies[9] or possibly to other, general "lifestyle" factors.[10]

And with respect to AIDS alone, yet another factor is pertinent—knowledge of one's own and one's partner's HIV status (infected or not infected) and how one acts in response. The best current estimates hold that about one out of a thousand adult Americans is now infected with HIV.[11] This is 0.1 percent of the adult population. Because roughly half the population is male and 2.8 percent of all males are homosexual, 1.4 percent of the adult population consists of homosexual males, which account for about 30 percent of all AIDS cases. Thus the likelihood of a randomly selected *heterosexual* man or woman being infected with AIDS is roughly 7 in 10,000 (0.07 percent).

But shockingly and frighteningly, yet consistent with the concentration of AIDS cases among high-risk populations, epidemiologists estimate that 30 percent of all twenty-year-old homosexual males will be HIV-positive or dead of AIDS by the time they are thirty.[12] This means that the incidence of AIDS among twenty- to thirty-year-old homosexual men is roughly 430 times greater than among the heterosexual population at large.[13]

It is also estimated that a single act of unprotected intercourse (not taking into account whether it is homosexual or heterosexual, anal or vaginal) with a known-to-be-infected male carries with it a transmission risk of roughly 1 in 500.[14] If we multiply this rough measure of the transmissibility of the AIDS virus by the average risk of encountering an HIV-positive heterosexual, this means that in the absence of any information about one's partner's HIV status, age, demographic group, and so on, a single act of heterosexual intercourse of any type carries with it an average risk of roughly 1 in 715,000 (calculated by 7 in 10,000 x 1 in 500 = 7 in 5,000,000). In fact it must be less, as acts of heterosexual intercourse are by far mostly vaginal, and the 1 in 500 transmissibility figure includes acts of anal intercourse as well. Of course, if the partner is a known IV-drug-abuser or prostitute, for example, the risk is much greater. But a single act of unprotected intercourse with a twenty- to thirty-year-old male homosexual carries with it a transmission risk of roughly 1 in 165.[15]

It is important under all circumstances to know or estimate the likelihood of one's partner being infected in a heterosexual encounter. But in homosexual encounters, this knowledge—and the willingness to act on it—is of life saving statistical importance. The sequence of life saving steps would include the following, for both partners:

1. Being tested for HIV
2. Knowing the test results
3. Communicating the test results to one's partner(s)
4. If infected, refraining from knowingly engaging in sex with an uninfected partner
5. If not infected, refraining from knowingly engaging in sex with an infected partner

But here, too, as with the degree of successful risk-reduction through avoiding unprotected anal intercourse, the insufficient regularity with which homosexuals take these steps is startling and grim.[16] Indeed, a body of opinion has recently arisen in the scientific literature arguing that the benefit (pleasure) of high-risk sex outweighs its risk (death).[17]

A Favored Activity

The correlation between male homosexuality and disease has been recognized for at least two thousand years. Thus the Apostle Paul, writing during the heyday of the Roman Empire when licentiousness was rampant, observed that "Men committed indecent acts with other men, and received in themselves [sometimes translated 'in their bodies'] the due penalty for their perversion."

Some claim, however, that the above problem is not with homosexuality, but with anal intercourse, and that to confound anal intercourse with (male) homosexuality is a deliberate ploy to tar homosexuals with something that is fundamentally different and irrelevant. Clearly, in some abstract sense, this is so. One could envision homosexual relationships in which anal intercourse plays no role. Perhaps there are a fair number of such relationships. One could also envision a widespread educational and cultural process reducing the significance of anal intercourse in gay male life to the same relatively minor level of importance that it plays in heterosexual life.

But is it realistic to claim that anal intercourse is *not* an essential part of gay male life—even if not for all gays? It has been throughout history, so this would be a very radical change indeed. And is it realistic to think that this specific behavior can be reduced in frequency to its level of incidence among heterosexuals? The research cited above, reflecting ten years of intense preventive measures, strongly suggests otherwise. Considering the risks involved, the continued practice of anal intercourse by some 80 percent of the male homosexual population[18] strongly suggests that this hypothetical approach is futile. Rather the research supports the tacit admission embedded in such centuries-old language as "sodomy"—that anal intercourse is a defining feature of male homosexuality.

Thus the authors of a major long-term study of 508 homosexual men in San Francisco report that even after extensive prevention programs, "non-monogamous individuals who in 1984 reported that unprotected anal intercourse was their favorite sexual activity were more likely to practice that behavior in 1988."[19]

The author of a Norwegian study examining this phenomenon notes:

> Safer sex is often experienced as emotionally colder, as expressions [sic] of distrust, and as a reminder of death. To receive the semen is traditionally valued as a commitment to the partner. Sexual acts compose a language of love and affection, and the protective measures destroy this language.[20]

The incidence and intractability of anal intercourse in a gay population, even in the face of illness or death, suggests its central, compulsive role in the lifestyle. The following research points more incisively to the central role of anal intercourse in male homosexuality:

> The core sample was a group of 106 men who had sex with other men before 1980. . . . The data . . . suggest that . . . the correct gen-itoerotic role distinction is not insertive vs. receptive behaviors, or even insertive vs. receptive anal intercourse, but receptive anal intercourse vs. all other behaviors.[21]

Dr. Charles Silverstein, author of the popular *The New Joy of Gay Sex,* presents a less scholarly and shockingly graphic description of this well-known dimension of gay male life. (Reader discretion is advised. The entire passage is provided in the notes.)

> As you become more sexually experienced, you will soon discover your preferred sexual activities and positions. You may find that you prefer getting f___ed no matter the time, place, partner or position. . . . When this happens, you have become a bottom, or bottom man. The name, of course, derives from the placement of the person being f___ed—i.e., on the bottom. . . . But we would be in error if we seemed to suggest that being a bottom is merely a matter of who f___s whom. It is, more importantly, a state of mind, a feeling one has about oneself in relationship to other men.[22]

Though not in every instance, in general male homosexuality and anal intercourse are inexorably intertwined.

Where Does the Road End?

Besides anal intercourse, another defining feature of homosexuality is the broad range of sexual appetites and behaviors that appear when people do not conform themselves to a code of behavior. Indeed, once people begin to "walk on the wild side," they have effectually broken one of society's strongest taboos. Other taboos then fall away easily and rapidly. For homosexual apologists, this feature of the gay lifestyle is not so much a mark of enslavement to sexuality as a sign of homosexuals' greater freedom from arbitrary and stifling social inhibitions, sexual and otherwise.

Keen observers of the gay scene—many gay themselves—have cogently argued that the gay lifestyle is not so much "homosexual" as "pansexual." And indeed, this observation suggests an important point: that there really may be no such thing as "homosexuality." There is rather mere "human sexuality," which in the "state of nature" is enormously diverse and polymorphous. Psychoanalysts have long argued the natural *bi*sexuality of human beings, but it would perhaps be more accurate to speak of natural *poly*sexuality. This protean potential of human sexuality may be constrained or it may be unconstrained.

What we call the "gay lifestyle" is in large measure a way of life constructed around *un*constrained sexuality. Thus it is more readily oriented toward sexual pleasure in all its many possible forms than is the "straight" lifestyle. Of course there are many heterosexuals who are oriented toward unconstrained sexual expression, but less commonly than among homosexuals. Instead of mirroring the boundaries and hedges of heterosexual marriage, the gay life comes much closer to displaying the innately multifaceted nature of human sexuality in its unconstrained state.

As Dennis Prager puts it:

> Human sexuality, especially male sexuality, is polymorphous, or utterly wild (far more so than animal sexuality). Men have had sex with women and with men; with little girls and with young boys; with a single partner and with and in large groups; with immediate family members; and with a variety of domesticated animals. They have achieved orgasm with inanimate objects such as leather, shoes and other pieces of clothing; through urinating and defecating on each other . . . ; by dressing in women's garments; by watching other human beings being tortured; by fondling children of either sex; by listening to a woman's disembodied voice (e.g., "phone sex"); and of course by looking at pictures of bodies or parts of bodies. There is little, animate or inanimate, that has not excited some men to orgasm.[23]

Thus in San Francisco a popular magazine is called, *Anything That Moves.*

"Intergenerational Intimacy"

Any discussion of pansexuality will lead quickly into a discussion of those forms of sexual expression that stand outside of even today's expansive boundaries of tolerance. Sadomasochists discuss the intricate variations of their sexual preferences on talk radio and on television; one may easily find partners for this and many other unconventional forms of sexuality in the personal advertisements of innumerable newspapers and magazines across the country. But the singular form of sexual expression for which we as a society continue to have little tolerance is adults having sex with children: pedophilia.

As sensitive as it may be to introduce the subject of pedophilia into a discussion of homosexuality, a full exploration of the pansexual nature of "the gay lifestyle" requires that we do, because when the constraints are loosened, they are likely to be loosened in this domain as well. It is important to preface this discussion, however, with a caveat. It is true (as we will document) that pedophilia is more common among homosexuals than among heterosexuals—and vastly more common among males, heterosexual or homosexual, than among females. But it is also true that the majority of homosexuals are not pedophiles.

Pedophilia *is* pertinent for two reasons: first, because it is statistically more closely associated with homosexuality than with heterosexuality; second—and more importantly—the dramatic shift of values that normalizes homosexuality must inevitably come to normalize all forms of sexuality. This is not a merely hypothetical argument. As the material that follows demonstrates, both here and abroad the normalization of homosexuality has been followed by a move to normalize all forms of sexuality, *pedophilia explicitly included,* and to lower the age of consent laws so as to make it legal as well.

My purpose here is not to warn against homosexuality on the grounds that homosexuals prey sexually on children—because the vast majority would not dream of such a thing (even if a vocal minority, as also their heterosexual counterparts, would). My purpose instead *is to warn against the general lifting of sexual con-*

straint, which the philosophy that undergirds gay activism necessarily promotes.

Recently *The Journal of Homosexuality,* a premier, broad-based, scientific[24] journal that addresses from an advocacy position all cultural, social-scientific, and historical issues pertaining to homosexuality, devoted a special issue almost exclusively to "the pedophilia debate." The editor of the journal, John DeCecco, also sits on the editorial board of *Paedika: The Journal of Paedophilia,* a Dutch publication that sponsors research on pedophilia, also for advocacy purposes.

This special issue reflects the substantial, influential, and growing segment of the homosexual community that neither hides nor condemns pedophilia. Rather they argue that pedophilia is an acceptable aspect of sexuality, *especially of homosexuality.* Indeed, the *San Francisco Sentinel,* a Bay Area gay-activist newspaper, published a piece arguing that pedophilia is central to the male homosexual life. Thus an advocacy group exists, the North American Man-Boy Love Association (NAMBLA), which actively promotes homosexual pedophilia as an acceptable alternative form of sex. Their contentions as to the naturalness, normalcy, unchangeability, and ubiquity of pedophilia mirror precisely the arguments used to support the naturalness, normalcy, and so on of homosexuality, as does their claim that the social condemnation of pedophilia is arbitrary and prejudicial.

Thus one author argues:

> Pedophilia is always considered by mainstream society as one form of sexual abuse of children. However, analysis of the personal accounts provided by pedophiles suggests that these experiences could be understood differently.[25]

Another states that:

> Contemporary concern over paedophilia and child sexual abuse usually rests upon uncritical and under-theorized conceptions of childhood sexualities. This article . . . outlines the "social-constructionist" alternative.[26]

And another author decries the constricted American view of pedophilia:

In recent years the general trend has been to label . . . intergenerational intimacy [as] "child sexual abuse. . . ." [This] has fostered a one-sided, simplistic picture. . . . Further research . . . would help us to understand the . . . possible benefits of intergenerational intimacy.[27]

Farther along than America in this process of radicalization, Holland has programs of psychotherapy that do not treat pedophilia itself as a problem, but rather the social difficulties that pedophilia is associated with. Like homosexual therapies in the United States, these facilitate adjustment to, not treatment of, pedophilia:

Male pedophiles are trained to talk effectively about common problems surrounding man-boy relationships. Counseling is based on the notion that the emotional, erotic and sexual attraction to boys per se does not need to be legitimized or modified.[28]

Sample results include:

Sixteen males were treated for sexual identity conflicts. For eight of them this ended in a positive self-labeling as pedophile. . . . Twenty males were . . . counseled how to handle their relationships with boys. Several modalities of interpersonal interaction in man-boy relationships are proposed. . . . [29]

Activists are aware of the adverse effects on the gay-rights movement that could result if people perceived any degree of routine association between homosexuality and pedophilia—as well as other forms of sexual expression that continued to be thought of as "deviant." They have denied this association by focusing instead on the (true) fact that—in absolute numbers—heterosexuals commit more child molestation than homosexuals.

But careful studies show that pedophilia is far more common among homosexuals than heterosexuals. The greater absolute number of heterosexual cases reflects the fact that heterosexual males outnumber homosexual males by approximately thirty-six to one. Heterosexual child molestation cases outnumber homosexual cases by only eleven to one, implying that pedophilia is more than three times more common among homosexuals.[30]

In spite of the potential political fallout, another author in the special issue argues that:

> The issue of man/boy love has intersected the gay movement since the late nineteenth century, with the rise of the first gay rights movement in Germany. In the United States, as the gay movement has retreated from its vision of sexual freedom for all in favor of integration into existing social and political structures, it has sought to marginalize cross-generational love as a "non-gay" issue. The two movements continue to overlap, amid signs of mutual support as well as tension—a state of affairs that also characterizes their interrelationship in other countries.[31]

As discussed above, the American Psychiatric Association normalized homosexuality in two steps: At first it only removed from its list of disorders homosexuality that was "ego-syntonic," comfortable and acceptable to the individual, leaving only "ego-dystonic"—unwanted—homosexuality as a disorder; later, it removed "ego-dystonic" homosexuality as well.

In a step strikingly reminiscent of what occurred in the seventies with respect to homosexuality, the 1994 edition of the DSM (DSM-IV) has quietly altered its long-standing definitions of all the "paraphilias" (sexual perversions). Now, in order for an individual to be considered to have a paraphilia—these include sadomasochism, voyeurism, exhibitionism, and among others, pedophilia—the DSM requires that in addition to having or even acting on his impulses, his "fantasies, sexual urges or behaviors" must "cause clinically significant distress or impairment in social, occupational or other important areas of functioning."[32] In other words, a man who routinely and compulsively has sex with children, and does so without the pangs of conscience and without impairing his functioning otherwise is not necessarily a pedophile and in need of treatment. Only the man who suffers because of his impulses is a pedophile requiring treatment.

The committee responsible for this change claims that their intent was not to "normalize" the paraphilias, but to give diagnosticians greater latitude in making the diagnosis. Nonetheless, that will certainly be its effect, as it was with respect to homosexuality. Race Bannon, coordinator of the "DSM Project" for a major sadomasochistic organization, notes that "For the first time, the leather S&M fetish community's style of sexuality is no longer considered necessarily pathological. . . . The new DSM-IV language means that we will no longer be considered sick unless our erotic play causes 'clinically significant distress or impairment.'" Bannon praised "kinky-friendly psychotherapeutic professionals" who lobbied for the changed criteria.[33] Gay activism has long made known its objections to the "pathologizing" of any form of sexual freedom.

Does it seem absurd to think that the taboo against pedophilia, too, will soon come under broad social attack? It is beginning already. The May 8, 1995, issue of the widely respected magazine *The New Republic* published a review of the movie "Chickenhawk." The movie's title is slang for pedophiles who hunt for children to have sex with. The author downplays the seriousness of NAMBLA (whose publications document locales in the Third World where children may be molested free of legal consequence); denies that the idea of mutual consent between boys as young as twelve and older men is necessarily unreasonable; and considers the pedophile perspective on age-of-consent laws to be "plausibly on the continuum of, say, a defense of children's legal autonomy." She notes: "There is some bravery in NAMBLA members keeping all their activities above board. . . . After all, it is still heresy to consider the possibility of the legitimacy of their feelings."[34]

Breaking Down the Wrong Barriers

We now turn to an examination of the reasons why male homosexual behavior is so dangerous as to produce the medical syndromes alluded to previously.

Even if condoms are used, anal intercourse is harmful primarily to the "receptive" partner. Because the rectal sphincter is designed to stretch only minimally, penile-anal thrusting can damage it severely. The introduction of larger items, as in the relatively common practice of "fisting," causes even worse damage. Thus gay males have a disproportionate incidence of acute rectal trauma as well as of rectal incontinence (the inability to control the passing of feces)[35] and anal cancer.[36]

Furthermore, anal intercourse, penile or otherwise, traumatizes the soft tissues of the rectal lining. These tissues are meant to accommodate the relatively soft fecal mass as it is prepared for expulsion by the slow contractions of the bowel and are nowhere near as sturdy as vaginal tissue. As a consequence, the lining of the rectum is almost always traumatized to some degree by any act of anal intercourse. Even in the absence of major trauma, minor or microscopic tears in the rectal lining allow for immediate contamination and the entry of germs into the bloodstream. Although relatively monogamous gay couples are at lower risk for AIDS, they tend to engage in unprotected anal intercourse more frequently than do highly polygamous single homosexuals.[37] As a result, they are at higher risk for non-AIDS conditions—if all other factors are equal, which is usually not the case because of the clustering of risk factors.

Because receptive anal intercourse is so much more frequent among homosexual men than among women, the dangers of this kind of sex are amplified among homosexuals. Furthermore, comparable tears in the vagina are not only less frequent because of the relative toughness of the vaginal lining, but the environment of the vagina is vastly cleaner than that of the rectum. Indeed, we are designed with a nearly impenetrable barrier between the bloodstream and the extraordinarily toxic and infectious contents of the bowel. Anal intercourse creates a breach in this barrier for the receptive partner, whether or not the insertive partner is wearing a condom.

As a result, homosexual men are disproportionately vulnerable to a host of serious and sometimes fatal infections caused by the entry of feces into the bloodstream. These include hepatitis B and the cluster of otherwise rare conditions, such as shigellosis and Giardia lamblia infection, which together have been known as the "Gay Bowel Syndrome." A major review article summarizes:

> Because of their larger numbers of sexual partners and sexual practices such as anilingus and anal intercourse, homosexual men are at particularly high risk of acquiring hepatitis B, giardiasis, amebiasis, shigellosis, campylobacteriosis, and anorectal infections with Neisseria gonorrhoeae, Chlamydia trachomatis, Treponema pallidum, herpes simplex virus, and human papilloma viruses.[38]

Another review article classifies the conditions homosexually active men encounter into four general groups:

> Classical sexually transmitted diseases (gonorrhea, infections with Chlamydia trachomatis, syphilis, herpes simplex infections, genital warts, pubic lice, scabies); enteric diseases (infections with Shigella species, Campylobacter jejuni, Entamoeba histolytica, Giardia lamblia, hepatitis A, hepatitis B, hepatitis non-A, non-B, and cytomegalovirus); trauma (fecal incontinence, hemorrhoids, anal fissure, foreign bodies, rectosigmoid tears, allergic proctitis, penile edema, chemical sinusitis, inhaled nitrite burns, and sexual assault of the male patient); and the acquired immunodeficiency syndrome (AIDS).[39]

How Great a Risk?

Gay activists have long sought to obscure the powerful statistical connection between AIDS and homosexuality by emphasizing the truth that the virus itself does not "seek" homosexuals, can infect anyone, and has already infected many other people. In such places as sub-Saharan Africa, where promiscuity is the cultural norm across much of the populations with a high intersection of homosexual and nonhomosexual circles, the virus has spread uniformly. In fact, the majority of people in the United States with AIDS are *not* homosexual—reflecting the fact that male homosexuals consist of such a small fraction of the population. Nonetheless, when most people think of homosexuality as risky, they think of AIDS because the statistical association is so self-evident.

Most people also have a fairly accurate impression about the effect of AIDS on the life span of individuals who suffer from it—they know that people with AIDS die disproportionately and terrifyingly young. But what about non-AIDS illnesses associated with homosexual practices? What effect do these have on life span? Here the average person is apt to presume that, apart from AIDS, the effect is minor. Certainly this is the message implied by the media, by publicly funded condom-distribution programs, and by sex education courses that emphasize "safer" sex with condoms. Even arguments that condemn an overemphasis on condoms *because of their failure rate*—breakage, slippage, improper use, the unwillingness of people to use them—tend to reinforce the notion that the major problem with homosexual practice could be solved with more perfect "protection" of a technical sort. But as we have seen, AIDS is far from the only risk associated with homosexual practices, and many of the other risks are inherent to anal intercourse itself, regardless of condom use. What are these risks, and how do they compare with the risk of AIDS?

In April 1993 three researchers presented a paper to the Eastern Psychological Association in which they analyzed the age of death for nearly seven thousand homosexuals and heterosexuals by obituary notices in a large number of gay and a smaller number of large non-gay newspapers.[40] They found that the gay male life span, even *apart from AIDS* and *with* a long-term partner, is significantly shorter than that of married men in general *by more than three decades*. AIDS further shortens the life span of homosexual men by more than 7 percent.

Because of the researcher's rough and ready methodology, these findings have to be considered preliminary. Their data for heterosexuals and for gay men with AIDS, however, are very close to similar data from other, more reliable and replicated sources, as are the differences found between the life spans of married and unmarried men and women. These findings should serve as a warning about the potential seriousness of the problems associated with homosexuality and the extent of the risk that people may be taking in entering into this way of life.

In the current political atmosphere the whole notion that homosexuality is dangerous must appear inflammatory. But consider for a moment: If these findings are true (and while the life span research has only limited value, the more rigorous medical findings are incontrovertible), how could anyone with a heart for the sufferings of others stand by in silence? Given the risks, the only ethical approach to assisting men and women who consider themselves homosexual—and especially youngsters still wrestling with their emerging sexual feelings—must at the least include a willingness to help them change not only the "high-risk behaviors" but the homosexual "orientation" itself. There is considerable evidence, presented in a later chapter, that homo-sexuality is actually no more difficult to change than the high-risk behaviors themselves.

4

Finding a Needle
in the Ocean

As you will recall, there are three disputed propositions at the heart of the debate over homosexuality today:

1. Homosexuality is normal
2. Homosexuality is innate, or inherited
3. Homosexuality is irreversible

In this chapter and the three that follow we will address the second point: "Is homosexuality innate and inherited?" As we will see, the very way the question has been framed—by gay activism and its media promoters—contributes seriously to our confusion.

Defining Our Terms

Let us start by defining our terms. When we analyze and discuss the *causes* of a given behavioral trait, we find that each cause belongs to one or more of the following categories:

Genetic

Genetic traits are those (like eye color, for example) that are coded for us by *genes*. We can think of each human gene as a book that provides a complex set of instructions for the synthesis of a single protein. These proteins are then responsible for forming and operating everything else in the body.

The entire collection of genes that provides codes for a human is vast. Therefore it is divided into twenty-three pairs of matched, physically distinct structures called *chromosomes*. We can think of them as matching libraries that contain and catalogue two copies of every required "book" (gene) in a specific order that does not vary from person to person. Chromosome libraries exist in pairs because each person actually has two instructional genes for every protein, receiving one of every gene from his mother and another from his father. The unvarying order in which the genes are catalogued allows each one of the millions and millions of genes to be matched to its proper companion during reproduction.

Any genetic trait inherited from our parents may be:

1. Expressed, as when the gene that codes for it is dominant and we have inherited the gene from at least one parent (brown eyes; brown is dominant); or as when the gene that codes for it is recessive and we have inherited the same gene from both parents (blue eyes; blue is recessive).
2. Not expressed, as when the gene that codes for it is recessive and we have inherited that gene from only one parent (brown eyes; blue is recessive and therefore not expressed).
3. Partially expressed, as when—whether the gene that codes for it is dominant or recessive—one or more other genes or other factors influences its expression. We may or may not have some or all of these other genes, or we may be only partially exposed to these other factors (green eyes).

Genetic traits are truly and directly *inherited*. All traits with which we are born tend to be put into this category, sometimes incorrectly, such as those that are innate but not genetic.

Understanding *behavioral* traits influenced by genetics becomes more complex. Unlike simple traits, such as eye color, that are close to being programmed by a single gene, most behavioral traits with a genetic background are programmed by multiple genes. Because these genes are rarely inherited together, their possible forms of expression fall into a complex spectrum. Behavioral traits that are influenced by genetics are therefore never either/or conditions.

Innate

Some traits may be merely *innate*, meaning the individual is born with them. But innate traits may be:

1. Genetic, as outlined above; or
2. Not genetic, but caused by *intrauterine influences*. These are traits (such as the degree to which a fetus develops masculine or feminine sexual characteristics) that are influenced by various aspects of the environment in the womb. Hormones, infections, exercise, general health, the ingestion of licit or illicit drugs, and many other variables influence this environment. Thus one may be born with a trait that is innate, but not *genetic*.

Familial

Other causes of traits may be *familial*, meaning that they tend to be shared by members of the same family. Familial traits may be:

1. Genetic. Because they have the same parents, brothers and sisters are more likely to share a high percentage of similar genes than would unrelated individuals.
2. Innate, but not genetic. Sharing the same mother, certain typical factors may remain constant or similar for all children born to her. Examples include the effect of her dietary habits on her unborn children, the fact that she smokes, or her general health.

3. Not innate, but environmental. To an extent greater than
   between individuals from different families, individuals
   raised in the same family share a similar environment.
   These include the physical, emotional, and moral influences. Thus family members may share some traits that are
   neither genetic nor innate but that are nonetheless transmitted from one generation to the next by influence.

Biological

Another term that may be used to describe a trait is *biological*.
A biological trait is rooted in an organism's physiology, rather
than its psychology. With respect to behavioral traits, this distinction suggests a dichotomy comparable to the difference
between "hardware" and "software" in the domain of computer
science. Biological traits may be:

1. Genetic.
2. Innate but not genetic.
3. Environmental and familial but not innate (for example,
   the effect of a virus that has taken root among the members
   of a household).
4. Environmental and not familial and possibly innate but
   maybe not (for example, the effect of a toxin in the environment at large, depending on whether its baleful influence is felt pre- or postnatally).

Environmental

Additionally, the cause of a trait may be purely *environmental*
but not biological—at least insofar as we do not attend to the biological dimension. Examples include the influence on behavior
of the values, standards, habits, economic status, and so on, of a
family or society.

Direct versus Indirect

Finally, any of these causes may be *direct* or *indirect*. That is,
the cause may:

1. Lead directly to the trait. Whether we are speaking of genetic or nongenetic, innate or noninnate, biological or nonbiological influences, the cause may directly produce the trait itself, as when genes cause blue eyes or when smoke causes a cough.
2. Lead indirectly to the trait. Because of what the influence causes directly, the individual finds it desirable to choose a particular trait. This is seen, for example, when tall athletic individuals become basketball players or when short athletic people become jockeys.

Furthermore, all of these causes may combine and influence one another in highly interdependent ways, mutually influencing each other throughout a lifetime. Behavioral traits, as opposed to simple, single-gene physiologic traits such as eye color, always interact in this way.

In summary, the question concerning all behavioral traits, such as homosexuality, cannot be "Is *such and such* genetic?" Rather we must ask, "To what extent, respectively, is *such and such* genetic and nongenetic, innate and noninnate, familial and non-familial, environmentally determined and not, direct and indirect? In the course of development, when do which influences dominate and how do their interactions affect one another?" We need to keep this sobering caution in mind as we clarify what medical science has and has not learned about the subject of homosexuality.

Unanswered Questions

Most mental states, normal or not, have long been presumed to be of *psychological* origin because we have not been able to understand the biology. We simply did not have the information or skills to intervene in a purported disease of the brain whose primary manifestations were psychological. But neuroscience research techniques have proliferated. We now can dissect out at least some of the specific mechanisms—down to the level of molecules—that play a role in many conditions previously thought to be purely psychological. Although this research has already produced many dramatic benefits, we are far from having a precise blueprint of the various causes of *any* psychiatric condition.

Demonstrating that any behavioral state—let alone one so complex, diverse in its manifestations, and nuanced as homosexuality—is not only biological but *genetic* is well beyond our present research capacity. One psychiatric researcher, who was tired of the overblown claims of people trying to label everything as "genetic," calculated what would be required to confirm a behavioral trait as genetic. He:

> projected that if the trait was 50 percent heritable and each family in the [initial] study had ten members (4 grandparents, 2 parents and 4 children), detecting one of the genes would require studying ... 2000 people. Replicating that finding would require studying ... another 8000 people. To find and confirm each additional gene (for a polygenic trait), researchers would need to go through the whole business again. "Suddenly you're talking about tens of thousands of people and years of work and millions of dollars."[1]

No study of homosexuality has come even remotely close to these requirements.

In the case of schizophrenia, for instance, such research efforts have only now begun to yield somewhat reliable results—after over forty years of effort. But even after so much research, the major questions—What causes schizophrenia? How does this illness affect the nervous system? What environmental cofactors are critical to its appearance? What interventions might be curative?—remain almost *entirely* unanswered.

Different studies claim to show anywhere from 40 to 90 percent heritability for schizophrenia. Researchers have made numerous claims to have found a meaningful "genetic linkage" to a particular chromosome, only being forced to retract them in every case.[2] The vastly more complex problem of finding the genes themselves or the specific DNA base-pairs among the millions on the chromosome has been compared to finding a needle, not in a haystack, but in the ocean.

What We Can Say

In the case of homosexuality, only a handful of barely adequate studies on a small number of people have been conducted in the past few years. We will explore these more fully in the chapters that follow. But first it is important to lay out three important limitations that are already beginning to emerge from this research. All are quite consistent with what we already know about the biological and genetic bases of other conditions.

First, like all complex behavioral and mental states, homosexuality is multifactorial. It is neither exclusively biological nor exclusively psychological, but results from an as-yet-difficult-to-quantitate mixture of genetic factors, intrauterine influences (some innate to the mother and thus present in every pregnancy, and others incidental to a given pregnancy), postnatal environment (such as parental, sibling, and cultural behavior), and a complex series of *repeatedly reinforced* choices occurring at critical phases in development.

Second, male and female homosexuality are probably different conditions that arise from a different composite of influences. Nonetheless, they have some similarities.

Third, "homosexuality" is very poorly defined. Our use of this one term creates the false impression of a uniform "gay" or "lesbian" condition and culture. It obscures the reality that what we are studying is a complex set of variable mental, emotional, and behavioral states that are caused by differing proportions of numerous influences. Indeed, one of the chief characteristics of the gay lifestyle is its efflorescence of styles and types of sexuality. Thus many of the more careful researchers in the field—usually nonactivist—refer to *"homosexualities."*

Do Brain Differences Make a Difference?

The belief that homosexuality is "genetic" tends to translate into a more positive attitude toward it. Gay activists know this and research studies confirm it:

To measure the relationship between beliefs about the determinants of homosexual orientation and attitudes toward homosexuals, we asked 745 respondents in four societies about their beliefs concerning the origins of homosexual orientation. Analysis indicated that subjects who believed that homosexuals are "born that way" held significantly more positive attitudes toward homosexuals than subjects who believed that homosexuals "choose to be that way" and/or "learn to be that way."[3]

Similarly:

105 ... subjects ... were exposed to one of three treatment conditions. Subjects in the experimental group read a summary article of current research emphasizing a biological component of homosexual orientation. Subjects in one control group read a summary article of research focusing on the absence of hormonal differences between homosexual and heterosexual men. Subjects in another control group were not exposed to either article. All subjects completed the Index of Attitudes Toward Homosexuals. As predicted, subjects in the experimental group had significantly lower[4] scores than subjects in the control groups.[5]

This "public relations" effect has precipitated a recent media outpouring on the biology and genetics of homosexuality. Starting in 1991, media all across the country have trumpeted the discovery of a series of supposed brain differences between homosexuals and heterosexuals. Commentators claim that these findings will halt any remaining uncertainty that homosexuality is either a choice or a consequence of factors in upbringing. In this light, to continue supporting anything less than full acceptance of homosexual behavior would be proof positive of prejudicial hatred.

The outpouring began in August of 1991 when a San Francisco neuroanatomist, Simon LeVay, published an article in *Science*. It reported his finding that a localized cluster (a "nucleus") of cells in the brains of "homosexual" men was twice as large by volume on autopsy as in "heterosexual" men.[6] ("Homosexual" and "heterosexual" are in quotations because in this study the definitions of each were extremely imprecise, nor was there any way of verifying sexual orientation as the subjects were dead.)

But this was not the first such discovery. One year before a group reported in *Brain Research* that they had found a similar difference—in both volume *and* number of cells—in a different brain nucleus.[7] The media, however, did not report this first study because *Brain Research*, unlike *Science*, is read only by neuroscientists. And in contrast to journalists, the neuroscientists understood the research—and its limitations—and refrained from grand pronouncements.

The specifics of these findings are not as important as realizing that unless group differences are dramatic, individual studies of such differences mean almost nothing. It would take hundreds, perhaps thousands, of such studies before meaningful trends emerge. Thus it is wrong for the media, or parties with vested interests, to argue the significance of something so complex as human nature on the basis of one or a handful of findings and then derive public policy implications.

Furthermore, even if such brain differences were convincingly demonstrated to be present, their significance would be on a par with the discovery that athletes have bigger muscles than nonathletes. For though a genetic tendency toward larger muscles may make it easier to become an athlete (and therefore such an individual will more likely be one), becoming an athlete will certainly give one bigger muscles. One researcher comments: "The brain's neural networks reconfigure themselves in response to certain experiences. One fascinating NIH study found that in people reading Braille after becoming blind, the area of the brain controlling the reading finger grew larger."[8]

Press accounts, in contrast, are often written so as to lead one to assume that brain differences must be innate and unchangeable—especially differences in the number of cells as contrasted with the simple volume occupied by a collection of cells. We tend to think of mind as "software" and brain as "hardware," the former plastic and changeable, the latter fixed at birth. We have used this analogy already to good advantage.

But the analogy breaks down at a certain point. Various processes go on throughout life: the selective death of brain cells in response to training or trauma, the establishment of new connections between cells, dramatic increases or decreases in the "thickness" of connections between cells as a result of learning, the loss of interneuronal connections through "pruning." Very unlike our modern computers, the brain's software *is* its hardware.

We know from animal studies that early experience and especially traumatic experience—this especially applies to the childhood histories of many homosexuals—alters the brain and body in measurable ways. Thus infant monkeys who are repeatedly and traumatically separated from their mothers suffer dramatic alterations in both blood chemistry and brain function.[9]

One major theory about why some people become depressed and others do not holds that under conditions of early trauma, a genetically based susceptibility to stress creates a greater likelihood of intense stress-responses later in life.[10] This "vulnerability" is represented physiologically as actual alterations in the brain. And because what is experienced as "stressful" depends on one's subjective interpretation of events, the brains in individuals with the same genetically determined biology may respond differently. One may demonstrate no brain changes; another may demonstrate very significant changes.[11]

Thus the editor of *Nature* commented on the LeVay research:

> Plainly, the neural correlates of genetically determined gender are plastic at a sufficiently early stage. . . . Plastic structures in the hypothalamus [might] allow . . . the consequences of early sexual arousal to be made permanent.[12]

And of course all this presumes that the research itself was of high quality. But two prominent geneticists, Paul Billings and Jonathan Beckwith, writing in *Technology Review* (published at the Massachusetts Institute of Technology) write: LeVay "could not really be certain about his subject's sexual preferences, since they were dead."[13] His "research design and subject sample did not allow others to determine whether it was sexual behavior, drug use, or disease history that was correlated with the observed differences among the subjects' brains."[14] LeVay's very method of defining homosexuality was very likely to "create inaccurate or inconsistent study groups."[15]

Because all human behavior is related in some way to genes, we can nonetheless guess that one day higher quality research *will* find genetic factors that correlate to homosexuality. But remember, one of the fundamental principles of research is that correlation does not necessarily imply causation. With respect to whatever genetic or biological factors are correlated to homosexuality we will need to be very careful to understand what they mean and, indeed, how limited the implications really are.

5

Two of a Kind

W hen we say that "we will find genetic factors that correlate to homosexuality," can we make this more precise? We can by exploring a powerful avenue of research into the genetics of behavioral conditions, namely twin studies.

The basic strategy of this research is fourfold. First is to consider the differing proportions of identical genes between two nonrelatives (very little similarity); then between two biological siblings with the same parents (some similarity); between two fraternal—"dizygotic" twins (same degree of similarity as non-twin siblings); and between two identical—"monozygotic"— twins (one sperm, one egg: 100 percent similarity).

Second is to compare the degree of *genetic* similarity between members of a given pair to the degree of *behavioral* similarity between members of a given pair.

Third, if possible, is to control for similar environmental influences acting on both twins by examining *only those twins who were both adopted away after birth into different families.* But *no meaningfully large studies of homosexuality in adopted-away twins have yet been performed.* All studies to date of sufficient size have examined twins raised in the same household, thus confounding any potential genetic factors with uncontrolled environmental ones.

It is extraordinarily difficult to locate both members of a pair of identical twins where at least one has the substantiating trait, where the trait is relatively uncommon, where both have been adopted away, and where both are willing to participate in a study. And so when adoption studies are not possible the fourth strategy applies: to examine the differences between pairs of twins and pairs of nontwin biological siblings and pairs of adopted siblings, hoping to control for the influence of family environment.

The best of the twin studies to date have been of this latter sort. Unfortunately, such studies are extremely difficult to perform well—none to date have been. Even when they are performed well, there are so many "links" in the chain of causal reasoning that leads to a conclusion that the conclusions are rarely solid. Indeed, in such studies different scientists routinely arrive at diametrically opposed conclusions from the same data set. Sometimes the very same scientist who conducted the research is forced to present contradictory conclusions. That is just what has happened in the twin studies on homosexuality.

If "homosexuality is genetic," as activists and their media supporters repeatedly claim, the *concordance rate* between identical twins—that is, the incidence of the two twins either both being homosexual or both being heterosexual—will be 100 percent. There would *never* be a *discordant* pair—a pair with one homosexual twin and one heterosexual twin. When we say that "eye color is genetically determined," this is what we mean. That's why identical twins *always* have the same eye color. If we were to find genuinely identical twins with different eye colors we would be forced to conclude that although genetics may exert an influence on eye color, it does not determine it. Eye color would be dependent upon some additional factor as well. An example of such a characteristic that is influenced but not determined by genetics is weight. And that is why identical twins are similar in weight, but not identical, especially after many years have gone by.

The Recent Few Studies

In the small number of recent identical twin studies that have been touted as proving "homosexuality is genetic," concordance rates turn out to be considerably less than 100 percent—less than 50 percent, in fact—even though all the sizable studies to date have examined only twins that have not been adopted away after birth. (In fact, the only study of adopted-away twins, which had a very small sample size, showed a concordance rate of zero.) This means that some proportion of the rate of concordance—which is anyway smaller than anticipated—is itself caused not by genes but by something else.

Recall that twin studies on non-adopted-away twins are very difficult to do well and are fraught with uncertainty even under the best of circumstances. For important conclusions about human nature—indeed life-changing ones—to be drawn from such studies is perilous to be sure. One would want a great deal of consistent, confirming research to be in place before committing oneself to any proposition (such as "homosexuality is genetic") that runs counter to both long-standing tradition and the accumulated clinical experience of the preceding eighty years. But in fact, there have only been three useful twin studies that examine the genetics of homosexuality. One study was published in the *British Journal of Psychiatry* and two in the American *Archives of General Psychiatry*.[1] The latter two were performed at Northwestern University by researchers who, as cited above, acknowledge that they are motivated by social-policy considerations to demonstrate that homosexuality is predominantly genetic, and to counter claims that it is largely environmental.

The press has taken these Northwestern articles as further "proof" that "homosexuality is genetic." But as we will see, the results of this research by activists with an acknowledged political agenda actually demonstrate no such thing. Indeed, the researchers themselves admit disappointedly—even apart from methodological problems that tend to weaken their findings altogether—that taken at face value their work demonstrated a far smaller genetic contribution to both male and female homosexuality than they sought.

Here, in brief, are the findings of the major twin studies.

Two by Bailey and Pillard

In one study by J. Michael Bailey and Richard C. Pillard, "A Genetic Study of Male Sexual Orientation," the authors found a concordance rate for homosexuality of approximately 50 percent among identical twins who were raised together where one twin identified himself as homosexual.[2] That is, half of the pairs of twins were both homosexual and half were composed of one homosexual and one heterosexual. If accurate, this finding alone argues for the enormous importance of *nongenetic* factors influencing homosexuality, because, as noted above, in order for something to be genetically *determined,* as opposed to merely *influenced,* the genetic heritability would need to approach 100 percent.

The concordance rate for *non*identical (dizygotic) twins was only 22 percent. This finding—the difference in concordance rates between types of twins—is consistent with the hypothesis that heritable factors influence some component of homosexuality—but not only with that hypothesis. It may also be because *identical* twins reared together share more significant environmental influences than *nonidentical* twins reared together. Thus, Theodore Lidz, a prominent psychiatric researcher at Yale University (and longtime critic of methodological weaknesses in the various adoption studies of schizophrenia) noted about Bailey and Pillard's findings: "Because the twins grow up with mirror images of themselves that can magnify their so-called narcissism, they are apt to be raised more similarly than DZ [dizygotic] twins."[3] Of course, the results are also consistent with the possibility that *both* factors have some degree of influence.

The finding of a potential genetic contribution to homosexuality is further weakened by the following five considerations:

First, the extreme similarity of environment in which twins— especially identical twins—are raised confounds the authors' claim that genetic factors were the determining influence in the finding that both twins were homosexual, when this was the case.

Second, the homosexual twin was recruited into the study by an advertisement in a homosexual magazine. A common problem in these kinds of studies is that concordant twins tend, in general, to respond to research advertisements more frequently than twins where one is a homosexual and the other a heterosexual. Furthermore, readers of homosexual magazines are in no way representative of homosexuals.

Third, sexual orientation of the nonrespondent twin or other sibling was mostly assessed *by report of the respondent,* which is an extraordinarily imprecise research approach. Here, too, many researchers have commented on the obvious potential for bias.

Fourth, when many genes are similar (in the case of identical twins all one hundred thousand genes and every single one of the many millions of DNA base pairs are absolutely identical), there is a so-called nonlinear or nonadditive dimension of genetic influence on a trait. In brief, this means that the sheer degree of similarity of twins can exaggerate the concordance rate, artificially inflating what appears to be the genetic contribution. This concept is discussed in somewhat greater detail below.

The results of the study of female homosexuality by the same authors, "Heritable Factors Influence Sexual Orientation in Women," are quite similar to the previous study. Again, the monozygotic twin pairs showed concordance rates of less than 50 percent—48 percent, counting bisexual twins as homosexual.

Furthermore, as noted above, in the only available study of monozygotic female twins *raised apart* the authors found a concordance rate for homosexuality of 0 percent.[4] That is, *none* of the co-twins were homosexual—but the sample size was so small that, if the genetic contribution to female homosexuality is actually as great as 50 percent, there would be one chance in eight that this finding was a fluke.

Fifth, Bailey and Pillard predicted that twin-pairs in which both were homosexual would report an early onset of "childhood gender nonconformity." They reasoned that a genetic determination of homosexuality would lead to its early onset in some form because if the cause is genetic, it must be present from birth. This would explain why many homosexuals recall such an early onset of being or feeling "different."

But just as the twin studies failed to demonstrate genetic causation, their twin pairs in which both were homosexual experienced "childhood gender nonconformity" no more frequently than did the single homosexual in a discordant pair. Although an early recollection of "being different" is thus common among homosexuals, the evidence suggests that this sense of difference is in fact *not* caused by something genetic. The authors report their unanticipated finding but do not draw the appropriate conclusion—namely that it weighs against their hypothesis of genetic causation.

One by King and McDonald

In Britain, Michael King and Elizabeth McDonald in "Homosexuals Who Are Twins: A Study of 46 Probands," found concordance/discordance rates for homosexuality that were lower than those found by Bailey and Pillard, but with a similar difference between monozygotic and dizygotic pairs (25 percent versus 12 percent). But unlike Bailey and Pillard, they conclude that:

> Discordance for sexual orientation in the monozygotic pairs confirmed that genetic factors are insufficient explanation for the development of sexual orientation.

Similarly, William Byne and Bruce Parsons, Columbia University researchers whose summary review of the research on homosexuality will be discussed in chapter 7, comment:

> ... what is most intriguing about the studies of Bailey and Pillard and of King and McDonald is the large proportion of monozygotic twins who were discordant for homosexuality despite sharing not only their genes but also their prenatal and familial environments. The large proportion of discordant pairs underscores our ignorance of the factors that are involved, and the manner in which they interact, in the emergence of sexual orientation.[5]

Recognizing that the evidence pointed more strongly toward the importance of nongenetic than genetic factors, King and McDonald also sought to discover what such nongenetic factors might be. They unexpectedly found, "a relatively high likelihood of sexual relations occurring with same-sex co-twins at some time, *particularly in monozygotic pairs*."[6] (One out of five same-sex twins had sex with one another.)

This finding hints at a principle that turns out to be quite important in understanding the development of any embedded pattern of behavior, namely the role of early experience and *subsequent repetition*. The fact that *identical* twins in particular tended to have sexual relations with each other also suggests that the experience of twinhood (a developmental peculiarity) itself can cause an increase in homosexuality as a factor in its own right, apart from the shared genes.

King and McDonald's study incidentally supports what investigators had actually noted as long ago as 1981: the role of childhood *incest* in fostering later homosexuality. As in the case of the obviously related role of childhood trauma,[7] incest is currently being downplayed or ignored as a significant determinant of homosexuality because it is a clear-cut environmental, not genetic, factor.

Contested Conclusions

Paul Billings and Jonathan Beckwith, cited in the previous chapter regarding LeVay, criticize the quality of much of this recent genetics research as well. In *Technology Review*, they write:

> In the nineteenth century . . ."phrenologists" claimed they could predict aspects of an individual's personality, such as sexuality, intelligence and criminal tendencies, merely by examining the skull's structure. . . . A look at recent studies seeking a genetic basis for homosexuality suggests that many of the problems of the past have recurred. We may be in for a new molecular phrenology, rather than true scientific progress and insight into behavior.[8]

Billings and Beckwith are specifically concerned about the biased conclusion Bailey and Pillard draw from their research, even if the concordance rates they reported were accepted as representative. Thus they note:

> While the authors interpreted their findings as evidence for a genetic basis for homosexuality, we think that the data in fact provide strong evidence for the influence of the environment.

More specifically:

> On average, both non-identical twins and non-twin siblings share 50 percent of their genes. If homosexuality were a genetic trait, the pairs in these groups should be homosexual a similar percentage of the time. They certainly should [both] be homosexual [if one is] more often than adopted siblings. But Bailey and Pillard's data do not fit those predictions.[9]

Here is what these geneticists are criticizing: In Bailey and Pillard's first twin study on male homosexuality the authors found a concordance rate for nontwin brothers of 9.2 percent. That is, roughly only one out of ten male homosexuals had brothers who were also homosexual. All the other brothers were heterosexual.[10] The concordance rate for nonidentical twins ("dizygotic") was two-and-a-half-times greater than this (22 percent or roughly one in five). But nonidentical twins have exactly the same degree of genetic similarity as nontwin brothers, because even though they develop at the same time in the womb, they start out from two different eggs fertilized from two different sperm, just as in the case of brothers who develop at different times. If we accept their data as meaningful—again, the very small sample size renders these findings quite weak—this finding points to the powerful influence of similar environmental factors found especially between twins, even nonidentical twins.

Note that when we compare the first two categories—identical twins versus nonidentical twins (genetic similarity of 100 percent versus genetic similarity of 50 percent) the concordance rates differ by a factor of 2.36.[11] But when we compare the second two categories—nonidentical twins versus nontwin broth-

Table 3		
Concordance Rates for Homosexuality in Brothers		
Type of brother (pair)	**Degree of genetic similarity (percent shared genes)**	**Concordance rate for homosexuality**
Identical twins (from one egg and one sperm)	100 percent	52 percent
Nonidentical twins (from two eggs and two sperms)	50 percent	22 percent
Nontwins (also from two eggs and two sperms)	50 percent	9 percent

Table 4		
No Difference in Comparative Concordance Rates		
Categories being compared	**Difference in degree of genetic similarity**	**Difference in concordance rates**
Identical twins versus nonidentical twins	Twice the number of identical genes	2.36
Nonidentical twins versus nontwins	No difference in number of identical genes	2.39

ers (genetic similarity of 50 percent is the *same* for both), the concordance rates *still* differ, by about the same amount 2.39.[12] Therefore either the finding that monozygotic twins are more likely to be concordant for homosexuality is less significant than environmental factors or it is of little significance altogether because of the sample size.

The importance of environment is further suggested by the fact that the concordance rate for biologic brothers with 50 percent genetic similarity (9.2 percent) and *nonbiologic adoptive* brothers with no significant genetic similarity (11 percent) were essentially identical. In their first study, Bailey and Pillard dismissed these puzzling findings as mere sampling errors—a function of the small sample size. In their later study on female homosexuality, the authors admit that the comparative concordance "rates for DZ co-twins and adoptive sisters did not differ significantly."[13]

When Two Plus Two Equals Ten

In the beginning of the chapter we alluded to yet another confounding factor in the twin study data that is neither precisely genetic nor environmental. None of these researchers has considered this factor—that because of their internal interaction with each other as well as with the environment, genetic influences do not simply add together. A high degree of genetic similarity can produce an outcome that mimics high heritability. It is as though under these conditions two plus two instead of making four, makes ten.

This nonadditivity is strongly suggested by the fact that the difference in concordance rates for homosexuality among identical twins is so much greater than for nonidentical twins, nontwin siblings, and nonrelatives. In the words of one behavioral researcher:

> The standard assumption of behavioral genetics is that traits run in families and that pairs of relatives are similar *in proportion* to their genetic resemblance. Yet there is evidence of traits for which the monozygotic correlation is high, indicating a genetic basis, when the dizygotic correlation *and other first degree relatives are insignificant.*[14]

Politically Expedient Science

Byne and Parsons comment on the discrepancy between Bailey and Pillard's data and their conclusions in the following manner:

> The increased concordance for homosexuality among the identical twins could be entirely accounted for by the increased similarity of their developmental experiences. In my opinion, the major finding of that study is that 48 percent of identical [female] twins who were reared together [and where at least one was homosexual] were discordant for sexual orientation.[15]

Similarly, Charles Mann, author of the lead article on genes and behavior in a special issue of *Science,* points to:

> the growing understanding that the interaction of genes and environment is much more complicated than the simple "vio-

lence genes" and "intelligence genes" touted in the popular press. Indeed, renewed appreciation of environmental factors is one of the chief effects of the increased belief in genetics' effects on behavior. "Research into heritability is the best demonstration I know of the importance of the environment," says Robert Plomin, director of the Center for Developmental and Health Genetics at Pennsylvania State University. The same data that show the effects of genes also point to the enormous influence of non-genetic factors.[16]

There is a story behind Byne and Parsons's comment, an all-too-typical illustration of the politicization and propagandizing that surrounds and distorts this subject. John Horgan, a senior writer for *Scientific American*, notes that two reviewers of the Byne and Parsons article accused Byne of having a "right-wing agenda." But in fact Byne has refused to address conservative groups who support the ban on homosexuals in the military because he himself is opposed to such a ban, supports "gay rights," believes that "homosexuality, whatever its cause, is not a 'choice,'"[17] and when asked was preparing a major article for the activist publication *Journal of Homosexuality*.[18] As Byne told the *Wall Street Journal*, "I'm told my criticism is not politically correct. . . . What they're saying therefore is that I should subjugate scientific rigor to political expediency."[19]

After examining the very few studies conducted on twins to determine a genetic influence on homosexuality, we can clearly see the bias that has existed not only in the research and execution of the studies, but in the interpretation and reporting of the findings.

6

A Cluster of Influences

I f homosexuality is not entirely genetic in origin, where does it come from? In exploring claims that homosexuality is genetic, the Columbia University researchers—Byne and Parsons—emphasize an extremely important point. In their own model, which they describe as "a complex mosaic of biologic, psychological and social/cultural factors,"

> . . . genetic factors can be conceptualized as indirectly influencing the development of sexual orientation without supposing that they either directly influence or determine sexual orientation per se. Similarly, one could imagine that prenatal hormones influence particular personality dimensions or temperamental traits, which in turn influence the emergence of sexual orientation.[1]

This last point concerning personality dimensions and traits is not an obvious one. The popular accounts of the biology of homosexuality uniformly avoid it. It is much easier to ask the meaningless, but subtly bias-inducing, sound bite question, "Isn't homosexuality genetic?" than to ask the much more realistic— but frustratingly complex—question, "To what degree is homosexuality (or any other behavioral trait) genetic and nongenetic,

innate and acquired, familial and nonfamilial, intrauterine-influ-
enced and extrauterine-influenced, affected by the environment
and independent of the environment, responsive to social cues
and unresponsive to these cues, and when and in what sequence
do these various influences emerge to generate their effects and
how do they interact with one another; and after we have put
these all together, how much is left over to attribute to choice,
repetition, and habit?"

One way to simplify and begin to approach at least part of this
very complex question is to note that, as we will explore in this
chapter, the genetic contribution to a given trait, behavioral or
otherwise, need not be direct; actually, when the trait is behavioral, the genetic contribution is usually *not* direct. In other words
genes often contribute to some other phenomenon that in turn
predisposes an individual to a given behavioral response.

An obvious example of this principle is basketball. No genes
exist that code for becoming a basketball player. But some genes
code for height and the elements of athleticism, such as quick
reflexes, favorable bone structure, height-to-weight ratio, mus-
cle strength and refresh rate, metabolism and energy efficiency,
and so on. Many such traits have racial distributions (which
makes the genetic connection evident), resulting in more men
of Bantu or Nordic stock (being taller) playing on professional
basketball teams than men of Pygmy or Appenzeller Swiss stock
(being shorter).

Someone born with a favorable (for basketball) combination
of height and athleticism is in no way genetically programmed
or forced to become a basketball player. These qualities, however, certainly facilitate that choice. As a consequence *the choice
to play basketball has a clear genetic component,* most evident in
the high heritability of height. Were scientists to undertake a
study of basketball-playing comparable to the studies that have
been done to date on the genetics of homosexuality, they would
find a much higher degree of apparent genetic influence. In summary, the strong genetic correlation does not mean that people
are forced to play basketball.

In an effort to counter much of the nonsense being promoted
nowadays in the press, the editors of *Science,* one of the premier

scientific research journals in the world, devoted a recent issue almost exclusively to "Genetics and Behavior." In the opening editorial, Torsten Wiesel, president of Rockefeller University, one of the leading international centers for genetics research, comments:

> The operations of the brain result from a balance between inputs from heredity and environment—nature and nurture—and this balance should also be reflected in research into the biological basis of behavior.[2]

Fight, Flight, or Drink

Before we examine these nongenetic influences on homosexuality we will look at the classic example of a similar phenomenon in the area of behavioral *problems*—alcoholism—and at some of the still tentative theories that are emerging to explain it.

It has long seemed that problem drinking has a genetic component.[3] Even after social and family influences have been taken into account, evidence remains that when a gene or set of genes are present in an individual or family there is a much higher risk for serious alcoholism. Furthermore, certain national and transnational gene pools (Irish, Scandinavian, Northern European in general) seem to be predisposed to alcoholism.

It turns out that the genetic makeup of Northern Europeans tends to stimulate an enhanced fight/flight response to a given stressor. The fight/flight response is an almost universal mechanism in animals; its nervous-system and chemical pathways are well-understood, and it is fundamentally a relatively simple process. Thus it is a good candidate for behavioral genetics research. Because their nervous systems are more "high strung," Northern Europeans react (on average) with an intense nervous system arousal to a perceived threat.[4] This is experienced subjectively as anxiety; alcohol is the original anti-anxiety agent.[5] People with this predisposition to intense anxiety responses are therefore more likely to find their way into greater alcohol use[6] because for them alcohol gives a greater degree of emotional relief than it does to the more laid-back "Mediterranean" type.[7]

Why might northerners have this disposition in greater proportion than southerners? The answer may lie not so much in the distinction between "north" and "south" or even "warm" and "cold" as in "Polar" versus "Equatorial." At issue is not the location itself but the differing cycles of light found close to and far from the equator. The harsher climate and reduced intensity of light found nearer the poles is not only associated with differences in body build and skin color but also with differences in the nervous system. The northern races have adapted to the harshness of their environment by developing more easily stimulated nervous systems than have the equatorial races.

In its pure form, this genetic type not only reacts subjectively, but also responds to stresses with intense physiologic responses such as increased heart rate and blood pressure, skin flushing, perspiring palms and soles, and so on. All these responses, subjective and physiologic, are mediated by the nervous system. Alcohol calms all of these by soothing the underlying nerves.[8]

Thus genetics strongly predisposes individuals toward alcoholism. And yet no genes specifically code for it. This seeming contradiction can be explained by the fact that some genes do code for the anxiety (fight/flight) response and under certain circumstances an especially intense response is adaptive. Those who carry such genes may be more likely to develop alcoholism than those who do not carry them. This does not mean, however, that alcoholism is itself directly genetic, natural, and a good thing (as activists claim of homosexuality)—nor that it is an illness in the strict sense of the word.

Of interest in comparing alcoholism to homosexuality is the fact that alcoholism is estimated to be between 50 percent and 60 percent heritable; homosexuality to be less than 50 percent even by activists, probably considerably less. This even greater risk for alcoholism does not lead to the conclusion, however, that alcoholics are not responsible for controlling, changing, or stopping the behavior. We should also note that early enthusiasm over alcoholism being linked to a gene that coded for the D_2 brain receptor proved to be as unfounded as all the other claims for behavioral genes.[9]

The analogy between, on the one side alcoholism and anxiety, and on the other homosexuality and some unknown intermediate trait, may be more than an analogy. For there is evidence that unusually intense anxiety responses are also associated with an increased tendency toward homosexuality. We will explore this possibility in greater detail in chapter 12 on treatment. For now, let us return to the recent research finding that homosexuality is mostly nongenetic.

What Is Normal?

The nongenetic factors that can influence the development of a behavioral pattern fall into five categories:

1. Intrauterine (prenatal) effects, such as the hormonal milieu (environment)
2. Extrauterine (postnatal) physical effects, such as trauma, viruses
3. Extrauterine "symbolic" effects, such as familial interactions, education
4. Extrauterine experience, such as the reinforcing effect of the repetition of behaviors
5. Choice

The lack of 100 percent similarity for sexual orientation of identical twins shows that the nongenetic factor(s) influencing homosexuality cannot be exclusively intrauterine. If they were, then the concordance rate for homosexuality would *still* be nearly 100 percent—because identical twins share the same prenatal environment. In fact, if there are any intrauterine effects, they would contribute to the 50 percent *apparently genetic* effect (concordance) that was described earlier.[10] Once these factors were identified and segregated out, the actual remaining genetic effect would be that much smaller.

But a vast body of research has emerged over the past decade that demonstrates how biological factors powerfully influence brain development. These factors therefore affect cognitive, emotional, and behavioral expression. Even small differences between individuals will result in statistically significant average differences between two large populations. But unexpectedly the most powerful effects on male versus female brain development do not occur directly from male versus female genetic differences, but indirectly by way of the maternal intrauterine hormonal milieu.

Put simply, the hormonal environment in which a baby develops is a balance of androgenic (male) and estrogenic (female) hormones. A genetically male baby signals the mother to generate a more heavily androgenic environment than does a female baby. The particular hormonal balance then determines whether the baby will develop typically male or typically female genitalia, bodily characteristics, and brain structures.

Because the maternal hormonal response varies, the masculinizing or feminizing influences are different for each developing baby. The resulting degree of masculinity or femininity is therefore a "bimodal" spectrum, having two somewhat overlapping bell-shaped curves with two separate average masculine and average feminine peaks. The curve does not show a strict dimorphism, that is, two perfectly distinct masculine or feminine spikes. This variable degree of masculine and feminine influences and results is especially so with respect to the brain. The secondary sexual characteristics (genitalia), however, take only two distinct forms, except in unusual circumstances.

Thus, in spite of the obvious general differences between men and women, a great many men have somewhat feminine physical features and a great many women have somewhat masculine features, all well within normal. Many women are actually more masculine than many men and many men are actually more feminine than many women; yet all these, too, are well within normal. Furthermore, some women are more masculine than the *average* man and some men are more feminine than the *average* woman, and these are also entirely normal. And yet it remains true that on average (which is to say, as a group), women are more feminine than men and men are more masculine than women. These differences should therefore show up in the *average* differences in behavior between the two groups.

To a less obvious but significant degree, these bimodal statistical differences (clustering about two somewhat separated points) extend to brain development as well. Thus the cognitive, emotional, and behavioral expressions of the male and female classes as a whole are affected to various degrees by masculine and feminine influences. Again there is much overlap. Therefore many normal men have rather more feminine behavioral characteristics and many normal women have rather more masculine behavioral characteristics. Little of this overlap, however, predicts homsexuality.

From time to time the chemical signals get crossed. The maternal hormonal milieu of, for example, a genetically male baby will then be very far to the feminine end of the spectrum. In these unfortunate cases, her genitalia, body type, brain, and behavior will develop physically as a normal-appearing female. She remains, however, genetically male and therefore infertile. We conventionally refer to such individuals according to their body type and not their genetic makeup, because they will live according to the former.

In other cases, the milieu is ambiguous. Regardless of the baby's genetic structure, the baby will emerge a hermaphrodite—one with variable proportions of male and female features. The parents will be obliged to choose a sex for their child to be defined surgically, which may or may not correspond to the genetic background.

The dramatic influence of the intrauterine environment on behavior is demonstrated well by a recent article in *Science* on spotted hyenas. In this species, maternal androgens are so elevated during pregnancy—in a twist, especially so when the fetus is female—that adult females are heavier and more aggressive than males, have fused vaginal labia that form a "scrotum," and have a clitoris that is fully erectile and as large as the male penis. As we might guess, the females in this species dominate the males. In this case genetics affects behavior not only directly on a species-wide basis, but also indirectly through hormonal mechanisms.

The typically masculine aggression that is "hardwired" into this animal (into both males and females, but especially females) is biologically determined and fierce. Unlike other carnivores, infant hyenas are born with fully erupted and efficient teeth, open eyes with fully functioning rapid tracking and focusing mechanisms, and the capability for perfectly coordinated adult-type motor action. Within an hour of birth a newborn pup can mount a full-fledged "bite-shake attack" in which she bites and grips the neck of her opponent, shaking it violently to death.

The unfortunate opponent in this case is usually the same-sex twin, especially when the twins are two females. In most cases, the first female twin to emerge will kill the second one just as she begins to emerge from the birth canal—before she can even leave the amniotic sac. Not surprisingly, the chief characteristic of members of this species is their extraordinary skill and efficiency as predatory killers.[11] They can even successfully chase off lions from a kill, failing only when the lion is an unusually experienced and dominant male. (Incidentally, however, female hyenas are not obligatorily "lesbian.")

Clearly an important determinant of at least certain behavioral predispositions is the hormonal environment. Thus some proportion of what appears to be genetic in homosexual behavior may actually be a nongenetic intrauterine effect on the parts of the brain that influence sexual behavior. This hypothesis is supported by the fact that although uncommon, homosexuality is not terribly rare in the population, the best estimate being 2.8 percent for males and 1.4 percent for females. Lower reproductive rates among homosexuals should lead to its diminishment and eventual elimination from the population—unless some relatively constant nongenetic factor(s) continued to influence its reappearance.

But if homosexuality were simply caused by a greater than average, but still normal, degree of opposing-sex influence of the prenatal environment, we would expect male homosexuals, for example, to have "female" brain structures. Many of the studies to date on the biology of homosexuality have looked for such a feminization of homosexuals' brains, but nothing convincing has been found. Indeed, LeVay and other researchers point out that a certain nucleus in the brain, the "Sexually Dimorphic Nucleus" (SDN), takes two distinct forms in men and women. This nucleus, however, is found in its typically masculine form in male homosexuals.

Nonetheless, two different sets of findings point to possible developmentally based hormonal influences on homosexuality. First is some evidence that male homosexuals perform more like average females than like average males on certain qualitative measures of mental functioning. This difference in performance may eventually be correlated to typical male-female brain differences. And yet it would still say nothing about cause, as changes in the brain could be caused by repetitively reinforced behavioral differences between homosexuals and heterosexuals.

Second are studies on females that indicate a correlation between a "masculinizing" intrauterine environment and subsequent female bisexuality, homosexuality, or transsexualism. Transsexuals are individuals whose internal self-image is opposite to their sex: A male transsexual feels himself to be truly female, a "woman trapped in a man's body"; a female transsexual to be a "man trapped in a woman's body." Transsexuals often seek and obtain surgical alteration of their sex. Because the subjective experience and objective marks of transsexualism are so different than of homosexuality, however, such studies that posit a common origin for both homosexuality and transsexualism raise more questions than they answer.

In 1991 Günter Dörner, one of the major researchers of the prenatal hormonal influences on sexuality, published a review of the studies on the subject to date. He concluded that a prenatal abnormality in hormones—perhaps caused by undue stress to the mother—will cause later homosexual behavior. In his words:

> The higher the androgen levels during brain organization, caused by genetic and/or environmental factors, the higher is the biological predisposition to bi- and homosexuality or even transsexualism in females and the lower it is in males. Adrenal androgen excess, leading to heterotypical sexual orientation and/or gender role behavior in genetic females, can be caused by 21-hydroxylase deficiency, especially when associated with prenatal stress. . . . Testicular androgen deficiency in prenatal life, giving rise to heterotypical sexual orientation and/or gender role behavior in

genetic males, may be induced by prenatal stress and/or maternal or fetal genetic alterations.[12]

But these conclusions have been vigorously disputed.[13] For one thing, as should now be clear, a "biological predisposition to bi- and homosexuality" is a dramatically different conclusion than to describe (within the same paragraph) "adrenal androgen excess [as] *leading* to heterotypical sexual orientation." Furthermore, no hormonal difference has ever been discovered between homosexuals and heterosexuals (as is dramatically the case between males and females) no matter how exquisitely sensitive the test.[14] In the words of Byne and Parsons: "Data pertaining to possible neurochemical differences between homosexual and heterosexual individuals are lacking."[15]

Other Prenatal Influences

At Harvard in 1974 the great behavioral neurologist Norman Geschwind and his colleague Ronald Galaburda first proposed the idea that homosexuality might be an intrauterine developmental abnormality that is not necessarily hormonal in nature. Geschwind and Galaburda had already hypothesized, and others have since confirmed, that at least one cause of left-handedness is an abnormal autoimmune effect during pregnancy. For reasons unknown, the baby's or mother's immune system responds to certain tissues in the developing brain as though they were foreign, attacking and destroying them. But Geschwind and Galaburda also noted, along with many other observers, that left-handedness appeared to be more common among male homosexuals than among heterosexuals. They therefore hypothesized that the same autoimmune problem might be responsible for both.[16]

In 1991 one research group concluded that although left-handedness seemed to be associated with autoimmune abnormalities, male homosexuality was not. The last part of their conclusion rested on their failure to find an increased incidence of left-handedness in the population of the homosexuals they studied.[17] But other researchers have confirmed this increased incidence in both men and women.[18] Thus the possibility that a homosexual disposition may at least partly be the consequence of a developmental autoimmune abnormality remains open.

Too Many People in the Room

If homosexuality were in fact directly genetic, and thus present in some form from birth (and before), it would likely be associated with an early onset of some form of "homosexual identity." But this presents an implicit conundrum, for homosexuality is associated with far lower childbearing rates than is heterosexuality. At present, and for the past thirty years, the childbearing rate for the United States as a whole has hovered around 1.05 children per adult. But 1.05 happens also to be the minimum "replacement" rate.

Because the total American rate is an average of the rate for both heterosexuals and homosexuals, the homosexual rate must therefore be considerably lower than the replacement rate. To whatever extent that homosexuality is significantly and directly genetic—and thus homosexuals would mostly discover their "orientation" prior to marriage—its presence in the population would shrink from one generation to the next. Unless it was continuously "redeveloped" by some nonheritable cause or causes, intrauterine or otherwise, it would eventually disappear:

> . . . one would expect that the role of a major gene in male homosexual orientation to be limited because of the strong selective pressures against such a gene. It is unlikely that a major gene underlying such a common trait could persist over time without an extraordinary counterbalancing mechanism.[19]

The fact that the incidence of homosexuality does not appear to be declining—a point the activists emphasize—is thus itself an argument *against* its being *directly* genetically determined. This argument would not hold if genes that merely indirectly increased the likelihood of homosexuality were directly associated with some other trait that enhanced survival and reproduction.

All of these human traits—a tendency to anxiety, stress-responsivity, the likelihood of alcoholism, hormonal dispositions in the mother, hormonal signals from the fetus to the mother, and many others—will have some degree of genetic background. And all may influence the likelihood of later homosexuality. It is not clear how much effect might be directly genetic and how much is indirect. Nor is it clear how many intervening levels of interaction are present between gene and behavior. Once again we need to remind ourselves that the discovery of a correlation between a gene or genes and a behavior is without significant meaning.

The Role of the Family

One of the most consistent findings from the studies of homosexuality is that a familial factor—or factors—strongly influences later sexual behavior. The more recent twin studies of homosexuality grew directly out of earlier ones that repeatedly confirmed an unequivocal family influence. In its decision that homosexuality was not an illness, the APA ignored nearly eighty years worth of psychoanalytic and psychotherapeutic observation. The gist of these practitioners' observations is consistent with what more rigorous scientific data demonstrates (even the biased studies such as by Bailey and Pillard), namely that the family environment plays a critical role in the development of homosexuality.

What did the psychoanalysts learn that activists want us to forget? That in the lives of their homosexual patients there was unusually often an emotional mismatch between the child and same-sex parent (such as a father who subtly or overtly rejects a son who has many "feminine" traits); or an emotional mismatch between the child and the opposite sex parent; or sexual abuse of a child by either the same sex or opposite sex parent; and most often the rejection of a child by same-sex peers.

Many excellent psychoanalytic and psychotherapeutic studies describe the complex interactions among these and other factors. Although these studies do not identify or describe any innate components that influence these environmental factors, they generate likely hypotheses to be further tested about the environmental influences on homosexuality evident in the genetics research.

Childhood Trauma

Besides the influence of the family, various other theories of homosexuality have evolved out of the extensive clinical experience of psychoanalysts and psychotherapists. It is not my purpose to provide or critique a detailed survey of these various theories; rather, my scientific purpose is served by demonstrating that the question regarding the precise causes of homosexuality remains open.

Nonetheless we will look at the "soft" consensus that has emerged over the years within the clinical community about how homosexuality occurs and changes. This consensus concerns a number of developmental events and sequences that lead to the habitual use of anxiety-reducing, self-soothing behaviors, including sexual deviations, promiscuity, homosexuality, and many other activities. Quite often an individual will use more than one such outlet. Thus, for example, homosexuality is commonly associated with both promiscuity and alcoholism or drug use. These activities all have a transiently soothing effect and the tendency to become first habitual, then compulsive, and finally addictive.

The developmental events and sequences that give rise to these later problems, though different from case to case, nonetheless share certain general features. These may be lumped together under the heading "psychic trauma." A typical clinical vignette reads:

> two clinical phenomena . . . are frequently related in analytic practice, namely sexual deviancy and inhibition in creative or intellectual work. The analysands in question seek psychoanalytic help not for their sexual acts and object-choices but because of blockage in their professional activities. In the author's opinion the roots of both sexual deviancy and creativity may often be traced back to early psychic trauma. The sexual "solution" and the creative activity both represent ways of attempting to overcome the traumatic situation of infancy. These propositions are illustrated by

the case of an author who sought help because her writing was completely blocked and because her homosexual love-relations caused tension and concern. The sudden death of her father when she was fifteen months old and her mother's disturbed way of handling the tragic situation were decisive factors in both the patient's sexual and professional life.[20]

"Psychic trauma" is a subtle concept that needs explaining. For one, actual physical trauma, including sexual abuse, may well be the source of psychic trauma. In the specific case of homosexuality it often appears to be the source. Nonetheless, actual physical trauma does not have to occur to cause psychic trauma. Also, individuals differ in their innate susceptibility to be traumatized. Thus, a severe, life-changing trauma for one individual may have little effect in another; conversely, what most outside observers rate as a trivial event could seriously wound someone with a particular disposition.

And so when we think of "trauma" we are apt to conceptualize it *objectively*, as a measurable outer event. This kind of trauma lends itself to quantitative research. One example is the studies that have found a disproportionate extent of sexual abuse in the childhoods of adult homosexuals.[21]

But psychic trauma is actually a purely subjective experience. The link between psychic trauma and measurable external influences can vary from tight and obvious to loose and invisible. Parental behavior, for example, can range from being, as many unprejudiced observers would agree, "bad" to being "good," while still being poorly matched to the needs of the child through no fault of the parent.

Thus "inner oriented" approaches to the concept of "psychic trauma" or "wounding"—whether secular (meaning psychoanalytic) or spiritual—provide a necessary additional perspective. For practical reasons, however, this perspective will remain almost invisible to rigorous scientific methods.

The kinds of traumas that can result in disturbed behavior are many and varied. Two specific traumas are most commonly associated with homosexuality.

The first is the trauma caused by the child's subjective experience of the same-sex parent's lack of availability, rejection, or even harsh verbal, physical, or sexual attack. By objective standards, the parent himself or herself may or may not be described in these terms. Rather the child's subjective experience of the parent creates the effect. This may give rise to the child's profound longing for love from that parent, a longing that he or she will likely enact in later relations with peers of the same sex. This longing may also become sexualized—that is, linked to the distress-relieving capacity of orgasm.

The results of a study by George Rekers reflect this:

> Significantly fewer male role models were found in the family backgrounds of the severely gender-disturbed boys as compared to the mild-to-moderately gender-disturbed boys. Male childhood gender disturbance was also found to be correlated with a high incidence of psychiatric problems in both the mothers and fathers and with atypical patterns of the boys' involvement with their mothers and fathers. . . . [22]

The second is the trauma caused by the child's subjective experience of the opposite-sex parent's lack of availability, rejection, or even harsh verbal, physical, or sexual attack. This may give rise to the child's fear of that parent, which will likely show itself later as a heightened wariness and avoidance of opposite-sex relations.

We must add a caution, however. Although these kinds of trauma are unusually common in the childhoods of homosexuals, they are not universal. And in many cases other, less typical traumas *are* present. This reflects the inherent complexity of homosexuality, a complexity stemming from the interactive or multiple genetic, intrauterine, environmental, family, social, psychological, and habitual influences on the course of development. Thus even common, quite general disturbances in family life, such as parental separation, are associated with a measurably increased incidence of homosexuality. Such general disturbances are more readily quantitated than the "inner" experience of "psychic trauma." A different study by Rekers reflects this:

> 56 boys diagnosed with gender disturbance, ages 3 to 18 yr. (mean age 8.4 yr.), were classified according to family structure. The proportion of gender-disturbed subjects separated from one or both parents (66 percent) was significantly higher than the 35 percent to 48 percent separated from one or both parents in comparable US general population statistics.[23]

Other possible causes of psychic trauma abound; thus the literature is filled with case studies that show many different kinds of childhood backgrounds. This diversity of experience does not mean that *all* possible childhood experiences lead to homosexuality and therefore that none do. It reflects, rather, that *the compulsive pursuit of pleasure (of all sorts) is the most common human response to distress.*

Clearly, a major factor that influences the final outcome of any developmental process is the partially innately determined, partially learned sensitivity of individuals to their environment. This affects the degree of distress they experience in response to it.

Rekers gives a sound general overview of the origins of homosexuality:

> At the present time, we may tentatively conclude that the main source for gender and sexual behavior deviance is found in social learning and psychological developmental variables . . . although we should recognize that there remains the theoretical possibility that biological abnormalities could contribute a potential vulnerability factor in some indirect way.[24]

7

The Gay Gene?

On July 15, 1993, National Public Radio reported a new study in *Science* due to be released the next day.[1] The tenor of the report was to celebrate the so-called discovery of the gene that causes homosexuality. Near the end, the necessary caveats were quickly added, but most laymen would have turned off the radio thinking that homosexuality is caused by a gene. But is there such a "gay gene"? The discussion in the preceding chapters should help us put the most publicly trumpeted scientific research on genetics and homosexuality into its proper, limited perspective.

In response to this research, the *Wall Street Journal* likewise headlined their report the next day, "Research Points Toward a Gay Gene."[2] A subheading of the *Journal* article stated "Normal Variation," leaving the casual reader with the impression that the research led to this conclusion. It did not, nor could it have. Indeed, the subhead merely alluded to nothing more than the researchers' own personal, unsubstantiated *opinions* that homosexuality, as they put it, "is a normal variant of human behavior." Even the *New York Times*, in its more moderate front-page article, "Report Suggests Homosexuality Is Linked to Genes" noted that researchers warned against overinterpreting the work, "or in taking it to mean anything as simplistic as that the 'gay gene' had been found."

At the end of the *Wall Street Journal* article, at the bottom of the last paragraph on the last page deep within the paper, a prominent geneticist was quoted for his reactions to the research. He observed that "the gene . . . may be involved in something other than sexual behavior. For example, it may be that the supposed gene is only 'associated' with homosexuality, rather than a 'cause' of it." This rather cryptic comment would be difficult to understand without the needed background information. Yet it is the most critical distinction in the entire article.

In the study the media was trumpeting, Dean Hamer and his colleagues had performed a new kind of behavioral genetics study now becoming widespread—the so-called "linkage study." Researchers identify a behavioral trait that runs in a family and is correlated to a chromosomal variant found in the genetic material of that family.

Insignificant Statistics

The authors of the Hamer study discovered that *in a small number of families the maternal uncles of homosexual men—but no other relatives—were disproportionately homosexual.* Because women have two X and no Y chromosomes (XX), while men have one X and one Y (XY), this finding seems to suggest that if a heritable factor contributes to *male* homosexuality it would have to be on the so called "X chromosome."

This is because mothers of male homosexuals would carry the gene on one of their X chromosomes but it would not be expressed in these mothers themselves. The lack of expression would either be caused by their having a second, normal X chromosome or because the specific trait in question would not express itself in females even if they carried two of its genes. Remember that male homosexuality and female homosexuality are not likely to be the same phenomenon.

The uncles of the homosexual men (their *mothers'* brothers) would be more likely to carry but also to express the gene because, like their sisters, they could have received an affected X chromosome from *their* mothers. (But as males, they would lack a second, "normal" X chromosome to compensate for the "abnormal" one.)

After finding a family sample in which the appearance of homosexuality seemed to follow a pattern of mother-son inheritance, the authors then examined the X chromosomes of the family members. The normal, multibanded appearance of the X chromosome is well-known. What they looked for was some variation in its typical banding pattern specific to this family, and especially to its homosexual males and their mothers. Such a variation was indeed found. The chromosome consists of some one hundred genes; the variation was found on the region known as q28 (Xq28, since it is the X chromosome).

To make the case that a gene or genes even *influence* male homosexual behavior several conditions must be met. The study must have been conducted with adequate care and its statistical assumptions must be valid. The variation in the chromosome must be present in most male homosexuals—not just in those male homosexuals whose families demonstrate a maternal-uncle pattern of male homosexuality. Or it must be present at least in many other families that demonstrate such a pattern. And the inheritance pattern itself must hold up when a larger family sample is examined. (Recall that to confirm the genetic background of a trait linked to but a single gene would require eight thousand individuals.)[3] If all these conditions were met, however, they would still not even remotely come close to the claim that "homosexuality is genetic"—for all the reasons discussed previously.

As it is, the Hamer study is seriously flawed. Four months after its publication in *Science*, a critical commentary appeared in the same publication. It took issue with the many assumptions and questionable use of statistics that underlie Hamer's conclusions, but not with his research methods and raw data, which met acceptable standards for linkage studies. Genetics researchers from Yale, Columbia, and Louisiana State Universities noted that:

Much of the discussion of the finding [by Hamer et al.] has focused on its social and political ramifications. In contrast our goal is to discuss the scientific evidence and to highlight inconsistencies that suggest that this finding should be interpreted cautiously. . . .

[The study's] results are not consistent with any genetic model. . . . Neither of these differences [between homosexuality in maternal versus paternal uncles or cousins] is statistically significant. . . . Small sample sizes make these data compatible with a range of possible genetic and environmental hypotheses. . . .

The hallmark characteristic of an X-linked trait is no male-to-male transmission. Because few homosexual men tend to have children, a study of male homosexual orientation will reveal few opportunities for male-to-male transmission, giving the appearance of X-linkage. In this context, examining the rate of homosexual orientation in the fathers of homosexual men is not meaningful. In the study by Hamer et al., there were only six sons of homosexual males, clearly an inadequate number for a meaningful test. Hamer et al. also present four pedigrees [four different families] as being consistent with X-linkage. Only one homosexual male in these four pedigrees has a child (a daughter). In the context of trait-associated lack of male reproduction, such pedigrees would be relatively easy to obtain. Thus the family data presented [by Hamer et al.] present no consistent support for the subsequent linkage results.

. . . Such studies must be scrutinized carefully and dispassionately.[4]

In response, Hamer responded as follows:

We did not say that Xq28 "underlies" sexuality, only that it contributes to it in some families. Nor have we said that Xq28 represents a "major" gene, only that its influence is statistically detectable in the population that we studied.[5]

Nonetheless, regarding the failure of their most important "findings" to achieve even statistical significance, they themselves agree—in a rather awkward circumlocution—that:

the question of the appropriate significance level to apply to a non-Mendelian [that is, polygenic, multiple factors influencing expression] trait such as sexual orientation is problematic.[6]

In lay terms, this translates as, "we have no idea how significant this finding is or indeed whether it is significant at all." And in a recent edition of *Science* devoted to behavioral genetics Hamer stated—to his fellow scientists—that:

Complex behavioral traits are the product of multiple genetic and environmental antecedents, with "environment" meaning not only the social environment but also such factors as the "flux of hormones during development, whether you were lying on your right or left side in the womb and a whole parade of other things. . . ." The relationships among genes and environment probably have a somewhat different effect on someone in Salt Lake City than if that person were growing up in New York City.[7] [For example, conservatives in Utah are less likely to become homosexual than liberals in New York.]

Needless to say, none of the disclaimers were given equal time in the press as the original overblown claims. And worse yet, Hamer himself testified as a sworn expert witness to the Colorado court that heard a motion to void the state's "Proposition 2," which would have disallowed sexual behavior as a legitimate basis for formal minority status on a par with race. On the basis of his research Hamer testified that he was "99.5 percent certain that homosexuality is genetic." The judge who heard the case ultimately struck down the law.

On June 25, 1995, reports surfaced and were later confirmed by *Science* that Hamer is under investigation by the Office of Research Integrity at the Department of Health and Human Services because he may have "selectively reported his data." There was no fanfare this time on National Public Radio.[8]

Conclusions We Can Make

What can we conclude about the biology of homosexuality? Let us turn in more detail to the most comprehensive review article—cited previously—on the subject of the biology of homosexuality, including genetics. "Human Sexual Orientation: The Biological Theories Reappraised" was written by William Byne and Bruce Parsons from Columbia University. This article was published in the same issue of *Archives of General Psychiatry* as Bailey and Pillard's study of female homosexuality, Lidz's response to their first article, and their response to Lidz.

The article reviews 135 research studies, prior reviews, academic summaries, books, and chapters of books—in essence the entire literature, of which only a small portion is actual research. The abstract summarizes their findings concisely and is by far the best available assessment of the current status of this research:

> Recent studies postulate biologic factors [genetic, hormonal] as the primary basis for sexual orientation. However, there is no evidence at present to substantiate a biologic theory, just as there is no evidence to support any singular psychosocial explanation. While all behavior must have an ultimate biologic substrate, the appeal of current biologic explanations for sexual orientation may derive more from dissatisfaction with the current status of psychosocial explanations than from a substantiating body of experimental data. Critical review shows the evidence favoring a biologic theory to be lacking. In an alternative model, temperamental and personality traits interact with the familial and social milieu as the individual's sexuality emerges. *Because such traits may be heritable or developmentally influenced by hormones, the model predicts an apparent non-zero heritability for homosexuality without requiring that either genes or hormones directly influence sexual orientation per se.*[9]

The desire to shift to a biologic basis for explaining homosexuality appeals primarily to those who seek to undercut the vast amount of clinical experience confirming that homosexuality is significantly changeable, as we will soon discuss.

We can summarize the conclusions about the biology of homosexuality in ten points.

First, a certain genetic constitution may make homosexuality more readily available as an option, but it is not a cause of homosexuality. Without that constitution it would be unlikely for an individual to choose homosexuality freely. With that constitution, it may be more likely that he or she would.

Second, if we accept proponents' research uncritically, this predisposition contributes no more than 25 to 50 percent to the likelihood of an individual actually becoming homosexual. But a realistic assessment of the research shows that the genetic contribution, though not zero, is likely to turn out to be far smaller than that—perhaps between 10 percent and 25 percent.

Third, when the actual incidence of homosexuality in the population is higher, the apparent influence of this possible genetic predisposition will be lesser and the influence of nongenetic factors greater. This is because the arithmetic used to assess probable genetic influence in twin studies requires a baseline estimate of prevalence in the general population. The rarer the trait, the more meaning a given level of concordance will have. That is, if the trait is almost universal, two twins are just as likely to share it as two unrelated individuals. If the trait is extremely rare, the twins will likely share it only if they share some factor common to both (such as a gene or genes, environment, experiences).

Fourth, the incidence of homosexuality depends on its definition. Using definitions that activists prefer, in some cultures male homosexuality—especially between older men and adolescents—is universal. With an incidence of 100 percent, the *measurable* genetic contribution in such a culture would be zero.

This huge cultural variability in incidence—from 1 to 100 percent—suggests the possibility that many strains of homosexuality could exist. At a minimum two classes exist: one class linked indirectly to a complex genetic component of the limited sort previously discussed, such as in the relationship of height to basketball-playing; the other would be almost entirely influenced by culture. The former would tend to be present in some measure even when culturally taboo and would be associated with a very low incidence rate. The latter would predominate in cultures where the taboos against homosexuality were nonexistent or relatively weak and would be associated with a relatively high incidence rate. In cultures such as ours where the taboo is weakening there is likely to be a mixture of types present.

Raw statistics about incidence from a cross section in time are meaningless when the two or more types are not separated out. We cannot say that the incidence of 2.8 percent for male homosexuality is necessarily the minimum—that is, the rate that would exist if the cultural type of homosexuality was eliminated. (See the discussion in chapter 14 on homosexuality in modern Judaism.) This fact renders meaningless any heritability estimates, because they all depend on meaningful general incidence rates.

Fifth, given that such cultures have existed where the incidence of homosexuality is far greater than at present, the incidence of homosexuality is clearly influenced by mores. Where people endorse and encourage homosexuality, the incidence increases; where they reject it, it decreases. These factors have nothing to do with its genetics.

Sixth, some yet-to-be determined proportion of any apparent genetic influence on homosexuality is actually a nongenetic, though innate, prenatal influence. This influence may be hormonal, autoimmune, from some undiscovered factor or factors, or a combination of all these. The proportion of this seemingly genetic but actually intrauterine and nongenetic influence is neither "all" nor "none." It may well be closer to the former than the latter if certain European studies on hormonal effects prove correct. This intrauterine influence may be an abnormality that could eventually prove to be correctable. Nonetheless, the practical influence of such an intrauterine predisposition can be at most no more than the maximum degree of seeming heritability—that is, considerably less than 50 percent.

Seventh, of the remaining 50 to 90 percent of the extrauterine, noninnate causes of homosexuality, a substantial but not yet quantifiable portion represents the individual's *response* to both environmentally reinforced attitudes and behaviors as well as to innate predispositional pressures.

Eighth, whatever genetic contribution to homosexuality exists, it probably contributes not to homosexuality per se, but rather to some other trait that makes the homosexual "option" more readily available than to those who lack this genetic trait (as in the correlation between height and basketball). The homosexual option may be selected for personal reasons, such as a response to trauma, or social reasons, such as overcrowding or subcultural mores, or both. It is reinforced each time it is selected. Therefore it is even more likely to be reselected the next time.

Ninth, in light of population genetics and the importance of replacement rates, the fact that homosexuality continues to exist suggests strongly that: (a) genetic influences are far from sufficient to cause homosexuality, though they may increase its likelihood; (b) the genes that influence the appearance of homosexuality do not code for homosexuality per se, but rather for other traits that themselves do not adversely affect heterosexual reproduction.

And tenth, most studies to date have many flaws. Some are caused by the intrusion of political agendas into what should be objective research, and some are due to the complex nature of the subject. These flaws must temper any conclusions we make. It is premature (and will almost certainly prove to be incorrect) simply to state that homosexuality "is" or "is not" genetic, innate, psychological, chosen, or social. It was extremely premature to pronounce it not an illness decades ago.

My primary aim in part one has been to demonstrate that hard science is far from providing an explanation of homosexuality, let alone one that reduces it to genetic determinism. My purpose so far, thus, will have been well served if the discussion helps to guard against the grossly overblown claims of interest groups who misuse science for political ends. As we have seen in the case of homosexuality, for all the public fanfare, science has accomplished almost nothing we did not know from common sense: One's character traits are in part innate but are subject to modification by experience and choice.

PART 2

Straight Mores

I do not understand what I do. For what I want to do I do not do, but what I hate I do.

—St. Paul

8

Wired to Be Free?

As we enter part two, the tenor of our discussion changes dramatically. For here we will look at choice and free will as they relate to homosexuality—and to other behavior as well. When speaking of choice and free will by necessity we enter into the domain of moral choice—not only for ourselves but for our society. As we will see, science—with its rigorous need to restrict itself to data, logic, mathematical precision, and probabilistic conclusions—can say nothing about morality. For morals have to do with how things should be, whereas science can at best only tell us how things are.

Furthermore, once we begin to consider how things should be, we find ourselves in the domain of religion. Notwithstanding the fuzzy modern impression that morality can be contrived apart from transcendent absolutes, religion is the originator of all morality. As Fyodor Dostoyevsky in *The Brothers Karamazov* had his most reflective character observe, "Without God, all things are permissible."

Thus as we move forward in our discussion we will also in a sense move back. The language and concepts we will be using in the second part may sound—by contrast to the first part—

ancient; to some readers archaic. One goal is to retrieve certain older understandings that have largely been lost to the illusory conviction that scientific advance is the same as moral progress; another, secondary, goal is to demonstrate that some of these "archaic" sources are keen in their understandings about human nature.

Cultural Rebirth or "The Great Death"?

The modern scientific framework has slowly emerged in the West over the six or seven centuries since the beginning of the Renaissance, which means rebirth. This era is so-called because it was characterized by a rebirth of classicism—and because of the long-standing consensus that the preceding ages were "dark."

But here "classicism" to a great extent means *paganism*. In fact, art historians have long focused on the reemergence of pagan motifs in the art of the Renaissance,[1] just as philosophers have studied the appearance of Neoplatonic philosophy at the same time. But few seem to reflect on how reintroducing a pagan outlook on life into the West might have caused negative long-term effects on *morality*—on the standards by which we live.

We should remember that until monotheistic Judaism emerged in the ancient Near East, all the world was pagan; people were subject to the determining influences of a multiplicity of gods. No single universal standard of morality was presumed to exist nor generally sought. Individuals were instead driven to worship that which they most craved. Not surprisingly, pagan worship was directed largely toward power, aggression, and sexual pleasure.

The Renaissance could have just as easily been called "The Great Death," for it marked the beginning of a massive dying-off of the cultural synthesis first based on Judaism and subsequently on the Christian faith. In the previous two and a half millennia this Judeo-Christian synthesis had largely conquered paganism and thus dominated much of the civilized world.

Among the human accomplishments that emerged from the Renaissance transformation of human thought, science—and the technology that derives from it—is certainly one of the most powerful to which we are heir. And modern scientific psychoanalysis, psychology, and psychiatry remain in keeping not only with the Renaissance spirit itself but with what amounts to the deification of that spirit at the time of the Enlightenment. Thus the primary goal of these disciplines as *sciences* has been to understand human subjectivity, motivation, choice, and behavior in terms of prior causes—including those areas that touch on morals, meaning, purpose, and value.

Free to Choose?

In the domain of psychology or psychoanalysis, this search for causes inevitably involves reductionism—as in the various hypothetical causes of homosexuality that we have been discussing. Scientists claim that what appears to be a freely acting or choosing agent—man—is actually a passive entity driven by prior, more elementary influences, such as psychological complexes, structures of the psyche, family influences, earlier experiences, social trends, and molecular biology, that is, genes. In the domain of biological psychiatry, this same reduction occurs at ever finer levels of purely physical detail. The primary cause of all things human may be found, it is said, at the organic foundations of the brain and in the genes that form the brain's blueprint.

From within this truly *analytic* framework ("analysis" consisting of the *lysis* or breaking down of a whole into its constituent parts), all areas of seeming autonomy within human experience are illusory. They are seen as the residue of our ignorance of the true influences that lie beneath our experience and cause our behavior, which only for the time being remain obscure to us.

Unwittingly, the scientific study of man thus aims ultimately at his abolition[2] as man—as free agent—and his reconstruction as biomolecular machine. In this view, the mystery of being human is nothing more than sheer complexity.

The psychotherapist who is heir to a scientific psychology is apt to object to this characterization. He would admit that he explains his patients' behavior in terms of the conflict among various forces at work in their psyches. But he would also insist that whatever "mechanisms" may be invisibly at work guiding a man in one direction or the other, there is always a free "sector" of the mind or the personality that is not subject to such influence.

But on closer examination this notion of free—indeed creatively free—choice that remains somewhere outside the scope of analytic reduction is merely a comforting illusion, at least from the point of view of rigorous science. What actually occurs is that at some point we merely stop the process of analyzing our behavior and decide to examine what remains no further. From a therapeutic perspective this makes practical sense: The surgeon cuts away the diseased tissue and allows the healthy tissue to remain, better functioning after the operation than before.

But the analogy quickly breaks down, for the "surgery" of self-knowledge does not consist in physically eliminating a section of the psyche. Rather we "see through" our behaviors and motivations and dissolve them into their origins—in which state we readily no longer take them seriously. Once we believe we have mechanically explained the parts of our selves we have trouble with—say, our homosexuality or our workaholism—we tend to explain everything else similarly—for example, our moral choices.

The scientific method applied to people thus sets the explanatory ball rolling in one inevitable direction, and it cannot be easily stopped. If our choices prior to scientific analysis and explanation were thought to be free, but actually resulted from family influences or unconscious conflict or biochemistry or genetics or mass opinion, then why should our current choices be anything more than the result of yet other still-invisible influences? And thus why should we be held responsible for them?

Put in statistical language, as the number of studies of any aspect of human behavior increases, ever stronger correlations will be found with an increasing number of factors external to "free will." The behavior, sexual or other, that remains unaccounted for by known factors will thus shrink to an ever smaller proportion, leaving less and less attributable to choice.

As more and more factors account for various behaviors, the plausible suggestion will inevitably arise that with sufficient effort and advances in technique, *all* remaining behaviors will be accounted for with *nothing* left to choice. This is the end point implied by such broad statements as "Studies Find Homosexuality Genetic," or as *Time* put it, "Born Gay." And even if this the-oretical end point is never achieved, what is left unexplained is apt to be so small that it can be easily dismissed. The analytic, scientific method in its very essence is reductive without limit. Applied to man, it is the universal solvent.

The alchemists, who first conceived such a thing, of course never found it, and were fortunate not to. For they never considered what would happen if ever they laid hands on it: Nothing could contain it; it would eat its way through everything, devouring even its creators. The scientific study of man thus often inspires not just resistance but dread and even revulsion, for its end point is appalling: the destruction of the very idea that there is choice, meaning, and purpose in human existence. From the scientific perspective, "meaning" and "purpose,"[3] like "free will," cannot but be illusions of human subjectivity that are ultimately reducible to other, prior causes. This not only wounds man's pride but demonstrates that the object of his deepest longings is utterly illusory, and therefore that his longings are utterly unfulfillable.

And yet, the example of homosexuality has one stunning feature that sets it apart from much of this discussion: Most of the gay activists in the United States *do not want* to find any freedom and choice involved in their way of life, and they are fiercely determined to prove that there is no way out of it either. Thus the debate is lined up in the reverse way of most debates over the medical bases of human behavior. People usually *resist* the idea that their behavior is driven by unchangeable, biological factors, as in feminist arguments over innate differences between men and women, or in the firestorm over the genetics of IQ and a potential correlation to racial groupings.[4] But in the case of homosexuality, many people rush to embrace scientific research, however flimsy, that seems to reduce this particular behavior not only to prior causes, but even to the end point that no choice is involved at all.

We should see the fallacy in the claim that homosexuality is not immoral *because* it is (supposedly) genetic. The claim that "homosexuality is genetic" is certainly false as a scientific statement, as we have seen. But whether it is true or false is also irrelevant. Science cannot distinguish between moral and immoral behaviors on the basis of the predetermination of these condi-tions, because from the scientific point of view all behaviors are treated as though predetermined. If they are not predetermined by our genes then they are predetermined by our families, and if not by our families then by our education, and if not by our edu-cation then by some other factor, and so on.

In truth, from a scientific perspective, there is *never* a place for freely acting agents because complete reductionism is the very premise on which science proceeds. At most, a given analysis only leaves us with remaining areas for which we have not yet discovered the true, prior causes. To the extent that the analysis of any agent's behavior is successful, science demonstrates that the agent's behavior is no longer free, but determined. To the extent that an agent's behavior appears free, science considers its understanding incomplete.

Once we recognize this fact, we realize that science cannot contribute to *any* moral question, because moral questions always presume an agent capable of freely choosing good or evil. Science does not—and should not—say anything about good or evil because it must presume that such apparent choice is an illusion.

Filling a Triangle

Picture the field of individual human action—or more pre-cisely, of the motivation to action—as a triangle resting on its base. At a certain stage of our understanding this triangle is empty, signifying our working assumption that all human action is determined by choice and free will. Put in statistical language: We know of no factors whatever that account for any differences in actions from one person or group of people to another. Note the subtle corollary that, with respect to cause, an utterly 100 per-cent unpredictable (or "random") event cannot be distinguished from one that is freely willed. Were it not free, the action would be predicted by correlation to some other factor.

Now draw a line across the triangle about a quarter of the way up from the base and fill it in with a certain color. Let us say that the area below this line represents genetic influences—the bio-

logical differences among individuals that account for a significant proportion of their variability in action. The remaining area,
still blank, represents what is left to choice and free will.

Next draw a second line, perhaps another quarter of the way
up, and fill that space in with a different color. This second area
will represent, say, family influences. Again, the remaining, even
smaller area that is blank presumptively constitutes what remains
of free will and choice.

Now draw a third line yet further up and fill in this space with
a third color, representing nongenetic biological factors: intrauterine influences, diet, the effect of pollutants, viruses and bacteria,
and so on. Then draw a fourth line to demarcate the area of social
influences, and so on. Each successive space accounts for less and
less of the remaining variability because the analyses grow
increasingly complex and costly to perform and contribute less
and less to our explanatory model. Slowly and relentlessly the area
remaining to "free will and choice" grows smaller. Will it perhaps
disappear altogether?

It may disappear; but even if not, it will grow less and less significant, approaching ever closer to invisibility as our scientific
analysis grows ever more precise. Perhaps it will never quite get
to zero. But when it comes to actions that matter most to us, no
matter how small this space becomes—this tiny remnant of free
will—even if it shrinks to a mere point, we all—including the most
rigorous, rational, insistent scientist—will live our lives just as
though that tiny point were dense as a neutron star, weightier by
magnitudes than the weight of all the rest of the triangle.

And when that tiny point at the very peak of the triangle finds
itself in a struggle against the pressing impact of all the other factors, and the odds seem hopeless and the struggle ordained to
fail, we will continue to wrestle. Our fellows will cheer us on as
well, sometimes with tears barely choked back at this quintessential manifestation of the human spirit. Under what circumstances do we experience this sense of higher triumph? Do we
really deeply cheer, say, the man who gets rich? Do we applaud
in our deepest heart the man who in spite of his physical unat-
tractiveness, succeeds as a Don Juan? Hardly. Rather we cheer—

from the depths of our being—the triumph of good over evil, over the evil that lies outside ourselves and also the evil that lies within.

Perhaps this insistence on free choice is mere sentimentality. Maybe we only kid ourselves into thinking that free will is at work, when actually everything is predetermined. This is one possibility. But we also must realize that although the various influences on our actions may be combined in an equation that shows the relative importance of each, no such weighting is even theoretically possible with respect to free will. Either will is truly free in each individual case or it is not. If free, it outweighs all the combined effects of prior causes, producing an utterly unpredictable outcome; if not free, then it is utterly subject to these prior causes and the "agent" is therefore predictable. In brief, either there is such a thing as free will, in which case anything less than 100 percent predictability leaves the agent totally free; or else there is no such thing as free will, in which case we are not free agents.

The Still Point of the Turning World

The scientific study of behavior thus subtly but inevitably tends to support not only a view of man that sets him outside the realm of free will and choice, but outside the realm of morality as well. Some scientists have had the courage—or at least the intellectual consistency—to claim that if the scientific view of man is not only true and complete then it indeed leads necessarily to the abolition of "man" as embodied in such moral categories as "freedom" and "goodness" (and therefore also of "dignity" and "nobility of character"). Scientific maturity—liberation from illusion—therefore demands that we should do away with such concepts entirely, as the famous American psychologist B. F. Skinner, the dean of behaviorism, has proposed. (Behaviorism asserts that all human behavior can be understood in terms of stimulus-response mechanisms.)

Nonetheless, Skinner too tries to pull himself up by his bootstraps to an Archimedean point of personal leverage above and outside his own assertions about being.[5] When asked who will lead us into this brave new world, he chooses *himself.* And when asked to what end will he save humanity, he replies that it will make a *better* world. Note how the moral concept of "goodness" has smuggled itself back in again—as also has "vanity."

This tiny, empty point at the apex of causality is indeed, to use T. S. Eliot's well-suited phrase, "the still point of the turning world."[6] And toward this infinitesimal point of ultimate weight an inverted, invisible, triangle emanates downward. Unlike its counterpart below, this triangle has no topmost dimension; it is an illimitable world of spirit that is utterly irreducible to the material world of causation below.

The essential feature of this view of reality, which actually is the traditional Jewish and Christian view, is that all of reality turns on the question of good and evil. This view claims that the overarching principle of existence—and therefore especially of all dimensions of man's existence, sexuality included—is the revealed moral law. From this upper triangle, the invisible realm of the moral dimension of life, is poured out the only *living* water to slake our thirst for meaning.

Invisible and intangible, this dimension nonetheless exerts the greatest possible impact on our lives. Not only does it affect the myriad of tiny decisions that make up our everyday existence, but it also influences the rarer moments of genius that define a culture, regardless of prior causes.

From a rigorous point of view concerning morality, therefore, one that maintains a clear-eyed perspective on the centrality of choice and freedom in human action, scientific evidence concerning the roots of behavior is irrelevant. It is clear that although individuals differ in the strength of their impulses because of many variables—some genetic, most not—do not fully account for activity, homosexual activity included.

Writing from a very different perspective, John DeCecco, editor of the *Journal of Homosexuality*, thus observes ". . . the sexual act shapes erotic desire as much as desire precedes it."[7] This leads us into the next chapter on choice, habit, compulsion, and addiction.

9

The Devil's Bargain

In earlier chapters we observed how gay activists and the media have reduced the question of a genetic contribution to homosexual behavior to such meaningless oversimplifications as "the gay gene" or "I am 99.5 percent convinced that homosexuality is genetic." But the oversimplification on the traditionalist side is also wrong—not only scientifically, but morally, because it leads to the harsh condemnation of homosexuals. For it is equally untrue to claim that people "choose to be homosexual" in the simple and simplistic sense that such a phrase inevitably evokes. Clearly no one sits down before a smorgasbord of sexual lifestyle choices and simply decides to be gay. The following fable illustrates not only the journey by which people become ensnared in the gay lifestyle, but indeed the process by which we are *all* prone to compulsive behavior.

One day long ago, over the hot sands of a middle-Eastern country, a white skylark flew in joyous loops about the sky. As she swooped near the earth, she heard a merchant cry out, "Worms! Worms! Worms for feathers! Delicious worms!"

The skylark circled about the merchant, hungry at the mention of worms, but puzzled as to what the merchant meant. Little did the skylark know that the merchant was the devil. And seeing that the skylark was interested, the devil motioned her nearer. "Come here, my little friend. Come! See the lovely worms I have!"

Cautiously, the skylark landed and cocked her head at the merchant. "Come! Taste the juicy worms!" The skylark became aware that she was, indeed, quite hungry. And these worms looked bigger and tastier than any she had ever dug for herself out of the hardscrabble ground of the desert. The skylark hopped closer and put her beak up close to the worm. "Two worms for a feather, my friend. Two worms for one!"

The skylark was unable to resist. And she had, after all, so many feathers. So, with a swift motion, she pulled out a feather—just a small one—from beneath her wing and gave it to the merchant. "Take your pick, my little friend . . . any two, your heart's desire!" And so the skylark quickly snatched up two of the plumpest worms and swallowed her meal with delight. Never before had she tasted such wonderful worms. With a loud chirp, she leapt into the air and resumed her joyful flight.

Day after day the skylark returned. And always the merchant had wonderful worms to offer: black ones and blue ones, red ones and green ones, all fat and shiny and iridescent. But one day, after eating her fill, the skylark leapt again into the air—and to her horror, she fell to the ground with a thud. She was unable to fly!

All at once, with a shock, she realized what had happened. From the delicious worms she had grown fatter and fatter; and as she plucked her feathers one by one, first her body, then her tail, and finally her very wings had grown balder and balder. Horrified, she remembered how, slowly, imperceptibly, day by day, it had been getting harder and harder to fly; and how she had told herself it was no matter; she could always stop before it was too late. Now, suddenly, here she was, trapped on the ground. She looked up and saw the merchant looking at her. Was that a small, sly grin spreading across his face?

In terror, the skylark ran off into the desert. She ran and ran and ran and ran. It took her hours and hours. Never in her entire life had she walked nor run so far. Finally, she came to the softer ground near the desert springs where, before she met the merchant, she daily had come to dig for herself the small, dusty brown desert worms that could be found around the springs.

The skylark dug and dug in a frenzy. She piled up worm after worm until it was nearly dark. Then, wrapping her catch in a small fallen palm frond, she dragged it off back across the sand to where she saw the merchant, closing up his stall for the night.

The skin around her beak had grown bruised and tender; her small feet were bleeding from the great distances she had been forced to walk. "Oh, merchant! Oh, merchant! Please help me! Please help me! I cannot fly anymore! Oh, dear what shall I do? Please, please, take these worms from me and give me back my feathers!"

The merchant bent down and peered at the terrified skylark. He threw back his head and roared with laughter, a gold tooth glinting in the red and setting sunlight. "Oh, I'll take those worms all right, my friend. A few weeks in this good soil and they, too, will be fat and green and glistening." He unwrapped the worms and tossed them into a jar of black and humid soil. "But feathers?" He laughed again. "What will you do with feathers? Glue them on with spit?" He wheezed and cackled at his little joke.

"Besides my friend," the merchant reached down and grabbed the already plucked and fattened skylark, "that's not my business—'feathers for worms.' Oh no . . ." He threw the skylark into a cage, ". . . my business is 'WORMS FOR FEATHERS!'" The merchant slammed the little cage door shut, smiled hungrily at his victim, and with a loud SNAP! of his fingers, he vanished into the desert air.

As our fable tells us, each time we behave in a certain way—each time the skylark exchanges a feather for worms—there is an important sense in which we *choose* to do so. And each time we do, we tell ourselves the truth that we are free to choose not to. Yet it is also true that with each successive step we progressively lose the ability to turn around, and yet are unaware of this worsening, insidious moral incapacitation. This is the devil's bargain we make with each successive step we take. At the end, it seems we are completely trapped, and can no more undo the changes in ourselves we have thereby allowed to develop—indeed, changes in the very brain—than can the leopard change his spots or the skylark buy back her feathers. From this trap there may eventually become no escape—none, that is, without the help of God.

The story of the skylark, which is based on a Jewish and Christian view of reality, tells us something quite specific and important about who we are: We were not meant to spend our lives pursuing shiny worms, however glistening or brilliant; we were meant to fly. Thus, there is a special poignancy to the fate of so many homosexuals trapped in the "gay lifestyle," and a special wonder in the stories of those who have become free.[1]

Those people who have successfully left the gay lifestyle have done so with difficulty—not because homosexuality is inborn, but because typical gay behavior is very compelling and, more precisely, *compulsive*. All compulsive behaviors are very difficult, at times seemingly impossible, to change; they will also lead people to do things over and over, irrationally, that have an extremely high cost associated with them—even death.[2]

Another element of confusion has thus been introduced into the general debate between science and free will, and into the political debate over homosexuality, by the imprecise use of the term "choice" as applied to *habitual* behavior. For another important influence on will is *habit*. And habit, as outlined in this chapter, also has an explicit biological basis in the brain that is different from the biological basis arising from genetics or prenatal influences. Once we understand the biology of habit, we will also have a better understanding of why habits, compulsions, and addictions are so resistant to change, yet not impossibly so.

The Highly Complex Brain

Perhaps the most common analogy used to understand the relationship between the brain and the mind is that between computer hardware and its software. In both the lay and scientific literature references abound to innate, brain-based phenomena as "hardwired."[3] The analogy is quite useful to convey how some mental states may be related to such phenomena as a loss of neurons or a chemical insufficiency—Alzheimer's disease and (some kinds of) depression, for example, are both "hardware" problems. Other states, in contrast, represent responses of normally functioning "hardware" to "software" events such as confusion caused by lack of information or grief in response to loss.

But the brain, as a kind of computer, operates very differently than the desktop computers we are familiar with. Conventional computers have a fixed hardware configuration into which any number of software programs may be swapped electronically. The hardware merely implements the rules preprogrammed into the software. In contrast, the "hardware" in biological computers—our brains—is *not* fixed. The "software" is simply the sum of the changes that occur over time in the hardware—that is, in the nerve cells and in the connections ("synapses") between nerve cells. There is actually little *pre*programming; what may loosely be called "programming" occurs over time through tacit learning from experience. In brief, repetition alters the brain itself.

A good example of this kind of learning is the way that a child spontaneously learns to articulate words, starting out with crude approximations and "zeroing in" with ever greater precision on the correct pronunciation. The changes in the connections between neurons that mediate the learning of language have been modeled—that is, simulated—on conventional computers running special "neural network" programs. These duplicate the neurons of the brain and their interconnections. When these models are run, we can actually listen to a computer "learn" to articulate simply by repetitive experience. The researchers at Princeton who first developed one such model started the program running at say 4:00 p.m. At 5:00 p.m. the computer sounded like an infant babbling, by 1:00 a.m. like a toddler, by 8:00 a.m. like a first grader, and by noon the next day it was speaking adult English.[4]

This description of the brain as a computer is, of course, an oversimplification. In fact the brain literally from bottom up is more like a hierarchy of types of computers. The lower nervous system functions quite like an archaic, standard, one-program hardware chip while the higher nerve cells function almost purely as a neural network-type computer, as described above.

This hierarchy parallels the stages of complexity of the nervous system in animals as we move up the various levels of the animal kingdom. Thus invertebrates, such as worms, have spinal cords and little else; simple vertebrates, such as eels, have spinal cords and brain stems; higher vertebrates, such as frogs and reptiles, have spinal cords, brain stems, and paleocortexes (somewhat more primitive cortical tissue that supports rather complex functioning, but not planning, reasoning, or language); higher vertebrates, such as dogs, human beings, and dolphins, have spinal cords, brain stems, paleocortexes, and neocortexes (cortical tissue that supports planning, and in the case of humans, reasoning and language).

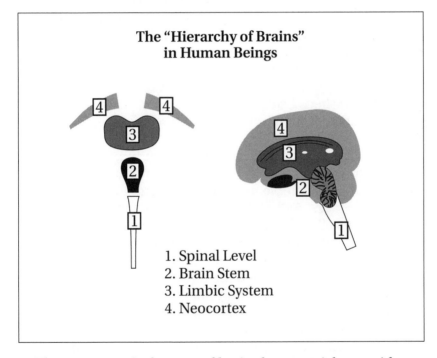

The "Hierarchy of Brains"
in Human Beings

1. Spinal Level
2. Brain Stem
3. Limbic System
4. Neocortex

The neocortex is the part of brain that we might consider as the seat of the will. Through its neurons this part of the brain mediates (this is not to say "determines") the act of selectively choosing among various options, acceding to specific impulses and resisting others. The cortex is arranged in large clusters of densely interconnected neurons. Each cell establishes connections, sometimes at great distances, to as many as a hundred thousand other cells.

It is also the part of the brain whose connections between neurons will be slowly modified over time, strengthening some connections, weakening others, and eliminating some entirely—all based on how experience shapes us. This ongoing process embeds the emerging pattern of our choices ever more firmly in actual tissue changes. *These changes make it that much more likely for us to make the same choice with less direct effort the next time—and that much more difficult to make a different choice.*

The neocortex of the young child allows him to reach out his hand to touch a hot, glowing object. No inhibitions are yet embedded in the neural network of his brain to counter the natural fascination with light and sparkle. But after sufficient experience—in this instance once may be enough—he will grow less and less likely to do so. There is thus a specific physical basis to learning that sheds light not only on the nature of habit, compulsion, and addiction but also on the relationship of each of these to choice.

In response to inputs to the cortex from the external world (such as touch and sight), as well as from internal stimuli (such as fear or hunger), nerve impulses travel from cell to cell over these connections. At first they travel in a random pattern, "activating" each cell to various, likewise random, levels of electrochemical excitation. The output—the thoughts and behaviors—generated by these excited cells is therefore also initially random. We easily see this kind of random output in the relatively disorganized and uncoordinated movements and sounds a newborn infant makes in response to being handled or hungry.

By contrast, behaviors that arise from lower, more primitive levels of the nervous system are quite well-organized. Such behaviors include breathing, crying, swallowing, the "startle reflex" (the way an infant suddenly extends its arms and legs in response to a sudden stimulus), or the "snout reflex" (the way an infant turns its head toward an object that touches its cheek—to orient its mouth toward the nipple). These behaviors are usually the most basic and life-sustaining and are therefore also common to lower animals as well. By comparison to behaviors organized at the neocortical, or higher, level, they are the most rigid and stereotyped, are fairly simple, and are also the least "plastic"—that is, the least subject to modification by learning and repetition.

Eventually, most of these innate behaviors become subject to selective suppression by learned, intentional behaviors mediated by the neocortex. Put differently, innate, primitive, preprogrammed, "hardwired," lower-level impulses are modified by the higher, plastic, learned configurations of the brain. One example is when youngsters learn to hold their breath under water. An infant is incapable of this act of voluntary suppression of the breathing mechanism. In similar fashion, some of these primitive mechanisms will be lost entirely.

When the neocortex is damaged, innate patterns reemerge in their primitive, unmodified form because they are truly "hardwired." Thus we see the painfully sad reemergence of primitive responses in people with Alzheimer's disease, which slowly destroys cortical neurons to cause both a psychological "second childhood" and the reemergence of primitive neurological reflexes such as the "startle" and "snout." Of course, if the neocortex is not taught properly to begin with, the innate behaviors will remain in relatively primitive, unmodified form.

As certain connections gain in strength and others lose strength, the pattern of the nerve cells being activated in response to stimuli becomes progressively less random and more well-organized. In this way learned behaviors start out quite chaotic and ineffective and become progressively more targeted, precise, and efficient. Anyone who has mastered a difficult sport or learned to play the piano has experienced this process. Indeed, we all have in most areas of life, so central is this process to human learning and action.

It is important to emphasize that the strengthening of connections between nerve cells involves an *actual increase in tissue.* This occurs as more and more neurotransmitter (the chemicals that signal from one neuron to another) is stored at the point of connection and more and more protein receptors for these neurotransmitters are synthesized. The weakening of connections between cells likewise involves a loss of tissue. This occurs both in the diminishment of neurotransmitter and receptors and eventually also in the actual dissolving of those parts of the cells involved in connections that are rarely used and reinforced. This dissolving is known as "pruning."

Furthermore, throughout development many new cellular connections are established for the first time. These new connections are stimulated by and come to embody physically learned behaviors. Beyond that, a selective loss of whole neurons relating to behaviors not being used takes place. These processes not only extend into adolescence, but are especially heightened then, probably under the influence of dramatically altered hormones.

Our Second Nature

The above section explains why it becomes ever more difficult—though not impossible—to teach a dog new tricks as the dog grows older. Unlike our modern computers, the brain's hardware and software are one. Therefore an old program cannot simply be swapped for a new one to be run on the same hardware. Complex patterns of behavior become progressively more "embedded" in actual physical changes in the brain itself.

This also illustrates one of the reasons why anatomical differences in adult brains are of limited significance with respect to genetics: The differences can be acquired; they need not be innate. This point is easily missed—even by presumably well-educated writers. Regarding homosexuality, a reporter at the *Wall Street Journal* wrote dismissively that, "Some religious fundamentalists even suggested that homosexual activity somehow could have caused the structural differences [in the hypothalamus, according to LeVay]."[5]

But recall that the editor of *Nature* (the English counterpart to *Science*) himself remarked that, "Plainly, the neural correlates of genetically determined gender are plastic at a sufficiently early stage.... Plastic structures in the hypothalamus [might] allow... the consequences of early sexual arousal to be made permanent."[6] It is worth noting that the hypothalamus is a relatively primitive part of the brain. Even such primitive parts, where most "hardwiring" is located, are subject to significant modification.

Clearly, new patterns of behavior can be learned "on top of" old ones, but the old ones will not be eliminated. Furthermore, the new ones will be acquired with much greater difficulty than the old; they are not being learned off of a random, only slightly configured base, but off of a base already converged into a physically, biologically shaped form.

Behaviors become increasingly strengthened through repetition. This strengthening physically alters the brain in a way that cannot be entirely undone, if at all; it is modified with great difficulty. Such modification requires a greater effort of will, additional repetition of the new behavior, and more time the more deeply embedded in the brain the old behavior has become. Experiences of religious conversion also generate new patterns of behavior, sometimes quite abruptly. But even here, in this widely recognized but more mysterious process, it is well-known that the old patterns, and the potential for falling back into old behaviors, do not simply disappear.

Complex, multidimensional series of actions that have become habitual start out as single, individually considered, and selected choices. Later they develop into the automatic actions we call habits. Our responses, in other words, become "second nature," which is indeed an apt term. Nonetheless, we all wish to retain within the realm of choice final authority over these habitual responses, choosing to restrain and release them as best serves our interests, or more importantly, as we consider right.

Pleasure Centers

The difference between a simple habit and a compulsion is partly a matter of degree. But more pertinently, compulsions are also linked to innate, primitive impulses. We have no natural biological urge to drive a car (although we do have a biological thrust to locomotion); we do indeed to eat, fight, and to have sex.

Of all the biological drives, the sexual drive is the one linked most strongly to pleasure. Even hunger maintains its force primarily through regulatory systems in the brain that are less

strongly linked to pleasure centers than is sex. In the "eating disorders" or in certain forms of depression mediated by the neurotransmitter serotonin, however, eating can become so strongly
linked to pleasure that the pleasure of eating overrides the dis-
comfort of satiety.

But indeed, in light of the goal-directness of all biological systems, hunger *need* not be so strongly linked to pleasure as is sex.
Whereas food is absolutely necessary for the survival of every
individual, sex is not. Food is thus truly a need of the individual
while sex is not, strange as that may sound in our society. Sex,
whose biological purpose is to preserve the species, is actually
a need of the race, not really the individual. (A person can survive without sex; a species cannot.) Its pursuit therefore needs
to be strongly reinforced through mechanisms beyond immediate survival.

The incredible power of pleasure-related mechanisms in the
brain is fearfully illustrated in a recent experiment with rats. They
were given a lever to press that fed them simple water and cocaine—whose effects in the brain involve many neurotransmitter systems. The rats pressed the lever to the point of starvation,
physical exhaustion, and death, ignoring hunger entirely. This
controlled experiment with lower animals illustrates an outcome
not that different from the life- and relationship-destroying
effects of many compulsive pursuits to which men are prey—
chemical, sexual, and otherwise.[7]

The brain has certain areas whose primary function is to create a feeling of "pleasure" only under specific circumstances.
Thus, as a prime example, the pleasure areas of the brain are most
intensely activated at the moment of sexual orgasm. The mechanism whereby this occurs is chemical: Among the many physiological events associated with orgasm, one is the generation of
a signal sent to certain nerves that travel to the pleasure areas of
the brain. When the signal arrives, it causes little sealed packets
at the nerve endings to open up and release their contents onto
other cells. The surface of these other cells have specially
designed receptors that match the shape of the released chemicals in lock-and-key fashion. When the chemical binds to the
receptor, the receptor sends a signal to the pleasure areas to gen-

erate the feeling "intense pleasure." (Incidentally, although we know that this mechanism triggers pleasure responses, it does not explain our subjective *consciousness* of pleasure.)

In the case of pleasure, the chemical released from the nerve endings is a special type called an "opioid," meaning "opium-like." Of all behaviors, none would appear to be accompanied by so intense a burst of internal opioids as sex. Therefore, apart from the repetitive ingestion of such external opiates as heroin—the classic example of addiction—no experience is more intensely pleasurable. This fact sheds light on the ease with which repeated sexual behaviors are especially strongly reinforced.

The subjective experience of heroin addicts provides a rather startling confirmation of this chemical connection between addiction and sexuality: addicts invariably describe the pleasure of a heroin "rush" as, precisely, "orgasmic." Not surprisingly, heroin or cocaine addicts also quickly lose interest in actual sex.

The experience of pleasure creates powerful, behavior-shaping incentives. For this reason when biological impulses—especially the sexual ones—are *not* at least partially resisted, trained, and brought under the civilizing influence of culture and will, the pressure to seek their immediate fulfillment becomes deeply embedded in the neural network of the brain. Furthermore, the particular, individualized *patterns* by which we seek this fulfillment will also become deeply implanted.

Once embedded, sexual fantasy life in particular *cannot* be erased. New fantasies may be learned "on top of," so to speak, the earlier ones; we may become highly motivated not to act on our fantasies; we may learn new behaviors that prove as gratifying or even more gratifying than the old ones; the old ones will weaken and wither, yet they will always be there—the "old self" and the "natural man" does not die entirely in this life, even though we may die (though not all at once) to self. Few are so strong that, given sufficient duress, the old patterns of fantasy and behavior could not be provoked once again into near-overwhelmingly seductive strength.

With effort and sufficient motivation, the unaided will may master other, nondrive-related habits. But habits linked to drive-related pleasures often overpower the will. In short order, therefore, unregulated sexual tendencies become habits, then compulsions, and finally something barely distinguishable from addictions.

Another important but subtler point needs to be made. The brain-based mechanisms that mediate pleasure are closely linked to those that mediate pain. Often, a pleasurable experience—or at least one that arouses some aspects of our physiology to a state in which we are supposed to feel pleasure—may become linked to a painful stimulus. This occurs commonly, for example, when children are sexually abused, causing them to link sexual arousal to the "taking-in" of pain. People who have suffered in this way when young often find themselves as adults confused and anguished over what seems to be an irrational compulsion to "seek out" hurtful sexual experiences and relationships. Mechanisms such as these lie behind the high percentage of homosexuals who were molested as children.

The Road to Addiction

As has been observed by psychoanalysts, the so-called "perverse" forms of sexual expression (including those associated with pain) are especially likely to become compulsive: "The concept of addictive sexuality or neoneeds is . . . introduced in reference to the compulsivity that invariably accompanies perverse sexuality."[8] This observation is consistent with the enormously greater promiscuity that is typical of the gay lifestyle, documented previously.[9]

These extreme variants of compulsive sexual behavior as well as the repetitive use of pornography, prostitutes, masturbation, extramarital affairs, or even erotic fantasy have caused considerable distress to many in our society. From a quite mundane perspective, therefore, and without an understanding of the brain processes underlying these behaviors, groups have sprung up to help people free themselves from these behaviors. Within these groups these behaviors are wisely, if from a medical perspective somewhat imprecisely, referred to as "addictions." The term might better be limited to the body's physiological response to the absence of an externally supplied chemical on which it has become *dependent.*

Dependence in this context means that a normal state of physiological repose (as measured by normal vital signs: blood pressure, pulse, respiration rate, and temperature) will be disrupted, sometimes to the point of death, unless that chemical is reintroduced. (This is what a "hangover" is and why "the hair of the dog" provides temporary relief.) Dependence occurs when an external substance is regularly ingested that closely mimics the critical regulatory function of an internal chemical—as opiates mimic opioids. In time, the body is fooled by the external compound into shutting down its own natural production.

But the compulsive behavior caused by an addiction is actually little different in its power or in its effects on character than are the compulsive behaviors related to the way we fulfill our biological drives. As discussed above, because the reinforcement mechanism (cessation of pain, pleasure) for the biological drives is mediated by naturally occurring opioids in the brain, to rename as *addictions* those compulsions that fall within any of the biological drives—hunger, aggression, sex—is not far off the mark. It is especially accurate in the domain of sex. Most importantly, from a practical point of view, the methods that have proven by far the most effective in breaking true chemical addictions also prove effective in modifying compulsive behaviors.

Many people appeal to *education* as an element in the long-term prevention of AIDS and other sexually transmitted diseases. Education can be effective in preventing people from ever *beginning* the behaviors that lead down the slippery slope to habit, then compulsion, and finally addiction. But with those for whom the behavior is already a habit or worse, the educational approach is notoriously ineffective because rational ideas and recommendations carry little weight against an addict's drive for drugs or sex. Formal drug treatment programs have long abandoned exhortation and education as being useless except in a supplementary role. Addicts simply will not abandon their behavior except under unusual and specific constraints. Arguments that homosexuals should simply "choose" a different way of life are equally futile.

Summary

Let us summarize the picture we are left with of the human will in the light of science. The naive, prescientific view might picture men as essentially free in their choices, constrained only by obvious external physical circumstances. But the plasticity of brain structure and function confounds this simple picture. Over time, the choices we make fall into ever more predictable patterns because the pattern of choices tends to be self-reinforcing. As we practice certain behaviors, they become easier and easier and we become "better and better" at them. As they become easier, we also tend to choose them. The more we choose them, the more deeply embedded they become, and so on. What starts out relatively free becomes less so as time goes on.

The lower, more general physiological mechanisms for sexual arousal are primitive, hardwired, and very similar in animals and men; sexual preferences, however, linked closely to higher level mental activities such as fantasizing, are subject to tremendous variability and modification, especially at the level of the cortex. Because animals have only rudimentary neocortexes—if any at all—sexual variability among animals is limited. Because men have such extensive neocortexes, sexual variability among men is extraordinary.

In order to explain why some people behave one way and others differently, the scientific approach is to examine why we begin to do certain things in the first place. In order to do that, we turn not only to our genes and hormones but to our childhoods, the influence of parents, and the influence of society. And in order to understand fully why parents act the way they do and why society acts the way it does, thereby influencing us in a predictable way, we need to keep reaching for more and more distant and more and more complex chains of causality.

Because of practical considerations, we cannot actually perform such an analysis in much detail with respect to complex behaviors. In theory, however, that is how science examines the problem—squeezing down the tiny residual area of unaccounted-for action to a smaller and smaller point until free will can be thrown out altogether. As we have said before, in this view will is nothing more than a gloss for our temporary ignorance of causes.

Sufficiently keen observers might be able to guess how most of us *might* act in certain situations. In so doing, they would be suggesting that our actions are not free, but determined. And yet the reality is that we are free, and we hold others accountable for their actions as though they really were, too. This freedom is not demonstrable by science[10] but is an act of faith as much for the hyperrationalist as for the fundamentalist.

And yet, free will is only part of the problem. For once we have become convinced that—in spite of all the obstacles we place in our own way through habit, compulsion, and addiction—we are still, at bottom, free to choose, there immediately arises the question, "what shall we choose?" and "on what basis?" "Are there right choices? And wrong ones? How do I tell?" Thus we enter the domain of religion.

10

The Unnatural Natural

At first, sin is like an occasional visitor, then like
a guest who stays for awhile, and finally like the
master of the house.

—Rabbi Yitzhak
Genesis Rabbah 22:6

One sure lesson of the current discussion is this: Science
cannot tell us what is right and what is wrong; it can only
tell us what is and, with respect to human behavior, elu-
cidate for us the influences that will nudge us in this direction or
that *if we let them.* Understanding these forces will not tell us
whether we are being nudged rightly or wrongly, although that
understanding may help us go in the direction we choose.

It should not seem strange then to proceed from a science-
based discussion of what *is* to an ethics-based discussion of what
should be; in other words to move from a description of the neu-
rophysiological basis of habit, compulsion, and addiction to a
discussion of the Bible and its view of sin. The entire debate about
homosexuality is inextricably rooted in the Judeo-Christian concept of sin because the idea that homosexuality is wrong has
entered our culture from the Jewish and Christian faiths. In many

other cultures not rooted in the worship of the God of Israel—
such as the many pagan cultures of the world—homosexuality
is perfectly acceptable and normative behavior.

The Bible, of course, is unapologetically ethical. It does not
pretend to be scientific in the sense of explaining how things
work; it mostly explains how things should be. It begins with the
startling premise that the entire world is not as it should be—
nature itself is broken, right from the beginning. Nature itself has
become, if you will, *un*natural, human nature included.

In today's secular culture, the biblical word "sin" is simply
understood to refer to actions that are in some sense "wrong." It
carries with it the musty overtones of a moralism that is both
quaint and cruel. But the full biblical description of sin is far more
radical and illuminating than this. The Bible describes most sins
as *pleasurable, natural,* and *self-reinforcing to the point of compulsion.* They are, in effect, the *addictions.*

This view of sin contrasts sharply with modern, individualis-
tic morality that more or less asserts that nothing is sinful that
does not immediately harm someone else. The Bible certainly
agrees that harm to others is bad, but it also has a distinctive view
on self-harm that derives directly from the first and greatest commandment: "Thou shalt have no other gods before me."

Addiction specialists emphasize how any addiction slowly,
insidiously, and relentlessly removes addicts from real relationships with other people, reorienting them exclusively to the object
of their addiction. The Bible views the same process as characteristic of sin, but with an important added dimension: Sinners
are not only progressively removed from relationships with other
people as they increasingly focus on the sin and the pleasure it
affords, but also from a relationship with God.

The Bible thus sees a vital dimension to sin: It is not only
increasingly addictive but a form of *idolatry.* The object of the
sinful compulsion slowly erodes and replaces all other desires,
eventually even displacing God himself, the one who should be
the object of our deepest yearning. In this way we literally worship and fall into the grip of a part of creation instead of the Creator. Thus the primary criticism of human nature found in the

Bible is that, for example, of the apostle Paul, describing all fallen men in their violation of the first commandment:

> Who changed the truth of God into a lie, and worshipped and served the creature more than the Creator . . .
>
> Romans 1:25 KJV

What is true of men, the Bible claims, is equally true of whole civilizations. Thus in its repeated—compulsive—falls into the snare of idolatry, the spiritual history of Israel tells much the same story as that of all nations. And the idolatry warned against in both Hebrew and Christian Scripture is not some vague intellectual nodding to a wood or stone model, but rather the repeated attraction to an ecstatic, pagan, *orgiastic* form of nature-worship—involving both male and female ritual prostitution in an unlimited variety of sexual forms. The overwhelming power of sexual gratification is what makes it so susceptible to becoming a true compulsion. The Bible therefore most often condemns ritualized sexual compulsion as a quintessential act of idolatry. God's great patience in deferring judgment on Israel reflects his understanding that sin is more like an addiction than a simple choice—people cannot conquer it through mere moral suasion.

In Old Testament times in the Near East this idolatry took the form of the worship of Baal and Ashtoreth; in New Testament times in the Mediterranean basin it became the worship of other female deities, for instance Aphrodite.[1] A biblically informed perspective on our own era would consider it to be similarly idolatrous: dominated by materialistic sexual hedonism undergirded by a secularized, skeptical, or pop-spiritual, quasi-occult theology.

In the Christian continuation of the Hebrew Bible's presentation of sin, a unique and specific role is outlined for a savior: His atoning sacrifice is capable of effecting not only forgiveness, but genuine liberation from the compulsive grip of sin. This story makes even more explicit sin's power and the *impossibility* of mere willful change, first described in the eighth century B.C. by the prophet Jeremiah:

> Can the Ethiopian change his skin
>   or the leopard its spots?
> Neither can you do good
>   who are accustomed to doing evil.

Jeremiah 13:23

I but Not I

Many passages and stories in both the Old and New Testaments illustrate how sin is self-reinforcing, leading to an ever deeper entanglement. It is often referred to as a "snare," suggesting that, as with all habits that develop into compulsions, sinful pleasures present themselves first as *options*, only later revealing their true power over the will. Sinners deny the potential for entrapment, inadvertently ensuring that the snare will pull tight about them before they know they are trapped. The sin itself prevents resistance to it:

> The evil deeds of a wicked man ensnare him;
>   the cords of his sin hold him fast.
> He will die for lack of discipline,
>   led astray by his own great folly.

Proverbs 5:22–23

In like vein, the prophet Isaiah had warned:

> Woe to those who draw sin along with cords of deceit,
>   and wickedness as with cart ropes.

Isaiah 5:18

The Talmud explains these passages as follows:

Rabbi Assi stated, "The Evil Inclination is at first like the thread of a spider, but ultimately becomes like cart ropes."

Sukkah 52a

Rabbi Isaac stated, "The [Evil] Inclination of a man grows stronger within him from day to day, as it is said, 'Only evil all the day.'"

Rabbi Simeon ben Lakish stated, "The Evil Inclination of a man grows in strength from day to day and seeks to kill him, as it is said, 'The wicked watcheth the righteous and seeketh to slay him. . . .'"

And St. Peter notes:

A man is a slave to whatever has mastered him.

2 Peter 2:19

We know from the modern psychology of compulsions that when a man is "mastered" by his desires, "denial" takes over as a specific mechanism, subverting any residual suspicion that escape is even desirable. What is actually a frightening vice (and a *vise*) is disguised as a virtue. Jeremiah describes this state of blindness in a famous passage:

The heart is deceitful above all things, and desperately wicked [or "beyond cure"]: who can know it?

Jeremiah 17:9 KJV

If and when a man awakens fully to his true state, it is usually far later than he had realized, for his psyche has already become configured by his behavior, "burned into" the synaptic connections of the brain:

Judah's sin is engraved with an iron tool,
    inscribed with a flint point,
on the tablets of their hearts.

Jeremiah 17:1

Those sinners who at last awaken to the truth—like addicts who have broken through their denial—describe their state with brutal realism. For nearly two thousand years Paul's anguished description of human bondage to appetite has remained among the most eloquent ever penned:

I do not understand what I do. For what I want to do I do not do, but what I hate I do. . . . For I have the desire to do what is good, but I cannot carry it out. For what I do is not the good I want to do; no, the evil I do not want to do—this I keep on doing. . . . [I]n my inner being, I delight in God's law; but I see another law at work in the members of my body, waging war against the law of my mind and making me a prisoner of the law of sin at work within my members. . . . What a wretched man I am! Who will rescue me from this body of death?

> Romans 7:15–24

Paul, himself a Talmudic pupil of Rabbi Gamaliel, answers his own query: He will be rescued only by "Jesus Christ our Lord," echoing in Christian form the Talmud's similar response to the intractable problem of the Evil inclination, in a continuation of the passage cited above:

and were it not that the Holy One, blessed be He, is his help, he would not be able to withstand it, as it is said, "The Lord will not leave him in his hand, nor suffer him to be condemned when he is judged."

> Sukkah 52a

Keep in mind our own street phrase "a monkey on my back," which refers to addiction. In the context of a discussion of sin, compulsion, and addiction, Paul's figure of speech—"this body of death"—is especially apt. It refers to the way a death sentence was often carried out under Imperial Rome. A dead body was strapped to the back of the condemned man from which he could not free himself, however he struggled. In time, the putrefaction of the corpse spread and ate away his own tissues as well, slowly killing him.

All Too Natural

Unless we are careful, this line of thinking leads us heedless to a trap—viewing sin as "unnatural." As we all know, one of the most common epithets hurled at homosexuals and other people who practice sexual behavior other than heterosexual intercourse is that their practices are "*un*natural." Paul's letter to the Romans makes a similar accusation:

> Because of this ["worshiping and serving created things rather than the Creator"], God gave them over to shameful lusts. Even their women exchanged natural relations for unnatural ones. In the same way the men also abandoned natural relations with women and were inflamed with lust for one another. Men committed indecent acts with other men, and received in themselves the due penalty for their perversion.
>
> Romans 1:26–27

But Paul's use of unnatural here is only half the story. As implied in his references to "my sinful nature" and to "another law at work in the members of my body," the more basic issue in assessing the concept of sin from a scientific and biological perspective is the fact that *all forms of sin are natural.* Sin is even theologically natural *in a fallen world*—it is unnatural only in contrast to the nature of the world as it was intended to be—the ideal world whose perfection our minds but dimly perceive, our hearts desperately long for, and our actions but rarely attain.

The term *sin* points toward a standard outside of nature and thus outside the domain of science. Stealing is merely the natural extension of hoarding (widespread in animals who naturally steal each other's food whenever they can), murder the natural extension of self-protection and dominance, adultery the natural expression of the biological drive to propagate one's own DNA as widely as possible in preference to others ("It's in Our Genes!" trumpeted yet another meaningless headline—this time about adultery—in a major newsweekly), and so on.

Paul's use of the term "natural" in the passage above has a different meaning—one he takes for granted—namely that the "natural use" of sexuality is primarily for reproduction and that the sexual organs are physically designed for one specific type of sexual use.

Whether it filtered into the culture directly from this single New Testament passage or is spontaneously repeated because of its surface obviousness, the condemnation of homosexuality as "unnatural" and therefore "shocking" is widespread. But this simplistic condemnation carries two dangers: It easily leads to judgmentalism and it sets up a straw man that is readily knocked down by commonplace misunderstandings of the genetic bases of behavior. If homosexuality is genetically determined then it must be natural; if the Bible objects to it on the basis of its being "unnatural" then the Bible is clearly mistaken.

But the Bible is filled with many references that point not to the *unnaturalness* of sin (including homosexuality among many others), but to its *naturalness*. The Pentateuch's 613 commandments, the requirement of daily animal sacrifice for atonement, the terrible punishments meted out against certain sins—all these point to the ubiquity and deep-rootedness in human nature of what God calls sin.

The revelation at Sinai in particular, but earlier covenants as well, illustrate that God's ongoing involvement in the life of humanity represents a *disruption of the fallen natural order*. Sin is defined by God, not by nature. Sin is therefore not against nature but against God:

> Against you, you only, have I sinned
> and done what is evil in your sight,
> so that you are proved right when you speak
> and justified when you judge.

> Psalm 51:4

So natural is sin, and so unnatural are God's requirements, that almost the entirety of the Bible tells the story of man's inability to obey these requirements through his own natural effort. The Bible shows the desperate human need for supernatural assistance in even approximating a godly existence:

> There is not a righteous man on earth
> who does what is right and never sins.

> Ecclesiastes 7:20

Some passages directly suggest an understanding of what we now recognize as a genetic predisposition toward sinful impulse and behavior:

> Surely I was sinful at birth,
>   sinful from the time my mother conceived me.
>
> Psalm 51:5

We, like the ancient Jews, therefore anticipate that the conquering of sin ultimately requires someone whose origins and nature are *not* entirely natural:

> Therefore the Lord himself shall give you a sign; Behold, a virgin shall conceive, and bear a son, and shall call his name Immanuel. Butter and honey shall he eat, that he may know to refuse the evil, and choose the good.
>
> Isaiah 7:14–15 KJV

Even in Judaism, in which the promised redeemer is human, albeit extraordinary, tradition holds that he has existed with God since creation. And furthermore, it is the suffering of the righteous—not just of the sinners—which keeps the world from destruction. In the Christian faith, redemption is understood as possible because of supernatural intervention:

> But while he thought on these things, behold, the angel of the Lord appeared unto him in a dream, saying, Joseph, thou son of David, fear not to take unto thee Mary thy wife: for that which is conceived in her is of the Holy Ghost. And she shall bring forth a son, and thou shalt call his name Jesus: for he shall save his people from their sins. Now all this was done, that it might be fulfilled which was spoken of the Lord by the prophet, saying, Behold, a virgin shall be with child, and shall bring forth a son, and they shall call his name Emmanuel, which being interpreted is, God with us.
>
> Matthew 1:20–23 KJV

Because God knows how unnatural it is for us not to sin, he refrains from swift, talon-like judgment and tempers his response with patience and mercy:

> he does not treat us as our sins deserve
>> or repay us according to our iniquities.
> For as high as the heavens are above the earth,
>> so great is his love for those who fear him. . . .
> As a father has compassion on his children,
>> so the LORD has compassion on those who fear him;
> for he knows how we are formed,
>> he remembers that we are dust.
>
> Psalm 103:10–11, 13–14

The problem lies in the fact that after the Fall nature itself—including human nature—is sinful:

> God saw how corrupt the earth had become, for all the people on earth had corrupted their ways.
>
> Genesis 6:12

The Suffering One

In the biblical view, God sent his Word—the Torah—into the corrupted natural world. From this perspective the entire question of right and wrong cannot be addressed without an understanding of and dependence on this Word. Absent this, with a viewpoint that sees only nature, "right" and "natural" will soon collapse into one another. Man resists the sin that is natural to him only with the greatest of effort. He requires the guidance of this Word in order to achieve even limited success:

> I have hidden your word in my heart
>> that I might not sin against you.
> Praise be to you, O LORD;
>> teach me your decrees.
> With my lips I recount
>> all the laws that come from your mouth.

> I rejoice in following your statutes
>   as one rejoices in great riches.
> I meditate on your precepts
>   and consider your ways.
> I delight in your decrees;
>   I will not neglect your word.
> Do good to your servant, and I will live;
>   I will obey your word.
>
> Psalm 119:11–17

But even this was not enough; the Israelites repeatedly lapsed back into the orgiastic worship of idols and ritual killing. Eventually, in the Christian continuation of this great drama, in order to save his children from the overwhelming power of what, through the Fall, their own *natures* were, God made this *supernatural* Word literally flesh (John 1:14). He thereby began the process of transforming the flesh into his Word.

The redeemer's life thus tells the story of the One who completely refrained from that which is merely natural to do that which is right. Not only did he thereby lose his own life, he appeased the anger of a just God at all humanity's sins, an anger that was poured out on him during his death. In mercy God withheld his wrath from his all-too-human children:

> For God so loved the world that he gave his one and only Son, that whoever believes in him shall not perish but have eternal life.
>
> John 3:16

The idea that atoning sacrifice of an innocent, morally perfect individual is required to avert the just punishment of men in their natural state is central, of course, to the Christian worldview. It was present as well in the sacrificial system of the Old Testament. And although it seems not to play a major part in normative American Judaism today, something quite close to it remains an important tradition within Orthodox Judaism, linked to Messianic hopes and speculations:

> ... suffering and pain may be imposed on a Tzadik (righteous one) as an atonement for his entire generation. This Tzadik must then

accept this suffering with love for the benefit of his generation, just as he accepts the suffering imposed upon him for his own sake. . . . All this involves a Tzadik who is stricken because his generation is about to be annihilated, and would be destroyed if not for his suffering. . . .

Within this same category there is a class that is even higher than this. There is suffering that comes to a Tzadik who is even greater and more highly perfected than the ones discussed above. This suffering comes to bring about the chain of events leading to mankind's ultimate perfection.

They can therefore rectify not only their own generation, but can also correct all the spiritual damage done from the beginning, from the time of the very first sinners.[2]

The natural desires of the flesh are not only nor even primarily sexual desires but all the selfish cravings to which we are natively inclined. The power to overcome these finally cannot and does not arise from nature, nor from men themselves as a matter of simple choice, nor of complex technique. But rather:

> . . . to all who received him, to those who believed in his name, he gave the right to become children of God—children born not of natural descent, nor of human decision or a husband's will, but born of God.
>
> John 1:12–13

Because:

> Flesh gives birth to flesh, but the Spirit gives birth to spirit.
>
> John 3:6

In fact, the very ability to know the saving truth, to be convinced that God's Word is what he says it is, also does not arise from nature nor solely from human will, but is itself a gift from God:

> "But what about you?" he asked. "Who do you say I am?"

Simon Peter answered, "You are the Christ, the Son of the living God."

Jesus replied, "Blessed are you, Simon son of Jonah, for this was not revealed to you by man, but by my Father in heaven.

Matthew 16:15–17

The Battle between Flesh and Spirit

Sin is so natural to us, and we are so utterly helpless and unable to resist it by our own power, that we inevitably either deny that we sin or must depend upon God even to *know what we need to know* to begin to resist it. If God chooses not to help us, we are lost:

He told them [the Apostles], "The secret of the kingdom of God has been given to you. But to those on the outside everything is said in parables so that, 'they may be ever seeing but never perceiving, and ever hearing but never understanding; otherwise they might turn and be forgiven!'"

Mark 4:11–12

Indeed, to be allowed to do as we wish *is* God's punishment. It is precisely because men exchanged God for idols of their own devising that:

God gave them over in the sinful desires of their hearts to sexual impurity for the degrading of their bodies with one another.

Romans 1:24

Since they did not think it worthwhile to retain the knowledge of God, he gave them over to a depraved mind, to do what ought not to be done. They have become filled with every kind of wickedness, evil, greed and depravity.

Romans 1:28–32

This mind is deeply rooted in nature itself (it is "our" nature) and thus has a sinful disposition which finally is unconquerable by natural means:

... the sinful mind is hostile to God. It does not submit to God's law, nor can it do so.

Romans 8:7

Understanding the molecular mechanisms that undergird the impulses of the flesh will not illuminate the standards of the Spirit. Nor will it release us to operate in accord with those standards:

Are ye so foolish? having begun in the Spirit, are ye now made perfect by the flesh?

Galatians 3:3 KJV

For the flesh lusteth against the Spirit, and the Spirit against the flesh: and these are contrary the one to the other: so that *ye cannot do the things that ye would.*

Galatians 5:17 KJV

In other words, the natural is sufficient neither to point us toward what is right in God's eyes, nor to carry us there. This is not to deny the evidence for divine will both in nature and in human nature, but knowledge of the laws of nature is not enough for us to live a godly life, merely a natural one.

And, more to the point, the fact that our nature drives us toward certain activities does not mean that these activities must therefore *not* be sinful. In Christ's own words:

If your hand causes you to sin, cut it off. It is better for you to enter life maimed than with two hands to go into hell, where the fire never goes out. And if your foot causes you to sin, cut it off. It is better for you to enter life crippled than to have two feet and be thrown into hell. And if your eye causes you to sin, pluck it out. It is better for you to enter the kingdom of God with one eye than to have two eyes and be thrown into hell.

Mark 9:43–47

Moral Standards Are Unnatural

The morality that God demands of man stands in contrast to the standards of behavior that come to him naturally. Precisely because these standards go against our nature, we need to be reminded of God' s law every day of our lives; and every generation must recall this law and claim it anew for itself. Thus the ancient Israelites were commanded at Sinai always to wear specially woven *tzitzit* or "tassels." (Observant Jews wear them to this day; they are the "fringe of his garment" through which in the gospel accounts Jesus heals a woman ill for twelve years.) The LORD tells Moses why:

> Speak to the Israelites and say to them: "Throughout the generations to come you are to make tassels on the corners of your garments, with a blue cord on each tassel. You will have these tassels to look at and so you will remember all the commands of the LORD, that you may obey them and not prostitute yourself by going after the desires of your own heart and eyes."
>
> Numbers 15:37–39

Maintaining that morality is determined by nature is a specifically pagan error that we fall into when we argue either that homosexuality is right because it is genetic or that it is wrong because it is not. Ultimately, any rootedness of homosexuality in nature does not remove it one whit from the domain of moral choice. In its genetic, familial, or psychological influences, homosexual impulses and behavior are no different than the many other *natural* behaviors that God, in spite of their naturalness, calls sin.

The natural self, far from being worshiped because of being natural, is to be destroyed:

> For we know that our old self was crucified with him so that the body of sin [see above, "the body of this death"] might be done away with, that we should no longer be slaves to sin.
>
> Romans 6:6

Modern man reflexively revolts against the assertion that God's morality stands in opposition to his own natural self, and he gladly abandons such conceptions as archaic. But ancient man did likewise, as Paul observed around him:

But the natural man receiveth not the things of the Spirit of God: for they are foolishness unto him: neither can he know *them*, because they are spiritually discerned.

1 Corinthians 2:14 KJV

The modern mind sees the demand that we live to some extent against our own natures as merely foolish, or misinterprets it as implying a radical asceticism that rejects all forms of pleasure. But it sees as truly *cruel* the judgment that supposedly falls on us for not being willing to resist our genetic influences. To the modern mind, as to ancient pagans, our bodies are ours to do with as we please so long as we feel we harm no one else. This is not the biblical view at all:

Do you not know that your body is a temple of the Holy Spirit, who is in you, whom you have received from God? You are not your own; you were bought at a price. Therefore honor God with your body.

1 Corinthians 6:19–20

Of those who deny God altogether, in order to do as they wish, the Psalmist cries out:

The fool[3] says in his heart,
"There is no God."

And they are fools because of what their denial leads to:

They are corrupt, their deeds are vile;
there is no one who does good.

Psalm 14:1

Free, Yet Slaves

Circumcision is the seal of the primary agreement between Israel as carrier of God's standard and God himself. By its very nature it points to the unnaturalness of his law, showing how the law stands as a modification of, and even in opposition to, the purely natural impulses (perhaps especially so with regard to the sexual impulses):

> You are to undergo circumcision, and it will be the sign of the covenant between me and you.
>
> Genesis 17:11

With the establishment of this covenant—a covenant that is contrary to nature—humanity is put on notice of just what God's standards are:

> I had not known sin, but by the law: for I had not known lust, except the law had said, Thou shalt not covet.
>
> Romans 7:7 KJV

And yet the mere fact of this standard does not bring people into compliance with it. Thus the unfolding history of Israel over the fifteen hundred years following the establishment of the covenant is one of almost unremitting failure. Only divine intercession could reverse this failure:

> For what the law was powerless to do in that it was weakened by the sinful nature [KJV: "the flesh"], God did by sending his own Son in the likeness of sinful man [KJV: "of sinful flesh"] to be a sin offering. And so he condemned sin in sinful man. . . .
>
> Romans 8:3

From a certain perspective it might seem strange that God would establish a standard of behavior impossible for us to meet. This is the perspective of those who claim that a genetic component to homosexuality—or to any other impulse—contradicts its sinfulness. But from the Judeo-Christian point of view, when we honestly confront what our natures, left to their own devices, really are—and what in the way of suffering they produce—we can only be grateful that we have been granted a vision of genuine goodness, however beyond our grasp. In this state of sorrow at our inadequacy, we can turn from prideful dependence on ourselves to voluntary dependence on God. But of course, against this surrender our pride has always urged us, and continues to urge us, to rebel.

And indeed, from the very beginning, it is as we consider what *is* good and what *is* evil that our pride insinuates its own, independent, and natural standards:

> "You will not surely die," the serpent said to the woman. "For God knows that when you eat of it your eyes will be opened, and you will be like God, knowing [determining for yourself what is] good and evil."
>
> Genesis 3:4–5

The chief result of the Fall is that we now determine for ourselves what is right and what is wrong. But in this self-determination we are far less free and independent than the serpent's lie convinces us we are. In fact, to our natural, impulse-driven compulsions we are slaves and do not know it, comfortable in a state of bewitchment. In modern language, we are in denial.

Into this cold, Luciferian illusion of freedom from sin, freedom from the consequences of choice, and darkness masquerading as illumination, God shone on ancient Israel the true searchlight of a law above, outside of and prior to fallen nature.

But except insofar as God, knowing our fallen nature, had already planned how the intrusion of his law would unfold in history, this law has not accomplished what it seemed intended to. Rather than bringing about a transformation of character from the natural to the spiritual, it accomplished just the reverse, stimulating, it seems, an even worse rebellion. Thus, foretelling the destruction of Judah and the forced exile of the people by the Babylonians, God states through Jeremiah:

> but I gave them this command: Obey me, and I will be your God and you will be my people. Walk in all the ways I command you, that it may go well with you. But they did not listen or pay attention; instead, they followed the stubborn inclinations of their evil hearts. They went backward and not forward. From the time your

forefathers left Egypt until now, day after day, again and again I sent you my servants the prophets. But they did not listen to me or pay attention. They were stiff-necked and did more evil than their forefathers. When you tell them all this, they will not listen to you; when you call to them, they will not answer. Therefore say to them, "This is the nation that has not obeyed the LORD its God or responded to correction. Truth has perished; it has vanished from their lips."

Jeremiah 7:23–28

The light of God's law not only has made the darkness of human nature stand forth for what it truly is, but by contrast seems to darken it further. As Paul put it:

But sin, seizing the opportunity afforded by the commandment, produced in me every kind of covetous desire. . . . Did that which is good, then, become death to me? By no means! But in order that sin might be recognized as sin, it produced death in me through what was good, so that through the commandment sin might become utterly sinful.

Romans 7:8–13

Biblical history reveals that the attempt to establish by prescription alone a moral standard outside of nature is futile—even when the prescription comes from God. Within a few generations at most, the habit of obedience to such a prescribed standard will degenerate into little more than hypocritical conventions that hide the greatest degree of instinctive gratification possible. The God who prescribes those moral standards must be our redeemer as well. If not, argues the Bible, we are lost.

The Modern Basis for Morality

As it was in ancient Israel, so it is in the modern world. Today the most widely accepted philosophy of morals, which is more commonly implicit than explicit, comes from psychoanalysis as rooted in Freud. This view holds that conscience and guilt are culturally relative and derive from nothing more substantial or absolute than learned restrictions. Because these restrictions oppose the natural impulses they therefore engender emotional conflict, such as "internalized homophobia." Sometimes these emotional conflicts are accepted as a necessary price for social orderliness; increasingly often, as the quest for pleasure and immediate gratification spreads widely, they are held to be unnecessary. In this view, these internal conflicts are passed on from one generation to the next, foolishly and uselessly, with no absolute basis whatever in either biology or spirit,[4] until enlightened would-be liberators arise to free us from them: "Overpopulation has made [the Levitical injunction against homosexuality] as irrelevant as refrigeration has made the injunction against eating pork," states one pastor.[5]

Although many people claim to hold overtly to a Judeo-Christian philosophy, the psychoanalytic view has deeply reinforced a widespread, modern version of pre-Christian, pre-Judaic, pagan morals in our society. Some people recognize modern moral standards as pagan and even advocate them as such, considering the replacement of God's law by paganism as not at all going "backward," but "forward."[6] Many churches and synagogues now widely welcome paganism, too, sometimes naming it as such. Alternatively they welcome certain aspects of paganism but call them something else, such as nature or goddess worship, diversity, and so on.

Modern people thus deal with the problem of guilt on the one hand by loosening most restrictions as archaic, arbitrary, and unnecessary. On the other hand they reinforce only those restrictions socially and legally that the shifting tide of fashion—both lay and expert—deems minimally necessary to sustain social order. If morality, and therefore also conscience, has no absolute basis, then there is no just cause to restrict the private or, when more than one person is involved, mutually agreed upon gratification of impulse.

But this wholesale casting off of moral restraint and therefore of the reality of a gracious, forgiving God, has the inevitable, if on the surface, somewhat surprising psychological consequence of *increasing* deep-seated feelings of condemnation and guilt. This occurs for the simple reason that man does, indeed, have a conscience that is not reducible to merely natural functions. It is genuine, and it reflects in some measure, if imperfectly, the divine standard that is its source and prototype.

When we transgress this conscience, as we are more and more apt to do in the absence of belief in its transcendent source and reality, we suffer its pangs. To escape these pangs, we drive ourselves with increasing mercilessness to further deny its reality in the vain hope that we may thereby escape it. Like Euripides pursued by the Furies, the harder we run, the deeper into our souls are sunk the pursuing talons. And yet we will suffer almost anything, even death it seems, to avoid accepting the yoke of heaven. With the loss of a deeply held belief in a just God, and in his saving grace, God's standards thus become not only meaningless but actually tend to reinforce sin. The rebellious spirit is nowhere more powerfully stimulated than in the presence of authority, especially authority perceived as both arbitrary and vulnerable.

The fierce campaign to normalize homosexuality represents therefore not merely the weakened moral authority of church and synagogue, but more importantly a widespread loss of faith in a just but gracious and truly transcendent God. This is true however loudly it may be denied by those who claim as a sanctified way of life any form of mere hedonistic individualism:

> But, dear friends, remember what the apostles of our Lord Jesus Christ foretold. They said to you, "In the last times, there will be scoffers who will follow their own ungodly desires." These are the men who divide you, who follow mere natural instincts and do not have the Spirit.
>
> Jude 17–19

And without God and his grace—without a genuine way to transcend all aspects of our merely mortal and inevitably doomed existence, not just our sexual appetites—the judgment of homosexuality as immoral will indeed appear as but a hypocritical cruelty to individual homosexuals. It can only appear unjust to deprive individuals of such instinctive pleasures as life can offer and replace this loss with nothing. In the face of this kind of condemnation, most sinners will only be driven more deeply into their sin—ragefully, self-righteously, and under-standably.

Psychologically, the keenest solution to the problem of guilt—and to the problem of how the guilt and condemnation of self or others drives us ever more deeply into doing the very things that make us guilty—does not lie in the biological, social, or psycho-analytic direction of "analyzing." We cannot eliminate guilt by merely seeing through it to its supposed origins, convinced that we have thereby dissolved it into nothingness. That way leads inevitably to personal and social decay. Rather the solution lies in maintaining conviction of our sin, and yet, in a seeming para-dox, understanding that the judgment can be lifted. Paul de-scribes this state as follows:

> I care very little if I am judged by you or by any human court; indeed, I do not even judge myself. My conscience is clear, but that does not make me innocent. It is the Lord who judges me.
>
> 1 Corinthians 4:3–4

11

To Treat or Not to Treat

In May 1994, the day was typically hot and muggy in Washington, D.C. As delegates from local chapters nationwide of the American Psychiatric Association made their way indoors, they were startled. All about them stood rows of protesters holding placards, chanting their objections to what would take place inside.

Protests themselves are not startling; nowadays they are routine. What was extraordinary this time was the nature of the protest. For here were large numbers of men and women who identified themselves as *ex*-gays furious at the attempt by the gay lobby in the APA to prevent psychiatrists from helping homosexuals change. It is perhaps a sad comment that, in the wake of the corruption of scientific objectivity first initiated by this same gay lobby twenty years before, these protesting former homosexuals would indeed significantly influence the vote that was about to take place, helping to defer for at least one more year the cruel attempt to quash all who help homosexuals leave the "lifestyle" behind.

If homosexuality was once a taboo, what is taboo now is the notion that homosexuals can be healed, if they want to. Few articles in the popular press ever mention programs that aim to reverse homosexuality; those that do are derisive and uncritically repeat activists' claims that the programs are rarely successful. And almost no articles in the professional literature discuss the treatment of homosexuality as homosexuality. Rather, they discuss the treatment of homosexuals as a class of individuals who require a special approach, in the manner of cross-cultural psychiatry or "feminist" psychotherapy.[1] Treatment, if there is any, simply helps people adjust to their homosexuality and cope with the suffering caused by their "internalized homophobia."

Is this an exaggeration? For the years 1992, 1993, and 1994 (well after the APA decision to remove homosexuality from its list of disorders) the Medline database refers to 1,581 articles on homosexuality. Only two discuss the treatment of homosexuality. One, published in the *Journal of Homosexuality,* is a historical review of Freud's attitudes toward the treatment of homosexuality;[2] the other—from France—is the only one to discuss the treatment of undesired homosexuality.[3]

For the years 1975 through 1979 (the early years immediately after the APA decision) there were forty-two articles on the treatment of homosexuality, including articles that followed up on significant long-term success (61 percent) in sexual reorientation.[4] This is true even though during these years there were fewer than half the total number of journals published than from 1992 to 1994.

Earlier still, between 1966 and 1974, prior to the APA decision, there was an even smaller pool of journals, yet Medline lists 1,021 articles on the treatment of homosexuality. By 1976, the changing mores had so affected objective scientific research and treatment that one expert published a critical evaluation of the nature and meaning of the radical changes in sexual customs and behavior and their clinical consequences: "[M]any of the[se] revolutionary changes demonstrate a complete and disastrous disregard of knowledge gained through painstaking psychodynamic and psychoanalytic investigations over the past 75 years."[5]

Since the professional normalization of homosexuality, we no longer hear of the many successful programs that continue to "cure" homosexuality nor of the deeply moving stories of those who have successfully negotiated this difficult passage. We are all much the poorer for this censorship, for the inner journeys of these people are revealing for us all, regardless of our own particular form of distress.

In fact, many groups of substantial size across the country do "treat" homosexuality with remarkable success. As they are not formal research institutions, however, there is little "hard" data—only first-hand experience and reports. This fact helps hostile skeptics remain determinedly ignorant of their successes. Many, though not all, such programs are *ministries*, and their approach is unabashedly based on faith. In the light of our preceding discussion, we should not be surprised at the benefits of faith in helping to achieve success in any area that touches on the "snare" of compulsive behavior and addiction.

The Secret of AA's Success

For a long time, a similar divide of ignorance was true of attitudes to alcoholism. Mainstream mental-health professionals treated alcoholics with the same method they used for almost all other conditions: insight-oriented psychotherapy. The twelve-step approach of Alcoholics Anonymous (AA), a lay organization, had been around for nearly sixty years but was ignored. Professionals commonly derided it as a quasi-religious cult.[6]

But two forces converged to cause a dramatic shift in the attitude of professionals, who now routinely consider Alcoholics Anonymous an essential component in "recovery." First was the eventual acknowledgment that limitless individual psychotherapy rarely helped alcoholics stop drinking; they merely became psychotherapized alcoholics. Second was the fact that insurance companies began to examine results to determine whether to reimburse. Although far from perfect, Alcoholics Anonymous was the only approach that could claim a meaningful success rate—30 percent,[7] compared to around 1 percent for psychotherapy.[8] Nonetheless, professional literature rarely examines why AA is so successful.[9] The program is simply accepted because it works—and because insurance companies insist.

A central feature of AA is that three of its twelve "steps" encourage people to acknowledge their own personal powerlessness and therefore dependency on a "Higher Power": "God as we understand him" in AA's original formulation. Most people with experience of AA insist that "religious surrender"—whatever it may be called—is the key element to recovery in AA.

Though no formal studies have been performed to confirm it, the same is true of ministries that successfully treat homosexuality. But then, only now, sixty years after the founding of AA, have such studies been performed with respect to alcoholism:

> The results of this study suggested that agreement with AA's first three steps can be measured, . . . correlates with number of sober days posttreatment, . . . and provides support for AA's contention that total surrender to one's powerlessness over alcohol is part of the process of achieving abstinence.[10]

The first three steps in AA are:

1. We admitted that we were powerless over alcohol—that our lives had become unmanageable.
2. Came to believe that a Power greater than ourselves could restore us to sanity.
3. Made a decision to turn our will and our lives over to the care of God as we understood him.

Replace the word "alcohol" above with the word "sin" and we have the essence of the Judeo-Christian view of man.

Adam's Curse

Note, too, that the various twelve-step groups speak of "recovery" rather than "cure." This distinction points to an issue we have been skirting so far—namely, what does "treatment" mean?

Early on we accepted one aspect of the APA decision to consider homosexuality no longer a form of "mental illness." The reason was simple: Without the demonstration of some kind of brain abnormality, the term "illness" means nothing more than "undesirable."

Later we discussed the possibility that homosexuality is a kind of illness, perhaps genetic or at least intrauterine in nature. But we dismissed that possibility too, because the evidence of the innateness of homosexuality is too weak. There are simply too many other factors for us to make such an assertion. In any event, if homosexuality *were* predominantly innate and biological and we also considered it an illness, its "treatment" would likewise be biological, if one could be found.

We have also emphasized that, viewed from the perspective of the world as it is now, homosexual impulses are not unnatural. Quite the opposite. The biblical standard of morality is unnatural. How then can we speak of "treatment" at all? But if we don't, do we not come perilously close to the gay activist argument that homosexuality is not an illness, but is normal, and therefore to try to "treat" it—as though it were abnormal and an illness—is unethical?

The truth is that the mislabeling of homosexuality as "an illness," like the similar mislabeling of other features of human *character*, has introduced confusion into our thinking. For, like many other aspects of human character, homosexuality is not an illness except insofar as "illness" is meant metaphorically, referring to the spiritual condition of our human nature after the Fall. As T. S. Eliot expressed it in his *Four Quartets*:

> The wounded surgeon plies the steel
> That questions the distempered part;
> Beneath the bleeding hands we feel
> The sharp compassion of the healer's art
> Resolving the enigma of the fever chart.
>
> Our only health is the disease
> If we obey the dying nurse
> Whose constant care is not to please
> But to remind of our, and Adam's curse,
> And that, to be restored, our sickness must grow worse.[11]

Psychology has misused this metaphor of the illness of a human body to capture an essential quality of spiritual decay and death—spiritual "illness." It sought to cast out "spirit" altogether from its secularized conception of reality, yet was forced to give a name to the suffering it was attempting to "cure."

But what we can see today is that the psychology and psycho-analysis of the past hundred years set for themselves an impossible task: to cure a condition, using medical methods, that is not a medical illness but a spiritual state. As a spiritual condition, homosexuality may be considered an "illness" only because we speak of spiritual matters by using material "things" as metaphors. Indeed, we must, for the spirit is no "thing" at all.

Further, the mistake mental health professions have made with respect to homosexuality is the same mistake they have made with many other conditions of human character that are spiritual rather than medical illnesses. There are several lessons to learn.

First, homosexuality points to the reality of our spiritual life in the same way that all sin, once acknowledged as such, points to our spiritual life. We recognize that although they are not really "illnesses," many of the conditions so labeled by the mental-health professions are nonetheless sources of profound suffering. This is true even though there is no strictly scientific rationale for this suffering. Thus we become aware of a dimension of life that transcends the material, that "man does not live on bread alone." The mislabeling of homosexuality and other spiritual conditions as "illness," like the mislabeling of "health," obscures the reality of the immaterial spirit and subtly misdirects our longing for God into various aspects of the material creation.

Second, homosexuality should not be treated as unique among the varieties of human spiritual illness. "Homosexuals" are simply people; in what truly matters they are no different from anyone else, especially in their healing, the current rhetoric notwithstanding. Put differently, people should not be grouped according to the varieties of their sinfulness, neither by those who indulge nor those who criticize them. After all, sin is but our lowest common denominator: All sinners share sin, and all men are sinners. In acknowledging our own compulsions—we each have our own particular habits and flaws; these are the shadow-side of our God-given individuality—we recognize ourselves in others. Then we can begin the process of humbling our prideful isolation, avoiding the extremes of both judgmentalism and of communal indulgence.

Third, homosexuality underscores in its own sphere what is clear from many others: There is always an element of compulsion in what the Bible terms "sin." In learning that such a thing as spiritual suffering exists, in carefully distinguishing it from other forms of suffering, especially those caused by physical illnesses, and in recognizing that all spiritual suffering hovers around what God has taught us to call "sin," we have identified another factor common to all spiritual suffering: compulsion. Sin truly is compulsion.

Thus in the act of breaking loose from psychology's literalized application of the word "illness," we identify a whole class of non-illnesses that nonetheless make people sick at heart. This is what the Bible calls "idolatry," the central sin that wrought the destruction of ancient Israel—as it does of all people and nations—and requires for its "healing" a saving God.

True Compassion

Nonetheless, the term "illness" is used widely in the twelve-step movement to apparent good effect. There alcoholics (and other "holics") learn to step away from the moral condemnation that is characteristic of many nonalcoholics' attitudes toward alcoholics—and of their own attitude toward themselves. For no one is so disgusted with an alcoholic as he is with himself, especially as he emerges from his drunken stupor. This phenomenon parallels the shame many homosexuals feel upon emerging from a sexual binge—even those who claim no ambivalence over the fact of their homosexuality.

Rooted as Alcoholics Anonymous is in the psychological principles that derive from the Judeo-Christian religious tradition, it is not surprising that AA should be keenly sensitive to people's most typical initial reaction to awareness of their sinfulness: They sin all the more. This is why AA has picked up on the "disease" model—to minimize guilt and therefore reduce relapse.

Until 1973, that was the common approach to homosexuality as well. This strategy fosters two typical responses to the problem raised above—the way guilt leads to a worsening of the very condition that produces it—one in the alcoholic himself, the second in others around him.

The alcoholic's response goes like this: "I am suffering from an illness, rather than a morally defective choice, so I needn't feel guilty. And because I am now not guilt-ridden, I needn't rebel against that guilt by insisting on my right to continue as I was. I am now free to acknowledge that I have a problem because I have redefined the problem in such a way as to make it morally neutral." Nonetheless, this redefinition is not quite right: because unlike true illnesses, there is an important element of volition present every time an alcoholic decides to pick up a drink or not to.

The response of others goes like this: "If what *he* suffers from is an illness rather than the result of a morally defective choice, then *I* will find it much easier to feel compassion for him—since I have such a hard time feeling compassion for people who make defective moral choices. He will therefore not feel judged and condemned by me. Incidentally, this will also make it easier for him not to rebel."

We need to examine the logic of this second response too. Why will thinking of someone's problem as an illness make it easier for us to feel compassion? We see the answer immediately if we come at it the other way around: Why is it so *difficult* to feel compassion for somebody who gets into trouble through the choices he makes? The answer lies in our conviction that *we are superior to him* in this. This is the prevalent form of denial from time immemorial: the denial of our own moral depravity. In other words, when we label someone as suffering from an illness, we actually make it easier for us to avoid examining ourselves. By turning so intense a spotlight on it, gay activists have turned to their (political) advantage the element of condescension that so easily creeps into an illness model of homosexuality.

But we must never forget that addictions and deeply embedded compulsive behavior patterns differ from true illnesses in that their progressive alteration of the brain is directed by choices, especially initial choices. They are therefore reinforced by *the progressive erosion of the ability to choose differently*. The capacity for moral choice is slowly undermined as the compulsion tightens its grip.

The difficulty of altering long-standing compulsions, and the fact that they become deeply rooted in the tissue structure of the brain, do seem to give these conditions a quality that is "medical" or "illness-like." (And indeed, some compulsions may be weakened, even if not entirely broken, by certain medications.) AA sometimes also loosely refers to alcoholism as an "allergy," thereby suggesting (imprecisely) that some people have an innate predisposition to it.

Another problem with characterizing compulsions as illnesses is that the term obscures the sinful, idolatrous character of these conditions. Of course, this is in keeping with our secularized culture. We have lost a clear conception of idolatry because we have lost that which opposes idolatry and gives it its significance: our relationship to God. But in ridding ourselves of God, we are not more free but less. For now as we fall into one idolatry or another, we lack even an idea as to what is happening to us, and why we are therefore so unhappy.

Thus the compulsions are neither simple choices nor true illnesses. They are a category unto themselves that includes elements of both choice and disease. They are a *process*, a way or path by which a life—a free, moral life—is progressively, not all at once, undone. It is this erosion of moral capacity that makes these preeminently spiritual conditions. For if there were no morality to consider, what difference would it make what a man did?

And this of course *is* the great modern "solution" to guilt: Define it away. "Homosexuality is not a problem," gay activism proclaims, "the problem is the *defining* of homosexuality as a problem." Gratefully we assent, not noticing that we do so because we thereby relieve ourselves of the unacknowledged burdens of our own sins. Of course, this "solution" will not work with alcoholism; its destructive effects are simply too widely known. When used as a defense by individual alcoholics (as it commonly is) it is rightly called "denial."

The Apostle Paul explains the way out of the impasse—the necessity of being at once aware of one's sinful nature and of being forgiven for it. This seeming paradox, Paul further tells us, is only possible through an atoning Messiah.

This, of course, is orthodox Christian belief. But in part, at least, it was also once believed by Jews. Prior to the destruction of the second Temple in 70 A.D., complete atonement was accomplished through the repeated, sacrificial death of pure, unblemished animals. And Jews, too, looked (and still look) forward to an era of salvation when the power of sin in the world would be definitively conquered by a Messiah. The earliest Jewish Christians, however, believed that the two—atoning sacrifice and salvation—come together in the person of Jesus of Nazareth.

Often if a man becomes clearly aware of his true state—whatever his particular idolatry—and then turns, resolved to escape the grip of the compulsion, he finds that he cannot do so without enormous personal effort. It requires far more pain and time and suffering than he ever could have anticipated, as well as a humbling dependence on the love and assistance of others—and of God. Many never find their way to such humility and thus remain trapped forever. This is the cruel truth of sin and its tragedy. It is not simply "wrong"; it is that it seems benign at the start but turns out in the end to be Faust's bargain with the devil.

What is it then, that stands most firmly in the way of healing? Is it the "leopard's spots" that cannot be changed? In fact not. For were that the case then we would all best abandon hope of moral betterment in any domain and turn our mechanical selves over to the unconstrained pursuit of pleasure. No the greatest obstacle to healing is pride. On the other hand, "a broken and contrite heart," the God who heals will not despise.

And what then is the ground of true compassion? It is not the attempt to redefine sin out of existence. This is not compassion but guilty sentimentality. In fact, it is even worse than that, for in the name of being nice we hinder another's true self-understanding and thus his hope for healing as well. True compassion for another *requires* acknowledgment of what his sin consists in, but coupled to an unwillingness to condemn the person. To do this, we must unflinchingly acknowledge our own sinfulness. Anything less is hypocrisy—seeing the speck in the eye of the other when our own vision is blinded by a beam.

We understand ourselves best, and gain a true understanding of human nature, when we fully acknowledge our own nature—our own unique configuration not just of gifts but of sins. More importantly, we also obtain a realistic and more truly humane understanding of how difficult it is to refrain from sinning—each from his own.

12

Secular Treatments

One might not think so because of the powerful conspiracy of silence, but many methods for healing homosexuality exist and they all demonstrate varying degrees of success. The purpose of this chapter and the two that follow is not to present a detailed description and critique of these various approaches. It is rather to demonstrate that different kinds of assistance can be found. This chapter examines secular methods of healing homosexuality; chapter 13 examines spiritual approaches and chapter 14 the relationship between homosexuality and Judaism.

For many people who are themselves secular, only secular approaches will be acceptable. The record of purely secular "treatments" for homosexuality is far better than activists and the popular press would lead us to believe. But, in a parallel to AA, it is perhaps not as good as the record of those who approach the problem by attending to its spiritual roots as well. The fact that not all methods are successful, and that no method is successful for everyone, has been distorted by activists into the claim that no method is helpful for anyone. It is a tragedy that so many professionals have accepted this distortion. The simple truth is that, like most methods in psychiatry and psychotherapy, the treatment of homosexuality has evolved out of eighty years of clinical experience, demonstrating approximately the same degree of success as, for example, the psychotherapy of depression.

Psychoanalysis

As discussed earlier, formal psychoanalysis as a whole has had an at best modest track record in treating homosexuality. As homosexual activists point out, Freud himself did not believe that homosexuality was "analyzable." But neither did he consider it an illness. What he did think was that the "homosexual solution," as he saw it, had certain disadvantages as a solution to the conflicts of the Oedipal phase of development. He also believed that some homosexuals could be changed—but *not* by classical psychoanalysis alone. As one gay-activist researcher recently noted,

> Although [Freud] did not believe homoeroticism to be an inherent impediment to human accomplishment and fulfillment neither did he see it as having the full value of heteroeroticism. For these reasons he did not altogether rule out the desirability or possibility of conversion therapy for some individuals even if he did not believe that it could be psychoanalysis alone that could redirect sexual orientation.[1]

To the dismay of activists, many classically trained Freudian psychoanalysts quietly continue to treat homosexuals today, modifying their approach as Freud suggested. Richard Isay, M.D., a homosexual activist and psychoanalyst, has chaired two APA committees and has used his influence to link their activities: the Committee on Abuse and Misuse of Psychiatry in the U.S. and the Committee on Gay, Lesbian, and Bisexual Issues. In frequent letters to the *APA Psychiatric News*, Isay has accused psychoanalysts of never succeeding in changing homosexuals but invariably trying to force such change on them.

In an attempt to refute Isay's contention, Houston MacIntosh, M.D., a Washington, D.C., analyst, sent out a survey to 422 colleagues asking whether they had successfully helped homosexuals change and also asking them to respond to the statement, "A homosexual patient in psychoanalysis for whatever reason can and should be changed to heterosexuality—agree or disagree." Two hundred eighty-five analysts responded (a very high response rate for such a survey) concerning a total of 1215 homosexual patients. Of these, 23 percent changed to heterosexuality and 84 percent benefited "significantly." But only two analysts agreed that homosexuals "should be changed" regardless of their wishes.[2]

Thus it is likely that many analysts continue to treat homosexuality, but do not wish to become embroiled, even indirectly, in the politicized public debate. They are possibly intimidated as well by Isay's position on the Committee on Abuse and Misuse of Psychiatry and his dangerous histrionics: "Efforts to change homosexuals to heterosexuals, I believe, represent one of the most flagrant and frequent abuses of psychiatry in America today."[3]

But some analysts and analytically oriented psychotherapists have openly opposed the activists' assertions. In response to an ongoing attempt by gay activists within the APA to make it a violation of professional ethics to treat homosexuality (even when the patient wishes it), a number of professionals formed an organization called NARTH—the National Association for Research and Treatment of Homosexuality. Since its recent founding NARTH has rapidly grown to nearly four hundred members nationwide. Its purpose is to promote collegial interchange and honest public education in an increasingly hostile, closed-minded and thought-controlled environment.[4]

One of its founders is the most prominent medical psychoanalyst active in treating homosexuality: Charles Socarides, M.D., a Fellow of the American Psychiatric Association and a Clinical Professor of Psychiatry at the Albert Einstein College of Medicine in New York. Recently, Socarides has been involved in a heated exchange of letters with Isay in the APA press on the subject of homosexual change. Isay has openly asserted that although perhaps some psychoanalysts and psychiatrists who claim to have helped homosexuals change are naively deluded, most are bigoted, dishonest, and abusive. He has asserted that *all* claims of homosexual change are spurious; the literature on such change he dismisses as lies. In an attempt to turn the tables on *medical* concern over the lack of aggressive measures to contain AIDS through behavioral change (male homosexual behavior being the single largest risk factor for HIV infection), Isay wrote in a letter to the *New York Times* that "homophobia . . . is a psychological abnormality. Those afflicted should be quarantined and denied employment."[5]

The Official Actions section of the major professional publication of the APA, the *Journal of the American Psychiatric Association*, recently published the following from Dr. Isay's Abuse and Misuse of Psychiatry committee:

> Dr. Robert Cabaj [chair of the Gay and Lesbian Task Force] brought to the committee a statement on reparative (conversion) therapy, with three issues . . .
>
> 1. APA labeling reparative (conversion) therapy as unethical
> 2. A continuing effort to have reparative therapy labeled an abuse or misuse of psychiatry, and
> 3. Finding a way to isolate the National Association for Research and Therapy [sic] of Homosexuality (NARTH), a group whose members feel conflicted homosexuals can and should be changed to heterosexuals.[6]

Drs. Socarides and Benjamin Kaufmann, officers of NARTH, responded:

> We wish to express to readers of the *Journal* and to psychiatrists worldwide our strong displeasure at being labeled abusers of psychiatry. We are a humanitarian organization devoted to research of homosexuality and its alleviation through psychotherapeutic measures, when the patient so requests.
>
> There are many who do not wish to change their psychosexual adaptation, and we respect their wishes not to seek change. . . .

[The committee's action] carries with it the strong suggestion that we attempt to force homosexuals to be heterosexuals. Nothing could be further from the truth.

This implication of force in therapy is designed to turn individuals away from joining our organization, and to mislead patients and their families. If there is an abuse of psychiatry here, it is the use of psychiatry to advise patients and their families to "relax and enjoy homosexuality; you're only neurotic if you complain."

It is an abuse of psychiatry to abridge the freedom of patients to seek help for a condition that they may find intolerable. If they do not have psychotherapists to turn to, their despair increases. Not to offer them help is to be untruthful, cruel, and intellectually dishonest.

We believe that the intent to isolate NARTH is an effort to suppress intellectual freedom and promote the erosion of psychoanalytic knowledge of this condition.[7]

The contrast between APA politics and clinical experience could not be sharper. Edward Glover, a prominent British psychoanalyst, recently took part in a Portman Clinic survey on *short-term* psychoanalytic psychotherapeutic approaches to homosexual change. The surveyors concluded:

Psychotherapy [of homosexuality] appears to be unsuccessful in only a small number of patients of any age in whom a long habit is combined with psychopathic traits, heavy drinking, or lack of desire to change.[8]

Psychotherapy

Another founder of NARTH is Joseph Nicolosi, Ph.D. He is the author of a recent, comprehensive text on the treatment of homosexuality called *Reparative Therapy of Male Homosexuality: A New Clinical Approach.*[9] Nicolosi has worked individually with over two hundred homosexual patients. He reports:

Today, 70 percent of my caseload is men with unwanted homosexual feelings. I've developed a therapeutic technique which, unlike traditional psychoanalytic therapy, is pro-active and more involving of the therapist. . . . [M]ore than an identity problem, homosexuality is a disordered way of being-in-the-world. Gay is a false place, a place of hiding.[10]

It is worth highlighting that Nicolosi's approach, which synthesizes and advances much prior research, departs from strict psychoanalytic technique. This is consistent with what Freud himself predicted would be necessary, and with what many other therapists have found who treat homosexuality. It is consistent, too, with what clinical experience has generally shown to be necessary when treating other problems that are likewise related to deep and early childhood wounds.

In the same way that modern therapists will help their patients work closely with AA in the treatment of alcoholism, so too is Nicolosi's approach one that acknowledges the benefits of *ministries* in assisting those struggling to emerge from homosexuality. His theoretical framework for treatment in the psychotherapeutic setting remains strictly secular, however (except to the extent that the selective integration of certain Jungian ideas could perhaps be considered "spiritual").

In terms of origins, Nicolosi's overarching explanation for many (but not all) instances of homosexuality is that it is stimulated by severe problems in relating to the same-sex parent. Speaking of homosexuality in men, he describes it as often:

the result of incomplete gender-identity development arising when there is conflict and subsequent distancing from the father. This defensive detachment is the psychological mechanism by which the prehomosexual boy removes himself emotionally from the father (or father-figure) and fails to establish a secure male identity. Many homosexuals are attracted to other men and their maleness because they are striving to complete their own gender identification.

. . . Failure to fully gender-identify results in an alienation not only from father, but from male peers in childhood. . . . The resultant homosexuality is understood to represent the drive to repair the original gender-identity injury.[11]

More Impressive than Realized

As the following tables illustrate, homosexuality has long been recognized as treatable. The tables include a selection of reports dating from 1930 to 1986 that discuss a variety of treatment methods.[12] These tables are but a representative cross section of the entire sixty-year literature that activists condemn as wholesale "lies." Recall that in the eight years between 1966 and 1974 alone, just the Medline database—which excludes many psychotherapy journals—listed over a thousand articles on the treatment of homosexuality.

Table 5
Individual and Multiple Case Studies

Author	Method
A. Freud[1]	psychoanalysis
Stekel[2]	psychoanalysis
Wallace[3]	psychotherapy
Eidelberg[4]	psychotherapy
Ovesy[5]	psychoanalysis
Poe[6]	psychotherapy

1. A. Freud, "Some Clinical Remarks Concerning the Treatment of Male Homosexuality," *The International Journal of Psychoanalysis* 30, p. 195.
2. W. Stekel, "Is Homosexuality Curable?" *Psychology Review* 17 (1930), pp. 443–51.
3. L. Wallace, "Psychotherapy of a Male Homosexual," *Psychoanalytic Review* 56, pp. 346–64.
4. L. Eidelberg, "Analysis of a Case of Male Homosexuality," in *Perversions*, S. Lorand and M. Balint, eds. (New York: Gramercy Books, 1956).
5. L. Ovesy, *Homosexuality and Pseudohomosexuality* (New York: Science House, 1969).
6. J. S. Poe, "The Successful Treatment of a 45-Year-Old Passive Homosexual Based upon an Adaptational View of Homosexual Behavior," *Psychoanalytic Review* 39 (1952), p. 23.

Table 6
Descriptive Report

Author	Method
Whitener et al[1]	psychotherapy

1. R. Whitener and A. Nikelly, "Sexual Deviation in College Students," *American Journal of Orthopsychiatry* 34 (1964), pp. 486–92.

Table 7

Outcome Studies[1]

Author	Treated	Changed	Success rate (%)*
Bieber et al.[2]	106**	44	42
Birk[3]	29***	15	52
Ellis[4]	28	18	64
Freeman & Meyer[5]	11	9	82
Hadden[6]	32	12	37
Hadfield[7]	9	7	77****
Hatterer[8]	143	67	47
Masters & Johnson[9]	67	48	72
Mayerson & Lief[10]	19	11	58
Mintz[11]	10	6	60
Monroe & Enelow[12]	7	4	57
Ross & Mendelsohn [13]	15	11	73
Socarides[14]	45	20	44
van den Aardweg[15]	101	37	37
Composite	622	309	50

1. A detailed analysis of most of these studies, specifying strengths and weaknesses of each and the degree of change may be found in R. Goetz, *Homosexuality and the Possibility of Change*, New Direction for Life, 1998, http://www.execulink.com/~newdirec/fp_chang.htm.

2. I. Bieber et al., *Homosexuality: A Psychoanalytic Study of Male Homosexuals* (New York: Basic Books, 1962).

3. L. Birk, "The Myth of Classical Homosexuality: Views of a Behavioral Psychotherapist," in *Homosexual Behavior: A Modern Reappraisal*, ed. J. Marmor (New York: Basic Books, 1980), pp. 376–90.

4. A. Ellis, "The Effectiveness of Psychotherapy with Individuals Who Have Severe Homosexual Problems," *Journal of Consulting Psychology* 20, no. 3 (1956), pp. 191–95.

5. W. Freeman and R. C. Meyer, "A Behavioral Alteration of Sexual Preferences in the Human Male," *Behavior Therapy* 6 (1975), pp. 206–12.

6. S. B. Hadden, M.D., "Treatment of Male Homosexuals in Groups," *International Journal of Group Psychotherapy* 17, no. 1 (1966), pp. 13–22.

7. J. A. Hadfield, "The Cure of Homosexuality," *British Medical Journal* (1958), pp. 1323–26.

8. L. J. Hatterer, *Changing Homosexuality in the Male: Treatment for Men Troubled by Homosexuality* (New York: McGraw-Hill, 1970).

9. W. H. Masters and V. E. Johnson, *Homosexuality in Perspective* (Boston: Brown and Company, 1979).

10. P. Mayerson and H. I. Lief, "Psychotherapy of Homosexuals: A Follow-up Study of Nineteen Cases," in *Sexual Inversion: The Multiple Roots of Homosexuality*, ed. J. Marmor (New York: Basic Books, 1965), pp. 302–44.

11. E. E. Mintz, "Overt Male Homosexuals in Combined Group Individual," *Journal of Consulting Psychology* 30, no. 3 (1966), pp. 193–98.

12. R. R. Monroe and M. L. Enelow, "The Therapeutic Motivation in Male Homosexuality," *American Journal of Psychotherapy* 14 (1960), pp. 474–90.

13. M. Ross and F. Mendelsohn, "Homosexuality in College," *AMA Archives of Neurological Psychiatry* 80 (1958), pp. 253–63.

14. C. W. Socarides, *Homosexuality* (New York: Jason Aronson, 1978).

15. G. van den Aardweg, *On the Origins and Treatment of Homosexuality* (Westport, Conn.: Praeger, 1986), pp. 195–204, 252–58.

*From "considerable" to "complete" change
**of which only 64 sought change
***of which only 14 sought change
****30-year follow-up for many

Note that the composite of these results gives an overall success rate of over 50 percent—where success is defined as "considerable" to "complete" change. These reports clearly contradict claims that change is flatly impossible. Indeed, it would be more accurate to say that *all the existing evidence suggests strongly that homosexuality is quite changeable.* Most psychotherapists will allow that in the treatment of *any* condition, a 30 percent success rate may be anticipated. An implicit precondition of all such change, not just with regard to homosexuality, is commitment to that change on the part of both patient and therapist.

One of the last articles on homosexual change in a major journal was published in 1976 (before the chill effected by the APA) and is not included in the above sample. The researcher examined carefully not only the immediate results of combined behavioral and psychotherapeutic interventions, but long-term follow up. The author found:

Of 49 patients . . . 31 (63 percent) were contracted for follow-up. The average period since the end of treatment was 4 years. Nineteen subjects (61 percent) have remained exclusively heterosexual, whereas nine (29 percent) have had homosexual intercourse. Heterosexual intercourse was reported in 28 (90 percent), including the previous nine subjects. Three (10 percent) subjects have had neither homo nor heterosexual intercourse.[13]

In 1984, the Masters and Johnson program similarly reported a five-year follow-up success rate of 65 percent (included above).[14]

Medication

Of all potential therapeutic approaches to homosexuality, a pharmacological approach would be the most politically sensitive. One reason is that pharmacological treatment—especially *successful* treatment—seems to imply that homosexuality is a true illness. This implication does not necessarily follow but it would not be an unreasonable conclusion to draw.

A second reason is that pharmacological intervention has long been used to treat the so-called *paraphilias*, the technical name for *perversions*. Not only do activists take offense at the term, they do not like being lumped together with pedophiles, exhibitionists, fetishists, and so on, even though "paraphilia" is the diagnostic category into which homosexuality was last placed by the APA.

A third reason is that the use of medication to treat the paraphilias—mainly pedophilia—has long been confined to the use of anti-androgen compounds, which suppress testicular function and thus sexual drive itself. It has thus been "tainted" by a long-standing ethical wrangle over the appropriateness of using such drugs under any circumstances. (These compounds are most commonly used when perverse sexual activities have created legal problems.) Recall that although the largest *number* of pedophiles are heterosexual, by far the largest *proportion* are homosexual, as was noted before. Furthermore, as the DSM-IV itself notes:

> The recidivism [relapse] rate for individuals with pedophilia involving a preference for males is roughly twice that for those who prefer females. . . . The course is usually chronic, especially in those attracted to males.[15]

A diagnosis in which medication would be prescribed is generally one that meets the standards set forth in the DSM. As there is now no diagnosis for homosexuality, there tends to be no formal research on it, let alone research involving the administration of medication. To do so would invite the accusation that one is knowingly administering medications to normal individuals.

Timing has played an ironic role in forestalling the application of such research to homosexuality. The removal of homosexuality from the DSM roughly coincided with the development of new classes of drugs that have proven remarkably effective for many disorders, for example depression. These agents have been so effective, in fact, that the new school of "biological psychiatry" has almost entirely thrown over the dominance that psychoanalysis enjoyed for decades in academic departments of psychiatry.

In the past five years these same new drugs have also proved effective in treating or at least mitigating the perversions, and they lack the controversial effects of the drugs that suppress the male sex hormone. Indeed, because they are mostly anti-anxiety and anti-depressant medications, they are prompting a reevaluation of the perversions themselves. These are now sometimes thought to be not primary sexual disorders, as they were long considered, but the result of a lifelong pattern of relieving anxiety and depression through various forms of sexual expression (consistent with older psychoanalytic ideas.)

This formulation could be—and has been—applied equally to homosexuality. Thus Glover (the British psychoanalyst cited above) noted the significance of *social anxiety* in treating homosexuals.[16]

Although research on the use of medications to change homosexuality would be quite difficult to accomplish in the current environment, there are nonetheless some indications that such an approach might help. One consists of a small number of instances of unplanned, unanticipated, and (at first) unwanted change in homosexuality after medication was prescribed for another condition altogether; the other follows as an implication from using certain drugs to treat those perversions that are still accepted as such and routinely treated.

Thus in January of 1993 two authors reported a case of "Adventitious Change in Homosexual Behavior During Treatment of Social Phobia with Phenelzine."[17] The man who sought treatment was a painfully shy, awkward individual who was extremely anxious about the impression he made on others. He avoided speaking in groups and was prone to extreme blushing and anxiety, which he often controlled with alcohol. The authors describe him as:

> a homosexual man whose severe social phobia . . . responded . . . to . . . phenelzine. During treatment, however, there was an unexpected change in his sexual orientation.

> Upon seeking treatment at age twenty-three, the patient himself

> stated that he was "gay," that he was content with this, and that he did not want his sexual orientation to be a treatment issue. He

had been aware of his homosexuality since his mid-teens and was sexually active exclusively with homosexual males. He was not aroused by females, and had never experienced heterosexual intercourse, as his erotic fantasies involved males only.

The patient was placed on 75 milligrams per day of phenelzine. Four weeks later he reported being:

more outgoing, talkative and comfortable in social situations. He spoke spontaneously in groups without blushing.

But he also:

reported a positive, pleasurable experience of meeting and dating a woman. During the next two months, he began dating females exclusively, reportedly enjoying heterosexual intercourse and having no sexual interest in males. He expressed a desire for a wife and family, and his sexual fantasies became entirely heterosexual.

We may well wonder what has happened here. The fact that a medication caused this change, especially when there was no desire to change, might suggest that at least in this instance homosexuality was caused by a biochemical abnormality similar to that in depression or the anxiety disorders. The authors conclude that:

Social phobia may be a hidden contributing factor in some instances of homosexual behavior and that phenelzine . . . might facilitate heterosexual activity.

The author's speculations about the relationship between homosexuality and social anxiety are widely supported by clinicians who routinely treat homosexuality. And the young man's own assessment as to what had happened to him is especially instructive:

In retrospect Mr. A decided that the combination of his anxiety when approaching and meeting people, the teasing rejection by heterosexual males [which he had reported in childhood] and the comfortable acceptance by homosexual males who pursued and courted him had helped convince him of his homosexuality. Passive homosexual behavior allowed him to avoid the severe anxiety experienced when initiating courtship.

Note that he allowed himself these introspective reflections about the role of his childhood only after he had been convinced that his homosexuality was indeed not permanent. In line with this man's conclusions, Nicolosi observes:

Troublesome fears seem more common to homosexual than heterosexual men. One young man reported . . . a fear . . . about not going fast enough for the driver he saw behind him. . . . Another said, "I've got this fear of tall bridges or tall freeway overpasses. I get worried I might pass out. . . ." Another client said, "I have this phobia with the phone. . . ." One frequently found fear . . . is what gay men call "pee shy," that is, having difficulty urinating in public restrooms. . . . Of seven men I've seen who reported this problem, six were homosexual.[18]

A related event was noted in the earlier literature:

A case report is presented where homosexuality apparently "spontaneously remitted" . . . while the patient underwent treatment for stuttering. The change in sexual orientation [was] . . . possibly . . . induced through generalization effects from treatment of the relevant phobic aspects of the stuttering problem to the associated social aspects of the sexual problem.[19]

When viewed from a purely psychological standpoint, these symptoms (in men) are thought to derive from inner conflicts that developed in the context of a poor relationship with an absent or bullying father. From a biological perspective, an innately heightened anxiety response would make these individuals more likely to respond badly to such a father and therefore to develop anxiety disorders later in life—whether or not homosexual. Such an explanation including biology and environment is more sound than a model that points to only biology or only the environment.

It is important not to overvalue individual case studies. Although they open up a line of speculation consistent with other observations about homosexuality, the vast majority of homosexual men who use antidepressants for depression or anxiety disorders do not change their sexual behavior. Instances such as these also suggest—as noted earlier—that there may be many different "homosexualities." The underlying causes of some may be more responsive to treatment involving medication than others. These findings should not be taken to mean that men and women who want to leave homosexuality should immediately begin taking medication. But it should be taken as a plea to the disinterested research community to begin adequately controlled investigations in the hopes of helping those who struggle.

Anxiety, Antidepressants, and "Addictions"

Many men and women—including those who are predominantly heterosexual—report that homosexual experiences lack the anxiety usually associated with heterosexual courtship and intimacy. (Psychotherapy of this "opposite-sex ambivalence" forms the basis of many treatment programs.[20]) This lack of anxiety contributes to the ease and disinhibition that is characteristic of same-sex practices, including promiscuity. Furthermore, when sex takes place exclusively among males in particular, *both* (or all) partners share the typically polymorphous and interpersonally detached style of male sexuality in its unconstrained native form. If the normal anxiety associated with opposite-sex relations is heightened by other factors—whether environmental or innate or both—same-sex relations will become that much more attractive.

Findings in the treatment of paraphilias likewise suggest that a mood disturbance with significant anxiety might figure prominently in an early turn toward homosexuality. Thus numerous studies have demonstrated that antidepressants can diminish or even eliminate long-standing perversions.[21] Furthermore, these same drugs have also been found to be effective in treating those sexual compulsions or obsessions not categorized as perversions.[22] (The distinction here is between, for example, a compulsive need for exposing oneself, which is a perversion, by contrast to a man's compulsive but heterosexual need for prostitutes or an obsessional fantasy about them.)

Some of the specific conditions that have responded to treatment through medication include pedophilia, transvestic fetishism, persistent paraphilic rape fantasies, compulsive paraphilic masturbation, cross-dressing, and exhibitionism. All the conditions share the following two features: First is that the content, although individualized, is not particularly important (from a pharmacologic standpoint). What is important, rather, is the obsessive, compulsive, or addictive *form* of sexual life. Second is that the condition lies outside of generally accepted norms of sexual behavior.

These two features, in fact, are most commonly found together: that is, paraphilic behaviors tend also to be compulsive. The perversions, sexual addictions, compulsions, and obsessions thus end up being categorized and treated as illnesses rather than simply as alternative lifestyles.[23] This is especially because they interfere with the capacity to form relationships, especially with members of the opposite sex, or are directly harmful to others, as in the case of pedophilia.

A broad understanding is beginning to emerge from the current research on the treatment of the paraphilias and sexual addictions through medication. This is that paraphilic, addictive, and compulsive sexual fantasies or behaviors are all means of temporarily reducing anxiety and associated depression. They are, in other words, *self-soothing responses to internal distress.*[24]

These responses, being oriented toward the self, automatically create distance from others even when another person is involved. (The other person is not being related to; he or she is being used.) And because of the power of the sexual impulse, initial attempts at self-soothing quickly become self-reinforcing and self-generating—and therefore obsessive, compulsive, or addictive. Thus the beneficial effects on *all* these behaviors of treatment with certain medications may be closely related to the *generally* inhibiting effect of these agents on the compulsive nature of gratification-seeking. That is, perverse behavior may be engaged in less frequently because the overall level of anxiety, hence of need for sexual relief, is dampened.

This addictive quality is yet further enhanced by the fact that although the depression is initially alleviated by the sexual *quest* and the anxiety by reaching the goal of the quest—orgasm—the orgasm itself actually causes a postorgasmic increase in depression.[25] This vicious cycle is no different, in essence, than the reinforcement of cocaine addiction caused by the post-high crash or alcoholism by post-binge self-loathing.

Individuals who are prone to greater depression or heightened anxiety, or both, are thus at greater risk to develop a sexual perversion, compulsion, obsession, or addiction as a method of alleviating their distress than are those who are not. When we consider that there is no objective distinction between homosexuality and the other perversions, we can easily see how the development of a homosexual "habit" fits into this framework. In fact, some paraphilias are being successfully treated with fluoxetine (Prozac). Here, too, sexual reorientation is reported to have occurred incidentally.[26]

Indeed, we have come across this interconnection of predisposition, anxiety, and behavioral problem before: It is the same model that accounts for the potential genetic component to alcoholism. In fact, if we use a wide-angle lens to survey the whole of the mental-health landscape, we can see a large-scale pattern emerging. Namely, that *all* of the behaviors on the compulsive/addictive spectrum represent mere variants of a response pathway for the self-soothing of inner distress. A predisposition to depression and/or anxiety will not insure but will increase the risk that individuals will find their way into one or more such self-soothing habits, some sexual, many not.

Consistent with this hypothesis is the phenomenon that many such individuals—perhaps most—adopt multiple methods of self-soothing. Thus, for example, alcoholism, drug abuse, promiscuous sex, and binge-eating are commonly found together in women diagnosed as "bulimic." All these behaviors improve in response to treatment with antidepressants.

This use of multiple methods of self-soothing is likewise the case among homosexuals. As a group they are characterized not only by a strikingly disproportionate incidence of promiscuity, but also by a much greater incidence than among heterosexuals of alcohol or drug problems as well as of paraphilias.[27] According to the National Gay-Lesbian Health Foundation, drug and alcohol problems are three times greater among homosexuals than among heterosexuals.[28]

Real progress in the treatment of such individuals—regardless of the addictions or compulsions in question—only begins when *all* routes of self-soothing are effectively closed off. Relapses will, of course, occur. Put slightly differently: Change in all these behaviors can only begin to happen when all routes of soothing *that depend on actions of the self turning to itself* are closed off—and the turn is made instead to others and to God.

13

Christian Treatments

Secular psychology is far more effective in helping homosexuals to change than most people think and many professionals would like us to know—or know themselves. Nonetheless, even among those professionals who understand that homosexual change is possible, there is too little appreciation for either the spiritual dimension of homosexuality or for the spiritual dimension of its "cure."

This shortsightedness is not surprising given the secular orientation of most mental health professionals. A review of over two thousand research articles in four major psychiatric journals between the years 1978 and 1982 revealed only fifty-nine that included a religious variable of any sort. This variable was usually single and one-dimensional—such as "On a scale of 1 to 10, how religious would you say you are?" Other available religious research was seldom referred to. The authors conclude dryly that, "The academic knowledge and skills needed to evaluate religion have not been absorbed into the psychiatric domain."[1]

With this in mind, we are not surprised to find that the secular literature on homosexual change tends to ignore the dramatic effects of religious faith and belief. Consider the following findings from an article—of a type all too rare—in the *American Journal of Psychiatry*:

> The authors evaluated 11 white men who claimed to have changed sexual orientation from exclusive homosexuality to exclusive heterosexuality through participation in a Pentecostal church fellowship. Religious ideology and a religious community offered the subjects a "folk therapy" experience that was paramount in producing their change. On the average their self-identification as homosexual occurred at age 11, their change to heterosexual identification occurred at age 23, and their period of heterosexual identification at the time of this study was 4 years. The authors report 8 men became emotionally detached from homosexual identity in both behavior and intrapsychic process; 3 men were functionally heterosexual with some evidence of neurotic conflict. On the Kinsey 7-point sexual orientation scale all subjects manifested major before-after changes. Corollary evidence suggests that the phenomenon of substantiated change in sexual orientation without explicit treatment and/or long-term psychotherapy may be more common than previously thought.[2]

It is this phenomenon that we will explore in this chapter.

The Twelve-Step Approach

Across the country numerous Homosexuals Anonymous (HA) groups have sprung up spontaneously from the grass roots. Although HA is not the main approach to the spiritual healing of homosexuality (as AA is for alcoholism), it is worth discussing in some detail. It provides a "transitional" model that falls between secular psychotherapy and more fully faith-based approaches.

That a twelve (actually fourteen)-step model has arisen to help people deal with homosexuality reflects the important role in homosexuality of compulsive/addictive and self-soothing behaviors. As of yet there are no solid statistics to indicate overall efficacy rates for HA as there are for AA, although a major study is currently underway. But HA seems to be approximately where AA was twenty or thirty years ago. The major testament to its current efficacy is its continued existence and growth, which is impressive in the teeth of the public campaign to normalize homosexuality, a campaign never waged on behalf of alcoholism.

HA welcomes individuals who actively live the homosexual life as well as those who have committed themselves to abstinence as a precondition to conversion. As in AA, individuals who are uncertain that they even have a problem suffer a much higher rate of relapse than do those who are convinced of their need for change. Nonetheless, it is understood that, as with alcohol and all other addictions, *abstinence is not the cure, but merely its precondition.*

The principle that abstinence is a precondition for successful change is also one of the basic principles of psychodynamic psychotherapy. So clearly was this principle understood and adhered to in the early days of psychoanalysis that, until their treatment was completed, patients were required to agree not to move nor change jobs nor alter their marital status. The treatment was expected to release anxieties that could provoke patients to impulsive, self-destructive acts if they tried to react in any other way than with words.

So long as people allow themselves the habitual, compulsive, self-soothing behavior for which they seek treatment, they will have an escape from the underlying emotional distress that prompts the repeated acting-out in the first place. When they give up the behavior—if need be forcibly—the distress remains. Indeed, if anything, it is now heightened because the usual routes of escape have been sealed. ("To be healed, our sickness must grow worse.") Only under these somewhat artificial and deliberately more difficult conditions can they now acquire *alternative* means of dealing with the distress. They learn to turn to others or to God instead of alleviating the distress with alcohol, orgasm, or indeed any form of solipsistic, self-centered soothing.

Within the AA community, alcoholics who have not had a drink for many years still wisely refer to themselves as "recovering," not as "recovered." This admirably modest way of describing one's progress embodies two pieces of folk wisdom.

First is the well-known fact that, unlike many purely medical illnesses, an alcoholic's problem with alcohol is permanent: He may always be tempted to replace his spouse or his God with a bottle. This is not because it is impossible to change alcoholism, but because we are human. We can erase neither the knowledge that a quick fix is available nor, under sufficient duress, the craving for it.

Second, and more importantly, is the fact that the "problem" with alcoholism is subtler than simply the drinking itself. Properly understood, the act of imbibing alcohol is the outcome of alcoholism, not its cause. The cause of alcoholism lies in a certain attitude: the individual's heightened temptation and willingness to use alcohol as a solution to the stresses of being human. In Samuel Johnson's words, "He who makes a beast of himself gets rid of the pain of being a man." Put differently, alcoholism is an idolatrous solution to the spiritual suffering that is the essence of the human condition.

This is why *not* drinking is not the solution to alcoholism, but merely the precondition for seeking the solution. One reason is that if the drinking continues, the distress to which it is the response is lessened and even eliminated, at least temporarily. With the distress "solved" (dissolved, really), there is no motivation to seek other solutions except abstractly or while briefly in the grip of post-binge depressive guilt when such motivation is often fruitless. Another reason is that only when alcoholics are not drinking, and keenly aware of the now-free-to-emerge spiritual distress, can they work toward an alternative solution.

HA models itself on AA, substituting homosexual behavior in the place of alcohol. Again, two features are central to its method. One is an acknowledgment of powerlessness over homosexuality —the profound truth of which is, as we have discussed, supported by what we know of how the brain changes in response to experience. The other is the needed dependence on a "Higher Power." The sense of "cure" within HA is likewise appropriately tempered because no such term is ever used. Rather one is perpetually in "recovery." This description not only comports with the neurological fact that old habits are never entirely erased—just overwritten with new ones—it also expresses humility in the face of weaknesses, which is a precondition to any spiritual healing.

As with AA, the roots of the HA approach lie deep within the Bible, tapping its view of our common humanity, of our sinful nature, and of our utter dependence on God. Unlike most current AA groups, however, HA still uses recognizably Judeo-Christian language. To the extent that HA embodies a tacit understanding that compulsion is central to homosexuality, HA can be said to be "good psychology." But likewise, to the extent that it manages this compulsion through "fourteen steps," it is a useful—if somewhat condensed and simplified—version of traditional Western salvation, and in particular of Christian surrender.

The strength of HA lies in its emphasis on building up self-discipline and mutual accountability among group members. These are indeed important components in the management and treatment of all forms of compulsive and addictive behavior. Nonetheless, they are often insufficient by themselves. As we know from extensive experience in substance-abuse programs, when rigid discipline and accountability are uncoupled from hope, compassion, and love, they often collapse into abrupt episodes of relapse and rebellion. This is especially true with regard to homosexuality. A compulsion whose roots lie deep within the need to be loved and affirmed may be anticipated to maintain an especially firm and subtle grip on the soul.

Exodus International

Exodus International is the name of an umbrella organization representing over two hundred separate ministries nationwide that comprise a wide spectrum of openly religious approaches to the healing of homosexuality. At one end of the spectrum are those that, like HA, tend to emphasize accountability and self-discipline and downplay or are even hostile to direct supernatural intervention. These ministries tend, in general, to have an authoritarian cast to them and, for doctrinal reasons, usually reject psychology or psychotherapy as an adjunct to healing. Activists and the press frequently highlight some of these groups as representative of all ministries to the sexually broken, which they are not.

A particular problem arises with those ministries that lack a clear understanding of the healing process. No matter what the setting, there will always be people who seek to change but are not successful, even after many years of effort. Understandably perhaps, some of these relapse into a vocally gay-activist posture and become hostile toward the ministries they perceive as having failed, or even deluded, them. Mel White, the former evangelical ghost-writer and author of *Stranger at the Gate,* is a prominent example. The ministries without a solid grasp of healing can only assert that sufferers need to remain chaste, live holy lives, and submit to God's will. Although there is no gainsaying the truth of this as far as it goes (from a traditional Jewish or Christian perspective), it is also true that without a realistic hope of regeneration and change, many people will fall into hopelessness and despair or into rebellion.

In general the new Catholic catechism happens to fit in well with such groups because it comes close to accepting the claim that homosexuality is not changeable and is therefore a "cross to be borne." Without mentioning healing, it offers this counsel:

> Homosexual persons are called to chastity. By the virtues of self-mastery that teach them inner freedom, at times by the support of disinterested friendship, by prayer and sacramental grace, they can and should gradually and resolutely approach Christian perfection.[3]

"Courage," however, the major Catholic ministry to homosexuals, acts within the bounds of the catechism but has reached out both to interdenominational healing ministries and to the charismatic renewal movement within the Roman Catholic church. Both offer the possibility of successful change as well.

At the other end of the spectrum are those ministries that do emphasize healing. Most have arisen out of the charismatic renewal movement and depend on direct intervention of the Holy Spirit. Although these ministries certainly accept the importance of responsible choice, self-discipline, and accountability, they also believe in the possibility of profound and lasting change—regeneration. Most have integrated the insights of depth-psychology (psychology of the unconscious) into their approach, some with great sophistication and discernment. Alien as such a formulation may appear to secularists and others outside the charismatic tradition, this belief in the potential transformation of even extremely intractable problems is repeatedly borne out by experience.

Desert Stream/Living Waters

One of the most successful of the healing ministries operating under the umbrella of Exodus International is Desert Stream, headquartered in Los Angeles and led by Andrew Comiskey, himself a former homosexual. Comiskey also trains leaders to establish and run similar ministries in churches around the country through his Living Waters program.

Comiskey's book *Pursuing Sexual Wholeness*[4] provides an overview of a biblical approach to the healing of male and female homosexuality. It offers a compelling and realistic personal testimony to his own difficult journey out of the gay lifestyle into committed marriage and fatherhood.

Comiskey's insights and principles can be directly applied beyond homosexuality:

> ... does that healing extend only to those who come out of homosexual backgrounds? Gratefully, no! The struggler begins to recognize in his quest for intimacy and identity the struggle familiar to all. . . . Some face heterosexual brokenness, others the sterile temptation to isolation. Whatever the specifics, the struggle to emerge as a whole person upheld by whole relationships applies to every man and woman. . . ."The healing of the homosexual is the healing of all men. . . ." No one is exempt from sexual brokenness—no one is altogether whole in his capacity to love and to be loved. Therefore, no one is exempt from the ever-deepening work of healing that Jesus wants to establish in the sexuality of His people.[5]

A motif that is repeated continually in ministries such as Comiskey's is that the healing and regeneration process, although perhaps particularly striking in the lives of homosexuals (who become visibly and dramatically different), is applicable in anyone's life. Those with an open heart and mind who spend time around these ministries learn an important and moving truth: "Homosexuals" are just "us." The particular nature of each person's brokenness, while needing to be taken into account in the details of healing, is, in the end, of little significance. Rather the whole person we may be led to become—out of whatever brokenness—is the great and significant matter.

People who come to Desert Stream/Living Waters for help undergo a screening interview prior to participation. Those accepted must be strongly committed to change and in most cases may not give evidence of severe psychopathology. Their personal testimony to·the depth of their involvement in the gay lifestyle and their struggles to overcome their homosexuality show that they are not merely preselected heterosexuals who have mistakenly identified themselves as homosexual. The program is expressly designed for people who have committed their lives to Christ and actively desire the healing of their sexuality through the power of the Holy Spirit, but Comiskey reports that an increasing number of those who are not Christians now apply for admission to the program.

On average, about seventy-five to eighty individuals seek admission to each cycle. Of these, twenty or so are refused, primarily because of the nature of their motivation, such as shame in the eyes of others rather than their own clear, inner determination to change. These are frequently highly "religious" individuals who have stifled their homosexual impulses not so much out of inner conviction as in response to the internalized shame-based strictures of the authoritarian churches in which they were raised. Perhaps three or four others decide on their own not to participate. Thus fifty-five people participate in small groups in each thirty-week cycle. Of these, two-thirds are homosexuals and one-third have other sexual addictions. Of the fifty-five who begin, it is rare for more than three to drop out, and often none do.

Comiskey reports that 50 percent of those who start the program complete it with substantial progress out of homosexuality and into heterosexuality; about 33 percent clearly make little or no progress, frequently regressing back into active homosexual behavior upon leaving the program. The outcome for the remainder is uncertain. His long-term experience reveals that approximately 25 percent of the homosexuals in the program marry within eight years and have marriages that last at least as long or longer than the current national average. Many individuals who began the program in the early eighties are getting married only now—a testament to the often slow nature of the healing process. Case studies in his *Pursuing Sexual Wholeness* movingly illustrate the many twists and turns that this process takes before it can reach a successful conclusion.

Redeemed Life Ministries

Redeemed Life is a ministry to people with all forms of sexual brokenness founded by Mario Bergner, a former homosexual who had been deeply involved in the East Coast gay life. His story, as well as an explication of the combined psychoanalytic and religious principles that guide his ministry, can be found in his moving book, *Setting Love in Order.*[6]

Bergner notes that as a teenager he made two serious attempts at living a Christian life and foregoing his homosexuality. But because the churches he attended only preached sermons either on the condemnation of homosexuality or on its outright acceptance, he remained unaware of the possibility of sexual redemption. In his words, "For years, I had been caught in the homosexuality-versus-Christianity vice-grip."[7]

The dominant approach to the treatment of homosexuality today focuses on the critical role of the same-sex parent, as noted above. Bergner's work, while taking this into account, is more sharply focused on the complementary role played by ambivalence toward the opposite-sex parent in generating homosexuality.

The therapeutic approach in Redeemed Life combines depth-psychology in a primarily group setting with healing prayer. Participants make an eight-month minimum commitment to a small group, which is focused on sexual redemption in Christ. For individuals who continue on and remain committed to the process for the long haul, Bergner reports success rates of over 80 percent.

Pastoral Care Ministries

Pastoral Care Ministries is a healing ministry founded by Leanne Payne, centered in Wheaton, Illinois. Her work has deeply influenced many in the field, including Comiskey and Bergner. Although Payne's ministry reaches out well beyond "sexual brokenness," much of it deals specifically with homosexuality and other forms of compulsive sexual behavior.

Healing of Memories

An important influence on Payne's work is the Healing of Memories movement. Spiritual healing of the body has been associated with Anglicanism and Pentecostalism since the beginning of the charismatic movement early this century; "healing of memories" extends healing to the domain of the mind. Not since the first few centuries of its history has this kind of healing been a clear and distinct objective of the church. (A similar reawakening of a healing movement within Judaism occurred at the time of the Hasidic revival of the 1700s.) Its reappearance in the twentieth century parallels—but did not arise from—the discovery of the unconscious. Because of this congruence, and because depth-psychology seemed to offer a more scientific-seeming and morally neutral approach than traditional religion, the work of Jung in particular came to be a dominant influence in the healing movement, mostly not to good effect.

Thus, although the Healing of Memories movement did not explicitly join forces with depth-psychology, it tacitly shared the understanding that one may *consciously* hold one set of ideas, emotions, values, attitudes, beliefs, memories, and so on while *unconsciously* holding an entirely different set. Our deepest wounds—and our sinful and most guilt-inducing responses to these wounds—may therefore lie unrecognized and out of sight. Insofar as from a faith perspective *confession* is the first step in healing, such parts of the psyche—memories of trauma, memories of responses to this trauma, feelings of subsequent guilt— may all remain unconscious impediments to the ongoing work of healing and growth in the life of a believer.

Healing of memories can be thought of as a modern formulation of the ancient process of in-depth confession, the necessary first step toward wholeness before God. Twelve-step programs also recognize the need for the retrieval of such memories in requiring a thoroughgoing, honest inventory of sins (although not called that) and a subsequent confession of those sins both before God and to those who have been wronged. In a Christian framework, one of the primary functions of the Holy Spirit is to bring to the mind of the believer all those sins that need to be confessed: both those committed repeatedly as well as those forgotten.

From the perspective of depth-psychology, parts of the self are routinely split off from our conscious awareness primarily in response to early emotional wounds. This splitting is one of the most common ways in which we protect ourselves from the painful memory of the wounding itself and therefore from recognizing our sinful responses to that wounding.[8]

When the memories are healed, these wounds and our sinful responses to them are remembered, acknowledged, understood for what they are, and *then presented to God for forgiveness and healing*. Thus the retrieval of our wounds and sins by using a depth-psychological approach is a way to deepen the process of confession. But these activities are not themselves curative; they are preparatory. Healing of the memories therefore departs from secular psychological theory in two critical ways: healing is, first, made far more likely because of openness to God; and, second, healing itself is effected by God. Both of these processes depend on something even more fundamental, which is necessarily lacking in a secular treatment setting—the conviction that conscience is genuine and absolute and not merely the internalization of parental and societal norms.

In spiritual healing, it is also presumed that God is genuinely present and that he defines a certain standard of sinfulness. If we sin, we experience guilt. If we deny the absolute reality of conscience we have little choice but to repress that guilt. If we repress the guilt, we cannot confess the sin—indeed, we deny that it is sin altogether. But if we do not confess, then we cannot receive forgiveness, and without forgiveness, healing is impossible. The consequence, as noted before, is that we are likely to be driven that much deeper into the very thing we hate.

The progressive healing of the personality by the Holy Spirit can therefore be understood as dependence on the deliberate, ongoing presentation to God of the wounded parts of ourselves and thus the parts most vulnerable to the destructiveness of sin. Depth-psychological techniques can assist in the process of "retrieval," but a secular worldview is opposed to the acknowledgment of sin ("conviction").

Why are our wounds most vulnerable to sin? Because when we hurt, we try to assuage our pain, and almost every method that we use *by ourselves* conforms to what the Bible calls sin. For example, when struck by others, literally or symbolically, we either strike back—using revenge as a substitute for healing; or we strike back at our own hurting selves, soothing the pain with sex, drugs, or any form of heightened stimulation—substituting pleasure for genuine peace.

The secular psychoanalytic and psychotherapeutic view of human nature comes close to this understanding. Yet curiously, by itself it is at once too optimistic and too pessimistic, limiting its effectiveness. Secular therapists, too, believe that many of our most harmful behaviors, whether toward ourselves or others, arise in response to wrongs we have suffered, especially as children. But they are too optimistic because they also believe that through sufficient inner examination all these wounds and all their consequences can be undone—by human effort alone. And from this view flows the conclusion that in time, with effort and along with sufficient community support and proper social programs, all men can return to a naturally good state.

The Judeo-Christian view of human nature disagrees with this naive optimism. It knows that, though irreducible good dwells in human nature, so too does irreducible evil. It also knows that this evil can never be removed through unaided human effort, however well-intentioned and however helpful for some people.

Payne's work thus departs dramatically from a psychologically reductionist view of man and returns to the older, Judeo-Christian view, based upon the conviction that the key to healing is the forgiveness of sin. Her work pays careful attention to the specific origins of psychological brokenness but also to the necessity of genuine, healing prayer. Payne absorbs what is valuable in the modern, psychological point of view while discarding that which is not.

Healing Prayer

Pastoral Care Ministries' central activity for the healing of homosexuality and other forms of brokenness is prayer. A feature of *healing* prayer as applied to psychological difficulties is that it requires a deep and careful articulation of the problem to be laid before God. Healing prayer thus incorporates the kind of psychological insight that is at the heart of the best secular psychotherapy. These formulations are consequently not empty ritual (although they could be misused that way by subtly introducing the mistaken notion of magical efficacy into the idea of prayer). Those praying put into words what they become aware of as they explore and express their deepest wounds, as well as their responses to those wounds.

The more psychotherapy helps us strip away the veils of self-deception, the more we become aware of our profound longing for ultimate truth. A life lived without such truth may be free of overt conflict, but it will also be free of genuine meaning. Thus many people "choose" to remain neurotic and self-deceived in order to maintain an illusory sense of meaning. For we *all* worship something, however great the cost. Thus at the heart of much psychic distress lies a complex mixture of mundane neurosis, such as the fear of intimacy, and spiritual self-deception, as is generated by the fear of meaninglessness.

Healing prayer as thus described is different from secular psychotherapy. Deep personal articulations are laid out before God, not simply another person. Secular psychotherapies, by contrast, depend solely on the compassionate presence of the therapist (an effect not to be underestimated, however) and on the therapist's ability to help patients outline the complicated interweavings of self-deception, selfish desire, mental anguish, and noble if unfulfillable longings.

Why is secular therapy not as effective as healing prayer? As patients strip away layers of self-deception to arrive closer to the truth of their own situation, they experience a sense of relief. But such a method for uncovering truth cannot by itself answer the question, "How should we then live?"[9] That is to say, it cannot provide the ultimate truth that carries the healing power. But one way to describe the fly in the ointment of psychology is that it invariably tries to do just that. A pure product of modernism, it substitutes limited personal truths for ultimate ones because it is convinced that there is no absolute truth to be found.

From the perspective of healing prayer, however, the act of excising our self-protective lies is not the cure; it is merely the painful preparation for the cure. If at this crucial point when our deepest wounds are exposed we do not turn to God, we inevitably will take the step that follows so easily in a purely secular treatment. Namely, we invent a new lie for ourselves. Thus we turn the therapeutic quest into a quest for ultimate meaning and make psychology into a new religion. At the point of greatest vulnerability, healing prayer assists us to lay before the one true and miraculous Healer the otherwise unhealable wounds that make up the core of our ever-fallible human nature.

Of all the approaches to the healing of homosexuality, the approach of Pastoral Care Ministries, and other similar ministries (see resources), incorporates the best of the secular psychological approaches into its vital, spiritual, orthodox Christian healing. Payne's focus on sexuality is especially appropriate for our age. No symptom of our modern spiritual disorder more clearly reveals the depth of our affliction than the spreading destruction of divinely ordered love and of the stable family relationships that are its fruit.[10]

14

Homosexuality and Judaism

The preceding discussion of sin and compulsion and of the spiritual approaches to the healing of homosexuality has been conducted from a primarily Christian perspective. But obviously not all homosexuals are Christians or sympathetic to the Christian perspective. Homosexuality is a phenomenon that cuts across religion, ethnicity, race, class, and culture. Viewing it from the point of view of Judaism can add valuable, complementary insights.

In the United States, Jewish individuals are as visible in the homosexual subculture as they are in many other subcultures. Because of the well-known, high levels of achievement of both Jews and of homosexuals, and because most non-Orthodox Jews hold attitudes that are considerably more liberal than non-Jewish society at large, Jewish gay activists are unfortunately disproportionately visible. This may leave the false impression that Judaism itself—by contrast to some Jews—accepts homosexuality fully. In the words of one Rabbi, a clinical psychologist, the truth is that:

There has been too much publicity about the Jewish approach to the issue that has been nothing short of a gross distortion of

Judaism. Judaism is what Judaism is, however uncomfortable—
not what some would like it to be.[1]

Orthodox Beliefs in Two Camps

When we speak of "Christianity" or "Judaism" in this context
we are focusing on *orthodox* Christianity and *Orthodox* Judaism.
Orthodox Christianity here means "traditional" or "conservative"
and "biblical" as opposed to "modernist" or "liberal." And Orthodox Judaism here also means traditional in the more general
sense, but in this case also refers specifically to the Orthodox
denomination of Judaism and not to its Conservative, Reform, or
Reconstructionist branches.

Indeed in many respects Orthodox Judaism and orthodox
Christianity today have much more in common with each other
than each has with its modern, liberalized variants. Both Orthodox Jews and Christians often share the view—usually only voiced
quietly among themselves—that the liberal forms of either faith
are neither real Judaism nor real Christianity. They see these liberal variants as closer to each other in their liberalism than to
their Orthodox counterparts; they also see them less as religious
faiths than sociopolitical ideologies.

Equally, many liberals of both religions dismiss their Orthodox counterparts as "fundamentalists" who turn a blind eye to
the fact—as they see it—that in the last hundred years science
has effectively debunked their worldviews. Thus, liberal Christianity (mostly in the mainline churches) and liberal Judaism
(Reconstructionist, Reform, and many Conservative synagogues)
view themselves as having grown beyond theological positions
supported by Scripture. They treat biblical injunctions (in Old or
New Testaments) as but the culturally relative opinions of the
men of the time.

In contrast, the orthodox Christian faith remains theologically
dependent on both Old and New Testaments as received. And
Orthodox Judaism remains theologically dependent on the
Hebrew scriptures as received—especially the Pentateuch—and
the Talmud. With respect to their shared dependence on the
Hebrew Bible they therefore both maintain an unbroken chain

of belief, going back thirty-five hundred years, that homosexuality is a sin—even if, like all sins, an "unnaturally natural" one. Neither would view homosexuality as an illness in the medical sense.

This is not the place to dispute the recent activist theological arguments that radically reinterpret the pertinent passages in both the Old Testament and New in an attempt to present the Bible as never actually treating homosexual acts as sinful. Among other glaring errors and distortions, those who treat the biblical text in this fashion are invariably unfamiliar with the Talmud. The Talmud presents a canonical expansion and interpretation of the Hebrew Bible that even according to skeptical critics dates back more than five hundred years prior to the New Testament. (In Jewish tradition, the essential contents of the Talmud were given orally at Sinai along with the written Torah as an explication of the latter.)

A major portion of the moral theology of the church derives directly from the Talmud, and some of the early church fathers routinely consulted the Rabbis of their time for clarification of scriptural principles. Recall that during the earliest years of the Church, "scripture" meant the Hebrew Bible. The New Testament had yet to be redacted and canonized. Paul, for one, was a Talmudic scholar, and with few exceptions, his comments about homosexuality directly reflect Talmudic discussions of sexuality. These discussions, in turn, constitute a detailed explication of the rather more terse commandments found in the Pentateuch.

On the basis of the Pentateuch, the Talmud treats all sexual activity outside of marital relations, including masturbation, unequivocally as sins, though it makes careful distinctions concerning their varying severity. Lesbianism, for example, is treated as a less severe sin than male homosexuality; the various Talmudic discussions concerning lesbianism view it as less of a threat to family formation and stability than the always potentially rogue male sexuality. As unmodern as this asymmetry may appear, it is indeed accurately reflected in the many families tragically being torn apart by the decision of (chiefly) husbands to leave their families and enter the "gay life." It is also seen in the lower incidence of lesbianism than male homosexuality in America (1.4 percent versus 2.8 percent) and in the more severe medical consequences of male homosexuality, primarily related to anal intercourse and secondarily to the exchange of fluids in male to male sex.

Homosexuality and Orthodox Judaism

A casual observer may discern that the vast preponderance of Jewish homosexuals are liberal not only in their outlook on life but in their religious attitudes as well—if they have any. But although homosexuality does occur among Orthodox Jews, it is strikingly uncommon. Why this is so would take us far afield but is worth considering briefly.

Why is this? Most telling about Orthodox Judaism is that its marriages are among the most stable in the United States—in spite of the fact that divorce is not forbidden, only strongly discouraged. Further, Orthodox Jewish marriages are stable even though many marriages (especially in ultra-Orthodox or Hasidic communities) are arranged—a method that cuts directly across the "natural," desire-based method of selecting partners. Beyond that, lengthy sections of the Talmud are devoted to the precise obligations, including sexual ones, that each partner in a marriage owes to his or her spouse. The failure to meet these obligations is laid out in the Talmud as some of the legitimate grounds for divorce. For example, unless extenuating circumstances prevent it, a man must satisfy his wife sexually at least once every week. Interestingly, the reverse obligation does not apply.

The homosexual impulses that naturally occur in any population of human beings are constrained among Orthodox Jews by their way of life. These impulses only rarely interfere with the biblical mandate to marry, to fulfill one's spouse, and to raise many children. Given these mandates, it is inconceivable that large numbers of homosexuals could remain "closeted," and it would be extraordinarily difficult to carry off mere "marriages of convenience." What occurs instead is a self-reinforcing process: Stable family life reduces the incidence of the kinds of problems that increase homosexuality; reduced levels of homosexuality help stabilize family life.

America as a whole is now in the midst of an opposite, downward spiral. The widely decried destruction of families—especially of fatherhood—increases the likelihood of all forms of sexual pathology—father problems especially causing an increase in male homosexuality; the increase in homosexuality in turn contributes to the destruction of families in the next generation.

In contrast to Orthodox Jews, some relatively conservative Christians actively embrace homosexuality. A public example is Andrew Sullivan, editor of *The New Republic,* who openly describes himself as a conservative, gay Catholic. (In *Virtually Normal,* his otherwise reasonably argued defense of a moderate gay activist position, Sullivan remains determinedly ignorant of success rates in homosexual change. As always, this fact pulls the linchpin from the pro-gay argument.) An even larger number of traditionalist Christians struggle with their homosexual impulses: some secretly, and in great pain, in churches that condemn not just homosexuality but homosexual people; some, fortunately, in churches that embrace them and offer programs to help them change. But the Jewish population is even more sharply divided than the Christian, falling into two distinct camps: the majority being secularists and liberals among whom homosexuality is present and widely accepted; a large minority being Orthodox among whom homosexuality is uncommon.

For this reason, no active Orthodox groups or Jewish ministries have arisen to "treat" homosexuality, as do ministries in Christian churches and parachurch organizations. The rare Orthodox individual struggling with homosexuality will be referred instead to one of the psychiatrists or psychotherapists who continues to treat homosexuality as a resolvable mental-health problem. The non-Orthodox Jewish homosexual, on the other hand, commonly accepts the gay-activist positions. Jewish therapists from a secularized background also will likely adopt the activist position that the problem is not homosexuality itself, but the desire not to be homosexual.

As a result of these factors, and of a general wariness regarding the Gentile world, until recently Orthodox Judaism has refrained from speaking out in the current debate over homosexuality. To the extent that public discussion among the Orthodox exists, it has been aimed almost exclusively at fellow Orthodox Jews or those considering a return to the Orthodoxy of their ancestors.

The general "Jewish" position on homosexuality—if one even senses such a thing—is therefore likely to be identified as the monolithic voice of liberal Judaism. Yet the true, traditional, Jewish position on homosexuality, as handed down since the revelation at Sinai and abdicated by secularized Jews only in the last few years, is the very different, Orthodox one.

Recently, a change has occurred in the traditional posture of the Orthodox. They have become concerned that the rapid drift of the other branches of Judaism toward the secular left will pull an entire generation away from both Judaism and from God; and—like their Christian counterparts—they are extremely concerned about what they perceive as the dramatically degraded moral state of the nation. They have lost confidence that their Reform brethren can be counted on to maintain the ancient standards. In the words of Albert Vorspan, senior vice president emeritus of the Union of American Hebrew Congregations:

> Orthodox Jewish leaders . . . charge that radical changes such as
> . . . support for gay/lesbian rabbis and congregations have cast
> Reform beyond the pale of Jewish authenticity.[2]

Recently, an Orthodox Rabbi wrote a book on homosexuality articulating the traditional Jewish position for both Jews and Gentiles.[3] Interestingly, it has been published by a Christian house whose titles appeal most to Evangelicals. The same Rabbi was coauthor of a formal Orthodox Jewish statement on homosexuality put forth by the Rabbinical Council of America. This council represents all Orthodox Jewish communities in America in their relationship to the society at large. Insofar as Orthodox Judaism continues to see itself—in a continuation of the ancient view—as having an ongoing spiritual purpose not only for Jews but also for Gentiles, its interest in the question of homosexuality extends beyond interpreting Jewish law only for Jews. The Rabbinical Council's statement makes this clear:

The Rabbinical Council of America views with distress the con-
doning of homosexuality as a legitimate alternate lifestyle. Such
an attitude rejects a fundamental moral pillar of the Torah. The
Jewish community is a community because of the Torah. As such,
Torah principles must always be the guide for communal norms.

Additionally, the Jewish community has a responsibility to the
world. It must be in the forefront of assuring that the seven
Noahide commandments are incorporated into society.[4] Since
homosexuality is a breach of these Noahide laws, the Jewish community must be a light unto the world in assuring that moral principles are not compromised. The uncompromising rejection of
homosexuality as a legitimate alternate lifestyle does not mean
that the Jewish community endorses a witch hunt to weed out
homosexuals.

It is recognized that a homosexual tendency is at times rooted
in deeper considerations, which may include physical, genetic,
psychological and environmental factors. As such, the Rabbinical
Council of America calls upon its Rabbis to become familiar with
those therapists who are on record as willing to treat people with
homosexual tendencies who desire to lead a productive heterosexual lifestyle. The Rabbinical Council of America is preparing a
list of these therapists, which it will make available to the Rabbis.
Additionally, the Rabbinical Council of America strongly urges the
scientific community to work on improving the therapeutic
approaches to help those who are wrestling with homosexual feelings and who desire to live a heterosexual lifestyle.

The Rabbinical Council of America also compassionately calls on
all those whose desires lead them in this inappropriate direction
to seek professional therapy and spiritual guidance from appropriate therapists and Rabbis, with the goal of achieving the capacity for fulfilling a heterosexual lifestyle. The Rabbinical Council of
America recommends that its Rabbis do their utmost to help those
with homosexual tendencies. They can best help those with homosexual tendencies by convincing them to remain true to the Torah
stand on homosexuality, and showing compassion and Torah
guidance for those who seek their help.

The Rabbinical Council of America rejects the proposition that
a person's sexual preferences be foisted upon the community. It
neither seeks to find homosexuals nor to have homosexuals
impose their will on the community. Everyone is welcome within

the community, but no one is welcome to show contempt for the community by publicly proclaiming any private proclivity that is inconsistent with community standards, be it homosexuality, adultery, or other deviations from Torah norms.

The Rabbinical Council of America firmly believes that true compassion in this most sensitive issue is manifested in doing whatever possible to help individuals affirm and actualize Torah values.[5]

Levels of Compassion

The Orthodox Jewish and orthodox Christian positions on homosexuality have differences between them. But these differences are mostly in emphasis and reflect certain differences in their approaches to spirituality in general.

The particular difference in question is based on the fact that Orthodox Jewish tradition consists largely of the more than three millennia of extraordinarily specific, finely tuned distinctions in the "Halakha," or Jewish Law, which are meant to regulate human behavior in relationship to God and to other people. Some Christian critics of Judaism have superficially dismissed this twenty-plus-volume code and commentary as an obsessive legalism. Actually, however, the Talmud itself criticizes legalistic Pharisees in the same terms as does Jesus. In fact, one of the most interesting and easily missed dimensions of Talmud is its careful thought regarding the *actual, observed specifics of human nature* and its consequent realism and compassion in approaching moral obligations.

To make a broad generalization, both Jews and Christians believe that after death all people will be judged according to their deeds on earth and will be rewarded accordingly. Although this judgment serves as a moral spur to Christians, in large part Christian theology concentrates on the prior salvation by grace alone—that is, on one's escape from condemnation through a savior, inasmuch as no one can enter heaven merely on merit.

Judaism, however, pays closer attention to one's place in the "Olam Haba," the world to come, which (as in Christianity) is determined by the balance of one's good and evil deeds. Judaism's specific focus here can partly be attributed to its conviction that the vast majority of people will be saved, and have at least some portion in the world to come. Only a small minority of particularly heinous individuals will be damned entirely—which is to say destroyed forever.

Much of Jewish Law has therefore evolved into an extremely discerning discourse on the standards of practical morality in the here and now. Those Talmudic disputes that discuss such ceremonial matters pertaining to Jews alone such as what constitutes "work" on the Sabbath (for example, closing an electrical circuit) will indeed strike the unsympathetic outsider as mere casuistry. But the discussions about degrees of morality—and of degrees of moral obligation under varying circumstances—can be immediately understood, giving extraordinary insight, once the Talmudic method of argument is grasped.

Among the many sad consequences that have followed from the historical enmity between Christians and Jews has been the loss to Christianity of the good of the Jewish Law. This is not to say the Old Testament itself, because that remains a part of the Christian faith anyway, but of knowledge of the Talmud, which was the *largest part of the Law at the time of Jesus.* When Christ insisted that though he came to fulfill "the Law," not abolish it, and that not "one jot nor tittle" of it should pass away until the end of time, his Jewish hearers—pro and con—would have automatically understood him to be referring not to the Pentateuch alone (the "Written Law") nor to the Pentateuch and other Old Testament writings ("The Law and the Prophets"), but to the Pentateuch ("The Written Law") and certain parts of the Talmud ("the Oral Law").

Thus Rabbinic discussions of homosexuality begin with the fact of its sinfulness and moral unacceptability but quickly make two important points. First, as in all matters pertaining to human failings, a strict distinction must be maintained between the sin and the person. Although homosexual behavior is to be condemned, homosexual persons are as beloved of God as everyone else; they are to be treated with no less dignity than we want for ourselves. This is, of course, no different than what the Christian position is ideally—hating the sin but loving the sinner.

Second, the Rabbinic discussions make a refined distinction as to the degree of *culpability* that individuals bear for their homosexual behavior, depending on the situation. For example, someone who has been raised to believe that homosexuality is not wrong commits less of a sin than does someone raised in the knowledge of its sinfulness and who then deliberately rejects the Torah's standard of behavior. Similarly, someone for whom homosexuality has become a compulsion is now less culpable than someone in the early stages of developing homosexual behavior, for whom it retains greater willfulness.

Indeed this assessment of "degree of culpability" has a further implication:

> In actuality, the person who wrestles with the homosexual demon within and overcomes it is considered much more praiseworthy [and will be granted a larger portion in the "Olam Haba"] than one who never had to wrestle with such feelings.[6]

Nor is this mere sentiment. Those who have worked closely with men and women who have successfully emerged out of homosexuality cannot but be struck by the depth of their compassion and wisdom, acquired at great cost, and by their strength of character. In the words of the Talmud, "The greater the man, the greater his Evil inclination" (Sukkah 52a).

Another component of the Jewish point of view, with its focus on finely assessed evaluation of behavior, is the importance of behavior in itself shaping character: "One is likely to become what one does . . . . [D]oing, whether for good or otherwise, is habit forming and personality building."[7]

In Judaism, sexuality is recognized as an enormously powerful force. It needs therefore to be hedged about with many constraints—even arranged marriages. But it is therefore also understood as one that, when sanctified, is potentially holy to the highest possible degree. Indeed, the sanctified marital union (not sexuality in the state of nature) is poetically referred to in Judaism as the "Holy of Holies." According to Rabbi Moses Nachmanides in the thirteenth century, one of the greatest Jewish sages, there is *nothing* more holy and pure.[8]

Judaism does not deal with the potential evil inherent in man by rejecting the natural altogether. It lacks entirely any ascetic tradition, so much so that a great sage who does not marry is criticized as in some measure having failed.[9] Its approach, rather, has always been to sanctify the merely natural and to make it holy. It is the guideline of the Torah, written and oral, that teaches man how to do this. Such sanctification invariably involves constraint.

Because of the natural power of sexuality, those who fall prey to it are seen as less morally culpable than those who fall prey to less compelling temptations, such as speaking ill of another person. In fact, this latter sin is considered so severe that persistent indulgence in it can place one's portion of the "Olam Haba" altogether at risk; not so, however, for homosexual or other sexual sins. In this view therefore, he who condemns the homosexual *person* for his behavior, rather than the behavior itself, commits the far more grievous sin—a notion that strikes at the root of all judgmentalism.

Orthodox Judaism thus holds that, although homosexuality cannot be condoned, mitigating circumstances may exist that temper our condemnation of it. Put differently, on the finely differentiated scale of moral assessment, there are many different kinds of homosexuality; each single instance must be considered in the individual human context in which it appears.[10] And a great many other sins exist that are far worse than homosexuality.

Thus in spite of the apparent legalism of the Orthodox Jewish approach, it contains what we might view as a specific and precise scale of compassion from which we all could learn much. Although Orthodox Judaism unflinchingly calls homosexuality a sin, it does not condemn it with the at times cruel and self-righteous tone that some Christian groups exhibit. But we must also emphasize that this rigorous compassion bears little resemblance to what now passes for "tolerance"—its modern, liberal, standardless counterpart.

15

Putting the Pieces Together

I t may be difficult to grasp how genes, environment, and other influences interrelate to one another, how a certain factor may "influence" an outcome but not cause it, and how faith enters in. The scenario below is condensed and hypothetical, but is drawn from the lives of actual people, illustrating how many different factors influence behavior. Because homosexuality is twice as common among men as among women and because its consequences are more dangerous for men, the book as a whole has emphasized male homosexuality; so too does this scenario.

But although the specifics are different for women, the general principles of how genes, environment, and choice can all work together are the same. And I should note that the following is just one of the many developmental pathways that can lead to homosexuality, though a common one. In reality, every person's "road" to sexual expression is individual, however many common lengths it may share with those of others.

1. Our scenario starts with birth. The boy who one day may go on to struggle with homosexuality is born with certain features that are somewhat more common among homosexuals than in the population at large. Some of these traits might be inherited

(genetic), while others might have been caused by the "intrauterine environment" (hormones). What this means is that a youngster without these traits will be somewhat less likely to become homosexual later than someone with them.

What are these traits? If we could identify them precisely, many of them might well turn out to be gifts rather than "problems," for example a "sensitive" disposition, a strong creative drive, a keen aesthetic sense. Some of these, such as greater sensitivity, could be related to—or even the same as—physiological traits that also cause trouble, such as a greater-than-average anxiety response to any given stimulus.

No one knows with certainty just what these heritable characteristics are; at present we only have hints. Were we free to study homosexuality properly (uninfluenced by political agendas) we would certainly soon clarify these factors—just as we are doing in less contentious areas. In any case, there is absolutely no evidence whatsoever that the behavior "homosexuality" is itself directly inherited.

2. From a very early age these potentially heritable characteristics mark the boy as "different." He finds himself somewhat shy and uncomfortable with the typical "rough and tumble" of his peers. Perhaps he is more interested in art or in reading—simply because he's smart. But when he later thinks about his early life, he will find it difficult to separate out what, in these early behavioral differences, came from an inherited temperament and what from the next factor, namely:

3. For whatever reason, he recalls a painful "mismatch" between what he needed and longed for and what his father offered him. Perhaps most people would agree that his father was distinctly distant and ineffective; maybe it was just that his own needs were unique enough that his father, a decent man, could never quite find the right way to relate to him. Or perhaps his father really disliked and rejected his son's sensitivity. In any event, the absence of a happy, warm, and intimate closeness with his father led to the boy's pulling away in disappointment, "defensively detaching" in order to protect himself.

But sadly, this pulling away from his father, and from the "masculine" role-model he needed, also left him even less able to relate to his male peers. We may contrast this to the boy whose loving father dies, for instance, but who is less vulnerable to later homosexuality. This is because the commonplace dynamic in the pre-homosexual boy is not merely the absence of a father—literally or psychologically—but the psychological defense of the boy against his repeatedly disappointing father. In fact, a youngster who does not form this defense (perhaps because of early enough therapy, or because there is another important male figure in his life, or due to temperament) is much less likely to become homosexual.

Complementary dynamics involving the boy's mother are also likely to have played an important role. Because people tend to marry partners with "interlocking neuroses," the boy probably found himself in a problematic relationship with both parents.

For all these reasons, when as an adult he looks back on his childhood, the now homosexual man recalls, "From the beginning I was always different. I never got along well with the boys my age and felt more comfortable around girls." This accurate memory makes his later homosexuality feel convincingly to him as though it was "preprogrammed" from the start.

4. Although he has "defensively detached" from his father, the young boy still carries silently within him a terrible longing for the warmth, love, and encircling arms of the father he never did nor could have. Early on, he develops intense, nonsexual attachments to older boys he admires—but at a distance, repeating with them the same experience of longing and unavailability. When puberty sets in, sexual urges—which can attach themselves to any object, especially in males—rise to the surface and combine with his already intense need for masculine intimacy and warmth. He begins to develop homosexual crushes. Later he recalls, "My first sexual longings were directed not at girls but at boys. I was never interested in girls."

Psychotherapeutic intervention at this point and earlier can be successful in preventing the development of later homosexuality. Such intervention is aimed in part at helping the boy change his developing effeminate patterns (which derive from a "refusal" to identify with the rejected father), but more critically, it is aimed at teaching his father—if only he will learn—how to become appropriately involved with and related to his son.

5. As he matures (especially in our culture where early, extra-marital sexual experiences are sanctioned and even encouraged), the youngster, now a teen, begins to experiment with homosexual activity. Or alternatively his needs for same-sex closeness may already have been taken advantage of by an older boy or man, who preyed upon him sexually when he was still a child. (Recall the studies that demonstrate the high incidence of sexual abuse in the childhood histories of homosexual men). Or oppositely he may avoid such activities out of fear and shame in spite of his attraction to them. In any event, his now-sexualized longings cannot merely be denied, however much he may struggle against them. It would be cruel for us at this point to imply that these longings are a simple matter of "choice."

Indeed, he remembers having spent agonizing months and years trying to deny their existence altogether or pushing them away, to no avail. One can easily imagine how justifiably angry he will later be when someone casually and thoughtlessly accuses him of "choosing" to be homosexual. When he seeks help, he hears one of two messages, and both terrify him: Either, "Homosexuals are bad people and you are a bad person for choosing to be homosexual. There is no place for you here and God is going to see to it that you suffer for being so bad," or "Homosexuality is inborn and unchangeable. You were born that way. Forget about your fairytale picture of getting married and having children and living in a little house with a white picket fence. God made you who you are and he/she destined you for the gay life. Learn to enjoy it."

6. At some point, he gives in to his deep longings for love and begins to have voluntary homosexual experiences. He finds—possibly to his horror—that these old, deep, painful longings are at least temporarily, and for the first time ever, assuaged. Although he may also therefore feel intense conflict, he cannot help but admit that the relief is immense. This temporary feeling of comfort is so profound—going well beyond the simple sexual pleasure that anyone feels in a less fraught situation—that the experience is powerfully reinforced. However much he may struggle,

he finds himself powerfully driven to repeat the experience. And the more he does, the more it is reinforced and the more likely it is he will repeat it yet again, though often with a sense of diminishing returns.

7. He also discovers that, as for anyone, sexual orgasm is a powerful reliever of distress of all sorts. By engaging in homosexual activities he has already crossed one of the most critical and strongly enforced boundaries of sexual taboo. It is now easy for him to cross other taboo boundaries as well, especially the significantly less severe taboo pertaining to promiscuity. Soon homosexual activity becomes the central organizing factor in his life as he slowly acquires the habit of turning to it regularly—not just because of his original need for fatherly warmth and love, but to relieve anxiety of any sort.

8. In time, his life becomes even more distressing than for most. Some of this is in fact, as activists claim, because all-too-often he experiences from others a cold lack of sympathy or even open hostility. The only people who seem really to accept him are other gays, and so he forms an even stronger bond with them as a "community." But it is not true, as activists claim, that these are the only or even the major stresses. Much distress is caused simply by his way of life—for example, the medical consequences, AIDS being just one of many (if also the worst). He also lives with the guilt and shame that he inevitably feels over his compulsive, promiscuous behavior; and too over the knowledge that he cannot relate effectively to the opposite sex and is less likely to have a family (a psychological loss for which political campaigns for homosexual marriage, adoption, and inheritance rights can never adequately compensate). However much activists try to normalize for him these patterns of behavior and the losses they cause, and however expedient it may be for political purposes to hide them from the public-at-large, unless he shuts down huge areas of his emotional life he simply cannot honestly look at himself in this situation and feel content.

And no one—not even a genuine, dyed-in-the-wool, sexually insecure "homophobe"—is nearly so hard on him as he is on himself. Furthermore, the self-condemning messages that he struggles with on a daily basis are in fact only reinforced by the bitter self-derogating wit of the very gay culture he has embraced. The activists around him keep saying that it is all caused by the "internalized homophobia" of the surrounding culture, but he knows that it is not.[1]

The stresses of "being gay" lead to more, not less, homosexual behavior. This principle, perhaps surprising to the layman (at least to the layman who has not himself gotten caught up in some such pattern, of whatever type) is typical of the compulsive or addictive cycle of self-destructive behavior: Wracking guilt, shame, and self-condemnation only cause it to increase. It is not surprising that people therefore turn to denial to rid themselves of these feelings, and he does too. He tells himself, "It is not a problem; therefore there is no reason for me to feel so bad about it."

9. After wrestling with such guilt and shame for so many years, the boy, now an adult, comes to believe, quite understandably— and because of his denial needs to believe—"I can't change anyway because the condition is unchangeable." If even for a moment he considers otherwise, immediately arises the painful query, "then why haven't I . . . ?" and with it returns all the shame and guilt.

Thus, by the time the boy becomes a man, he has pieced together this point of view: "I was always different, always an outsider. I developed crushes on boys from as long as I can remember and the first time I fell in love it was with a boy not a girl. I had no real interest in members of the opposite sex. Oh I tried all right—desperately. But my sexual experiences with girls were nothing special. But the first time I had homosexual sex it just 'felt right.' So it makes perfect sense to me that homosexuality is genetic. I've tried to change—God knows how long I struggled— and I just can't. That's because it's not changeable. Finally, I stopped struggling and just accepted myself the way I am."

10. Social attitudes toward homosexuality will play a role in making it more or less likely that the man will adopt an "inborn and unchangeable" perspective, and at what point in his development. It is obvious that a widely shared and propagated worldview that normalizes homosexuality will increase the likelihood of his adopting such beliefs, and at an earlier age. But it is per-

haps less obvious—it follows from what we have discussed above—that ridicule, rejection, and harshly punitive condemnation of him as a person will be just as likely (if not more likely) to drive him into the same position.

11. If he maintains his desire for a traditional family life, the man may continue to struggle against his "second nature." Depending on whom he meets, he may remain trapped between straight condemnation and gay activism, both in secular institutions and in religious ones. The most important message he needs to hear is that "healing is possible."

12. If he enters the path to healing, he will find that the road is long and difficult—but extraordinarily fulfilling. The course to full restoration of heterosexuality typically lasts longer than the average American marriage—which should be understood as an index of how broken all relationships are today.

From the secular therapies he will come to understand what the true nature of his longings are, that they are not really about sex, and that he is not defined by his sexual appetites. In such a setting he will very possibly learn how to turn aright to other men to gain from them a genuine, nonsexualized masculine comradeship and intimacy; and how to relate aright to woman, as friend, lover, life's companion, and, God willing, mother of his children.

From communities of faith that turn to him in understanding, offering not only moral guidance but genuine healing, he will gain much in addition. Most importantly, the love he sought so vainly when young and finally turned away from he will find in the arms of a loving God. Those for whom this is no mere formula but a living reality are truly blessed, whatever their wounds. And he will find too that the presence of this love makes it possible to lay those old defenses down and face fearlessly the wounds that have inflicted so much pain and distorted so much of his life over so many years. For many, this is the only circumstance in which it is possible to lay their defenses down.

Of course the old wounds will not simply disappear, and later in times of great distress the old paths of escape will beckon. But the claim that this means he is therefore "really" a homosexual and unchanged is a lie. For as he lives a new life of ever-growing honesty, and cultivates genuine intimacy with the woman of his heart, the new patterns will grow ever stronger and the old ones engraved in the synapses of his brain ever weaker.

In time, knowing that they really have little to do with sex, he will even come to respect and put to good use what faint stirrings remain of the old urges. They will be for him a kind of storm-warning, a signal that something is out of order in his house, that some old pattern of longing and rejection and defense is being activated. And he will find that no sooner does he set his house in order than indeed the old urges once again abate. In his relations to others—as friend, husband, professional—he will now have a special gift. What was once a curse will have become a blessing, to himself and to others.

If he is fortunate enough to be able to place all this in the context of faith, then he will also find that he has traveled far along the ancient pathway toward sanctification. This is just as when the angel put Jacob's hip out of joint and then blessed him, transforming him forevermore into Israel. On this road he will always have as his companion the Great Companion. And perhaps because of this he will find his footing a little more surely than those who are skeptical that such a companion walks invisibly at their side, too.

16

The Pagan Revolution

A major question has hovered unasked over the preceding discussion: How have we as a culture come so close to abandoning the long-held consensus on sexual mores that discourages homosexuality? Of course, this change in attitude toward homosexuality is merely a piece of a larger change pertaining to sexuality and family life as a whole, and this in turn is but a piece of an even more sweeping change in our general worldview. This massive change in attitude appears to have occurred within the space of a mere twenty or thirty years.

But this appearance of suddenness is an illusion. Profound changes have been germinating and growing within Western civilization for far longer than a mere three decades. The 1960s' counterculture was only the first full populist flowering of these changes, among which changing attitudes toward sexuality are central. We cannot understand the dramatic transformation in sexual attitudes that is now upon us unless we grasp the large-scale perspective of history within which these changes fit. For these alterations are the consequences of a sea change in the domain of the human spirit, which has been underway for centuries. Put differently, the changes in our attitudes toward sexuality are only the indicator of far more important spiritual changes that affect every aspect of our lives.

More specifically, four hundred years of growing religious skepticism among our elites and of stupendous technological progress in which faith appears irrelevant has laid us open to *alternative spiritualities*. For a time, it seemed as if the materialistic worldview would triumph; that as we rested on the material comforts it secured for us, we could set aside our longings for spirit and meaning as the wistful fantasies of our collective childhood.

But in fact this spiritual desert did not produce a sense of mature comfort and spiritual abstinence; instead it generated an intense new thirst for the spiritual—any spirit that would slake our thirst. Thus the emerging, dominant spirit of our age is not the skeptical one that denigrates all religion, but rather a profoundly and perennially religious spirit that stands opposed to the ethical monotheism of the Christian faith and of Orthodox Judaism. The tenets of this newly emerging religion, whether articulated deliberately or merely at work tacitly in the background, are coming swiftly to dominate our public morality. But the religion itself is not really new, neither are its theological beliefs. It is simply the reemergence of paganism, and its beliefs are gnosticism. What these ancient terms mean today is the focus of this chapter.

Clearly this reemerging paganism is not merely a belittling of religion. Nor is it merely the religion of humanism, even though humanism is a visible and prominent aspect of it. For its followers the pagan spirit offers not only a meaningful answer but a *better* answer than Judaism or Christianity to the crisis of meaning that has followed the rise of the materialistic, scientific worldview. Part of paganism's appeal stems from the fact that pagan spirituality makes few moral demands on the individual, and is thus more "tolerant" of human differences—that is of "diversity." (In Joseph Campbell's words, "Follow your bliss.") But the reverse side is paganism's deficient concept of evil. It therefore lacks a way to distinguish between will and compulsion, between conscious intentionality and unconscious instinctive drive.

By contrast, a cardinal tenet of the Judeo-Christian tradition for thousands of years has been that *sin* is the central explanation for human suffering. In this view, our absolute need for God seems equally apparent. But for us now to turn away from exclusively scientific and humanistic principles on the one hand and from a "new age" multiplicity of differing cultural standards on the other to the unitary ancient biblical ones would seem to most moderns as a kind of regression. This is so in spite of neither science nor humanism bringing us closer to that for which we most deeply yearn—meaningfulness, serenity, love.

The commonplace answer to the question "How did we get here?" is thus "progress." This progress is at once scientific and yet has moral implications; the two are entangled in the modern worldview as detailed in previous chapters. Further, we see this confusion carried forward by the seemingly opposing, but in fact mutually reinforcing, claims of scientific analysis on the one hand and "new" spirituality on the other.

The Many versus the True One

What is called ethical, or radical, monotheism was introduced into the pagan culture of the ancient Near East by a single people, the Jews. The rather dry term "ethical monotheism" conveys two essential points concerning Judaism as a religion. First, that there is only one God, and because there is only one God, he is therefore the God of all men; second, that the central concern of this God, and therefore of his people, is morality and goodness. To the Hebrew mind the most distinctive feature of the character of God was not his philosophical attributes but his *holiness*. Thus, as we see in the Bible, the living God is so "utterly transcendent" that merely to glance directly at his glory and goodness is instant death.

But it was through Christians, not Jews, that ethical monotheism decisively influenced the pagan world. Or we might say, through the Christian faith as a variant of Judaism. As Franz Rosenzweig, an eminent Jewish man of letters, put it, "Christianity is Judaism for the Gentiles." As this ethical monotheism spread, it toppled many pagan dominions with astonishing force and speed and established a moral order that reigned until the

Renaissance. What are the essentials of the paganism that ethical monotheism replaced, and that is now, in turn, rivaling it?

1. Paganism is *polytheistic.* Each individual (or group) feels himself subject to his own god or goddess. At a practical level this means that the distinctive set of values, standards, goals, and laws of each deity governs the lives of that deity's worshipers.

2. Pagan society is therefore *polyvalent.* No single moral standard governs the lives of men, and except by the power of force, no god, and no corresponding set of human values, is superior to any other.

3. Consequently, pagan societies tend to become *inegalitarian.* Different standards for different groups lead inevitably to factional competition, and in time the will to power becomes the only rule. Might makes right and soon displaces the rule of law; Zeus rules because he is strongest, and for no other reason. He is certainly not the wisest; neither has he even a conception of fairness.

4. Pagan society is *pantheistic* or *animistic.* Gods and goddesses inhabit the natural world and are one with it; nature itself is therefore worshiped as divine; there is no serious distinction between creature and Creator. Again, on a practical level, this means that men worship not only the nature "out there" but also their own nature "in here"—their instincts, including hunger, sex, and aggression, and more generally, pleasure. In short, they worship themselves.

5. In thus spiritualizing the instincts, pagan worship therefore tends naturally to the *violent,* the *hedonistic,* and the *orgiastic.* Pagan religious ritual arouses the instincts to the keenest possible pitch, especially sexuality and aggression. In gratifying these instincts, the greatest possible pleasure is achieved and therefore the highest level of religious ecstasy. Violent intoxication, temple prostitution, the ritual slaughter of enemies, self-mutilation, and even child sacrifice: All these can be understood from within this worldview not as pathological but as predictable results of the unfettering of human nature. Are such practices ancient and utterly alien? We need only look to television, or to the abuse literature of the present, or a few years back to the Holocaust, or to the swiftly rising incidence of violent crime, or to our

comfort in disposing of unwanted children before they are born to understand how entirely unexceptional they are. The dark nightlife of the gay "walk on the wild side" (in the words of a popular song from a rock star celebrated for his "androgyny") is celebrated in pop culture; it is but one piece of this pagan transformation of the modern West.

6. In all of this, paganism is *idolatrous*. The pagan takes what is found within his own human nature as the measure of what is good and makes of it a god: man as the measure of all things. Is this unfair to the humanist credo? We should remember that the worst human sacrifices in history were performed on explicitly humanistic soil: in France, Russia, Germany, and China.[1] The startling juxtaposition of modern humanism with ancient paganism becomes entirely unexceptional once we recall that humanism in its scientific mode—the understanding of man by science—ends by eliminating man qua man, and reducing him to mere mechanism.

Ethical monotheism stands opposed to all of these beliefs and practices. Unlike paganism, it is utterly *un*natural. Its appearance over four thousand years ago, and its subsequent flowering in a uniformly pagan world, is beyond historical explanation. Frederick the Great of Prussia, a man tormented by his inability to sustain religious faith, once challenged his chaplain to point him toward God. The Bishop replied that he could do so with but a single word. "And what single word can possibly carry the burden of such illumination?" asked Frederick. His chaplain replied, "*Israel.*" To emphasize the contrasts:

1. Monotheism is *monotheistic*. There is one God and there is no God but God. Thus every individual and group, however different by nature, however differently inclined, gifted, or handicapped, is accountable to the one God.

2. A monotheistic society is therefore *univalent*. At a practical level this means that all men are accountable to one overarching set of values, goals, and laws. Before the God who establishes this uniform law all men are treated as equal, whether it is to their immediate gain, as they see it, or to their detriment.

3. Monotheistic societies therefore tend rather to be *egalitarian*, not in outcome, but in process. The monotheistic God is no respecter of persons or of offices and ranks.

4. Monotheism is *theistic*. It asserts a critical distinction between the Creator and the creation, and thus also between the Creator and his creatures, including man. Man, too, as man—not as biomolecular machine—is perceived to contain within himself an utterly unnatural capacity for spirit, and this spirit is not of the world, though in it. This means that man is a dual creature. He cannot be comprehended solely in terms of prior causes; and in some measure his moral choices stand opposed to his instinctive nature. Though monotheists recognize the value of every instinct, instinctive pleasure must be submitted to a single, overarching higher purpose—sanctified—and thereby modulated, restrained, and at times, eschewed altogether.

5. Monotheistic worship leads *away from the violent, hedonistic, and orgiastic*. Because instincts are creaturely and not divine, they must not be elevated as final arbiters of individual and social mores. In other words, instincts are not worshiped. The history of ancient Israel as laid out in the Old Testament is in large part the two-thousand-year struggle of the worship of the one LORD against all the various forms of pagan instinct worship that dominated the ancient Near East. Supremely, it is the story of the fight of God against Baal, the god of sacred sexuality—heterosexual, homosexual, and bestial; against his sacred consort Anath/Astarte/Ashtoreth, the virgin-whore who copulates and conceives, but does not give birth; and against Molech, the god to whom the unwanted offspring of these practices were sacrificed.

6. Finally, monotheism is *anti-idolatrous* and *anti-humanistic*. Out of faithfulness to the one, true God, it refrains from making idols—whether of the wood and stone or of the purely mental variety—of the elements of human nature.

Monotheism observes that although the satisfaction of instinctive drives gives pleasure, by itself it ultimately does not give joy. It knows, rather, that we are so constituted—because of our dual nature—as to require something that goes beyond mere pleasure; that the pursuit of pleasure apart from God leads inevitably to emptiness and despair; that to worship pleasure is ultimately to court despair and thus to seek death.

From this perspective, all our human longings for instinctive gratification point beyond themselves to something else, something that is neither found in nor reducible to mere humanity. This longing is so great that, when we are unable to attach it to its proper, eternal object and attach it instead to some form of instinctive gratification, the pursuit becomes compulsive, even addictive, and ultimately monstrous. In drugs the drug addict, in alcohol the alcoholic, in sex the philanderer, in winning the gambler, and in food the compulsive eater all seek the one God and know it not; all thus become idolaters.

The relentless opposition of the God of Israel and his prophets to idolatry and pagan worship must seem to the modern at best a strange archaic obsession, at worst an offensive manifestation of a nationalism and chauvinism that we are well off without. In the antiseptic conditions of modernism, it makes perfect sense to replace such monomania with the endlessly accommodating syncretism that now passes for "spirituality" in an ever-growing number of churches and synagogues.

Paganism's Theology: Gnosticism

The conflict between monotheism and paganism is neither recent nor merely natural; it is a recurring, age-old battle for the soul of man that has never ceased. We can trace a historical line that connects the pagan religions of the ancient Near East (including Canaan) to pre- and early Christian gnosticism, to the Manicheaism of the late Roman and Aryan Empires, to certain schools of medieval Kabbalah and Alchemy, through the transforming matrix of Renaissance Neoplatonism with its combined emphases on magic, humanism, and science. From there, it is but a short step to the modern reduction of spirit to psyche that has allowed the present pagan resurgence.

C. G. Jung, unaware of his own role in it, nonetheless clearly saw what was coming in the pagan revolution. Surveying the decadent conditions following World War I, he wrote in 1918:

As the Christian view of the world loses its authority, the more men-acingly will the "blonde beast" be heard prowling about in its under-ground prison, ready at any moment to burst out with devastating consequences. When this happens in the individual it brings about a psychological revolution, but it can also take a social form.[2]

As apocalyptic as was Jung in this reading of the pagan trans-formation that was overtaking the German-speaking world, his prophetic power was less than that of the German-Jewish poet and convert to Christianity Heinrich Heine, who had warned in 1892:

It is to the great merit of Christianity that it has somewhat atten-uated the brutal German lust for battle. But it could not destroy it entirely. And should ever that taming talisman break—the Cross—then will come roaring back the wild madness of the ancient war-riors of whom our Nordic poets speak and sing, with all their insane Berserker rage. That talisman is now already crumbling, and the day is not far off when it shall break apart entirely. On that day the old stone gods will rise from long-forgotten wreckage, and rub from their eyes the dust of a thousand-year sleep. At long last leaping to life, Thor, with his giant hammer, will crush the Gothic cathedrals! . . . And laugh not at my forebodings, the advice of a dreamer who warns you away from the Kants and Fichtes of the world, and from our philosophers of Nature. No, laugh not at the visionary who knows that in the realm of phenomena comes soon the revolution that has already taken place in the realm of spirit. For thought goes before deed as lightning before thunder. . . . There will be played in Germany a play compared to which the French revolution was but an innocent idyll.[3]

Gnosticism, as we have said, is paganism's theology. To the gnostic, salvation is neither the undeserved gift of God (as it pri-marily is in Christianity) nor the fruit of consistent moral effort (as it primarily is Judaism). It is rather a Faustian prize achieved through "secret knowledge" (the definition of the Greek *gnosis*). The gnostic is granted this secret wisdom in relation to one of the many gods or demigods accessible, in an intellectualized version of pagan worship, through mind and imagination.

The temper of gnosticism is spiritual and ascetic and it appealed directly therefore mostly to the intellectual classes of the Roman Empire. But in time its implicit divinization of the instincts led it into a relativization of good and evil, and into a fierce opposition to the Jewish, monotheistic ethos being propagated by the Christian faith. There is therefore no irony in the asceticism of the early gnostic sects degenerating so quickly into license. In fact, the development was predictable, and has been followed by gnostics throughout history—down to our day.

Over the centuries gnosticism has continued to lead a clandestine existence as a kind of perpetual spiritual counterculture. Now and then erupting into the open, it has always provided a secretive, psychic, man-oriented, polytheistic, and morally relativistic counterpoint to the God-oriented ethical monotheism carried forward by the Judeo-Christian tradition.

Despite its ever-shifting forms, gnostic thought has many common motifs. Chief among them are:

- The conviction that through gnosis—special knowledge available only to the initiated—the human mind becomes sufficient to solve its problems by itself, especially those of its suffering and of its own evil inclinations, and thereby to attain to the prerogatives of the gods.
- The conviction that the great events of the Judeo-Christian tradition, especially the Incarnation, have no significant material reality and are to be understood at most as spiritual (or symbolic, psychological, or psychic) events.
- From these motifs, therefore, has flowed the rejection of *atoning sacrifice* as necessary for "mental and spiritual health"—salvation. For if the gods are but manifestations of the mind, then there is no absolute basis for guilt or sin.
- Consistent with all this, therefore, is the conclusion that good and evil have either no significance, or—what is in practice the same thing—merely symbolic significance, unrelated to the ethical requirements and sacrifices of daily life; in either case they are balanced opposites.

There is a striking irony in this latter point, for gnostic thought is well-known for the attention it gives to the nature of evil. In its Manichean variant, gnosticism's latent tendency to overrate and divinize evil became explicit in making Good and Evil the two eternal principles of reality. One is reminded of C. S. Lewis's admonition: "There are two equal and opposite errors into which our race can fall about devils. One is to disbelieve in their existence. The other is to believe and to feel an excessive and unhealthy interest in them. They themselves are equally pleased by both errors and hail a materialist or a magician with the same delight."[4]

When Evil and Good are placed on the same plane, in the form of dualism, two things inevitably follow: First, on a theological level, we succumb to the dangerous fantasy that Good and Evil will be reunited in a higher oneness. Second, on a psychological and behavioral level, we tend to relativize good and evil and hence to increase our propensity to *choose* evil, considering *it* to be our good, since it often *feels* good.

At the sophisticated level modern gnostic philosophies such as Jung's emphasize the first point while inadvertently facilitating the second. At a more popular level, occult philosophies make the second point concrete and explicit. Both provide a theology of moral relativism. Because of his great influence in propagating gnostic philosophy and morals in churches and synagogues, Jung deserves a closer look. The moral relativism that released on us the sexual revolution is rooted in an outlook of which he is the most brilliant contemporary expositor.

A Self-Proclaimed Prophet

Modern depth-psychology in both the Freudian and Jungian schools has played the same role in relation to modern, materialistic, instinct-driven culture as ancient gnosticism once played to pagan society. By collapsing nature and meaning into one they provide the philosophical underpinnings to an amoral view of life. It could even be argued that the real purpose of gnostic theologies—then as now, wittingly or otherwise—is to provide an aura of respectability for what is at heart unbridled sexual expression.

Jung, in particular, blended psychological reductionism with gnostic spirituality to produce a modern variant of mystical, pagan polytheism in which the multiple "images of the instincts" (his "archetypes") are worshiped as gods. He presented his purportedly scientific theories as an updated and improved version of Christianity synthesized with the instincts. To an ever increasing extent, that is precisely how his theories have been accepted.

Jung perceived his own role in the development of this new, world-embracing religion as prophetic. Max Zeller, one of his followers and a Jungian analyst in Los Angeles, told Jung of a dream he had of people all over the world building a temple, himself included. Jung responded:

> "That is the temple we all build on . . . all over the world. That is the new religion. You know how long it will take until it is built?"
> Zeller responded, "How should I know? Do you know?"
> "I know. . . . About six hundred years."
> "Where do you know this from?" Zeller asked.
> "From dreams. From other people's dreams and from my own. This new religion will come together as far as we can see."[5]

Commenting on this exchange, Murray Stein, Jungian analyst and author of *Jung's Treatment of Christianity: The Psychotherapy of a Religious Tradition,* notes:

> From this report, it is unclear whether Jung foresaw this new religion as a transformed version of Christianity or as a completely new world religion embracing, or supplanting, all other religions. But insofar as Jung . . . regarded himself as a Parsifal . . . and a bringer of the Holy Grail back to Christendom, he would have hoped that the new religion would represent . . . partially Christianity's "child" and partially something quite different from it, its own unique religious tradition.[6]

Jung's direct and indirect impact on mainstream Christianity—and thus on Western culture—has been incalculable. It is no exaggeration to say that the theological positions of most mainstream denominations—in their approach to pastoral care as well as in their doctrines and liturgy—have become more or less identical with Jung's psychological/symbolic theology.

To the end of his life Jung maintained that an accommodation between "matter" and "spirit" could be worked out; that the "dark side" of human nature needed to be "integrated" into a single, overarching "wholeness" in order to form a less strict and difficult definition of goodness; that true illumination was not shone by a holy God into a darkened world, but rather that it was clever, brilliant "Lucifer" who was himself the true source of wisdom, the font and origin of "gnosis," or higher knowledge.

For Jung, Good and Evil evolved into two equal, balanced, cosmic principles that belong together in one overarching synthesis. This relativization of good and evil by their reconciliation is the heart of the ancient doctrines of gnosticism, which also located spirituality, hence morality, within man himself. Hence the "union of opposites." What poet William Blake called "The Marriage of Heaven and Hell," Jung called the "Self"—capital "S" to indicate its "divinity."

Jung explicitly identified depth-psychology, especially his own, as heir to the gnostic tradition, especially in what he considered its superior handling of the problem of evil. He claimed: "In the ancient world the Gnostics, whose arguments were very much influenced by psychic experience, tackled the problem of evil on a much broader basis than the Church Fathers."[7] But in fact, the gnostics fell quickly into the embrace of the very evil they thought themselves to be tackling, inevitably the consequence of an inclusivist position toward it:

> There can be no doubt that the original Christian conception of the imago Dei embodied in Christ meant an all-embracing totality that even includes the animal side of man. Nevertheless the Christ-symbol lacks wholeness in the modern psychological sense, since it does not include the dark side of things but specifically excludes it in the form of a Luciferian opponent.[8]

To embrace such a vision of God is to lay oneself open to moral blindness. Even though Jung believed that his form of depth-psychology would become the "new" gnostic child of Christianity, he was not entirely ignorant of the problems inherent in a gnostic worldview. Thus, on the one hand, Jung could say, "If anyone wants to know what are the ethical consequences of intellectualism pushed to the limit and carried out on a grand scale, let him study the history of Gnostic morals."[9] Yet on the other, for all his brilliance and prophetic insight, Jung was unable to foresee the dire consequences of the pagan awakening that was fueling Nazism. He thus did not come to renounce the menace of Hitler until long after many of his less gifted contemporaries had done so; indeed, not until people were actually dying at Nazi hands.

It is not surprising that with this kind of theology as its foundation, within one generation Jungianism should have wholeheartedly embraced sexual revolutionaries of every stripe. In spite of Jung's comment about gnostic morality, for example, Jung himself maintained an extramarital relationship with one of his patients for years. The primary aim of such ideas seems to be the removal of barriers to sexual expression of every type and to justify the consequent behavior in the language of the mystery religions. Such characterizations lend these ideas an aura of "spirituality" that effectively obscure their fundamental tendency toward hedonism and amorality.

What is bizarre is how many Christian thinkers and writers have been in the vanguard of popularizing Jungian ideas throughout the church—for example, Rev. Morton Kelsey has made a career of such compromise. Not surprisingly, Kelsey's latest book, *The Sacrament of Sexuality*, specifically addresses homosexuality from the "pluralistic" perspective.[10] He approvingly cites the 1973 APA decision to normalize homosexuality and skirts the issue of homosexual change, instead saying that such change is "extremely rare."[11]

But more importantly, Kelsey's Jungianism, implicit in his title, directly relates to our discussion, not just with reference to homosexuality, but to all forms of sex outside of marriage. For from the Judeo-Christian perspective, sexuality—an aspect of nature—cannot itself be "sacramental." It partakes of sacramental reality and is thereby elevated (sanctified) only in the context of the "sacrament of *marriage*." Sacramental sexuality, on the other hand, is the very essence of pagan worship.

Thomas Moore, Episcopal Priest and Jungian analyst wildly popular with a new generation of soul-seekers, was recently interviewed by *NetGuide,* a popular magazine for Internet users. After having noted that, given his own personal definition of "soul," William Blake was "its most eloquent spokesperson," he was asked to comment on the fact that:

> There's lots of pornography on the Internet. There are bondage newsgroups, group for bestiality, you name it.... Is this good, bad, healthy, unhealthy?

Moore responded:

> Can we stop categorizing sex, and moralizing about it...? Can we ask, "is sex, any kind of sex, deeply satisfying? Is it soulfully enjoyable...?" So forget right or wrong, they don't pertain.[12]

Nowadays even explicitly pagan ideologies and theologies are everywhere. They are replacing orthodox theologies in divinity schools; television shows presenting them in visual form are wildly popular; churches are rewriting their liturgies to accommodate them; books espousing their point of view are regular best-sellers. As I began this book, two such, written by Jungian analysts, were on the *New York Times* best-seller list. Yet another is entitled *The Sacrament of Abortion,* dedicated to the goddess Artemis. The author and Jungian analyst Ginette Paris makes fully explicit the link between modern morality and ancient paganism:

> It is time to call back the image of Artemis, the wild one, who despite her beauty refuses marriage and chooses to belong only to herself.... When we are constantly paying attention to another person, to a group, to relatives, colleagues and friends, how much time, energy and space are left... for being present to one's self? ... When the Artemis myth manifests itself in our lives, it can be recognized by a sense of no longer belonging to a group, a couple, or a family; it represents a movement away from ... fusion with others, the most extreme example of fusion being the connection between a mother and her young children. Artemis... invites us to retreat from others, to become autonomous.

In a chapter entitled, "The Cure for Guilt," the author continues:

Our culture needs new rituals as well as laws to restore to abortion its sacred dimension. . . . I've heard women address their fetus directly . . . and explain why it is necessary to separate now. Others write a letter of farewell and read it to a friend, a spouse, or indeed to their whole family. Still others invent their own farewell ritual, inspired perhaps by rituals from other cultures, like offering a little doll to a divinity as a symbol of the aborted fetus.

. . . the pro-lifers see the spiritual dimension but keep it imprisoned within official orthodoxies, as if no other form of spirituality existed. What if my religious beliefs are pagan?[13]

These bizarre-sounding ideas are not as distant as they might seem. In deliberately regressing to archaic modes of thought, morality, and behavior, they lead us along the descent of nature: They describe the dark practices into which human beings inevitably sink if left to their own devices.

Which Spirit?

All who read the Bible will be well aware that other gods and other forms of spirituality exist. The Scriptures record Israel's often losing battle against seduction by these other forms of spirituality, which have been with us for thousands of years. To people reacting to the dryness of secularism, it seems that all forms of spirituality are good, and that all offer a sense of meaning to fend off the fear of life as machine. But, in fact, the crucial question is not "whether spirit?" but "which spirit?"

You will recall the tiny, empty point at the apex of the triangle of causality, "the still point of the turning world" referred to in our earlier discussion of the will. And remember the second, inverted triangle above it. At the intersection of time and eternity turns the unnatural question of individual moral choice. With laser-like intensity, at every moment of our existence, the question of "Which spirit?" is aimed at the invisible apex of our being.

In answering this question repeatedly over a lifetime, in thought, word, and action, people discover who they are—and in this sense alone are co-creators with God of themselves. The Bible says, in effect, that the spiritual dimension of reality has little to do with "magic," altered states of consciousness, healthy ego-development, the goddess, *n*-dimensional parallel universes, the earth as God's body, or archetypes or instincts that have been turned into gods. It claims rather that the overarching principle of existence is the character of God and his revealed moral law.

The spirituality that developed under gnostic influences in the ancient past and is being redeveloped in our own time is marked by an absence of belief in the primacy of the moral dimension as presented in the Judeo-Christian tradition. But once this moral dimension is removed, relativized, or transposed to a cosmic sphere, the intense spirituality of gnosticism shades easily into an overtly amoral materialism. As it does so, worship of its many gods devolves into the quest for its many pleasures, regardless of cost.

Thus the Apostle Paul cried out to all those in the Roman Empire who would listen, calling them away from the sexual worship of their many gods to the worship of the Holy One of Israel. These "gods" were but the multicultural variants of the same Baal and Astarte and Molech against whose worship the earlier Israelite prophets had similarly cried out to the Jewish people, making clear the link between idolatry and unconstrained sexuality.

Leviticus 18:22 and 19:13 describe homosexual relations as *toevah*, "detestable" (NIV) or as an "abomination" (KJV). This Hebrew word is mostly used, however, to condemn ritual prostitution, magic, divination, and idolatry, as well as violations of specifically Jewish requirements (such as desecration of the Sabbath). Paul, presenting the same unpopular message, makes the same connection:

> Although they claimed to be wise, they became fools and exchanged the glory of the immortal God for images made to look like mortal man and birds and animals and reptiles.
> Therefore God gave them over in the sinful desires of their hearts to sexual impurity for the degrading of their bodies with one

another. They exchanged the truth of God for a lie, and worshipped and served created things rather than the Creator—who is for ever praised. Amen.

Because of this, God gave them over to shameful lusts. Even their women exchanged natural relations for unnatural ones. In the same way the men also abandoned natural relations with women and were inflamed with lust for one another. Men committed indecent acts with other men, and received in themselves the due penalty for their perversion.

Romans 1:22–27

Twelve Concluding Propositions

As we have seen, the subject of homosexuality is enormously complex, touching on many aspects of human existence: biological, psychological, and spiritual. Nonetheless, we can present our conclusions in the form of twelve propositions. These are:

1. The general condition "homosexuality" is a loosely defined aspect of the overall polymorphism of human sexuality.
2. Given the present state of human nature, sexual polymorphism is natural.
3. Each individual's homosexuality is the likely result of a complex mixture of genetic, intrauterine, and extrauterine biological factors combined with familial and social factors as well as repeatedly reinforced choices. These create a particular blend of impulses. The role of genetic influence is small, and in any event means very little in terms of compelling an individual to become homosexual.
4. The godly standard of moral sexual behavior is much more narrowly defined than the great variety and natural polymorphism of human sexuality. *Sexuality in the state of nature* is therefore commonly sinful. Sanctified, it is one of God's greatest gifts.
5. Homosexual behavior is difficult to modify because, like other forms of compulsive behavior, it involves innate impulses and reinforced choices by which sinful activities become embedded in the brain ("engraved on the heart").

6. Ethical demands require homosexuals, like all people, to resist their natural sinful impulses.

7. Homosexuality is not a true illness, though it may be thought an illness in the spiritual sense of "soul sickness," innate to fallen human nature. Its treatment thus opens directly into the domain of the "cure of souls."

8. Because deeply engraved behaviors are so difficult to modify, homosexuals, like all people, have two choices: to capitulate to the behavior and its consequences or to depend on others, and on God, for help.

9. Secular programs that modify homosexual behavior are more numerous and more effective than popular opinion is led to believe.

10. Spiritual programs that lead people into dependency on God, and support them there, are even more effective. The best of these integrate into their spiritual approach the best that is offered by the secular approaches as well.

11. A pastoral understanding of the "cure" of a soul, which unfolds progressively over a lifetime, is more than the alleviation of particular symptoms; it consists of growing ever more closely toward the divinely ordained configuration that God intended for us from the beginning—and which is largely "unnatural," not only in the area of sexuality. This process is without question a reality; it is a reality that occurs in secular settings as well as in religious ones. It is a reality no less pertinent—and lifegiving—to every person, whatever his particular brokenness, than to those struggling with homosexuality.

12. The modern change in opinion concerning homosexuality, though presented as a scientific advance, is contradicted rather than supported by science. It is a transformation in public morals consistent with widespread abandonment of the Judeo-Christian ethic upon which our civilization is based. Though hailed as "progress," it is really a reversion to ancient pagan practices supported by a modern restatement of gnostic moral relativism.

For individual homosexuals, for each of us in our own circle of brokenness, as well as for our civilization as a whole, the choices today are as clear as they were for the Jewish nation living amidst their pagan neighbors centuries ago:

> This day I call heaven and earth as witnesses against you that I have set before you life and death, blessings and curses. Now choose life, so that you and your children may live and that you may love the LORD your God, listen to his voice, and hold fast to him. For the LORD is your life, and he will give you many years in the land he swore to give to your fathers.
>
> Deuteronomy 30:19–20

Postscript

It has been over fourteen years since I stood in that New York apartment reading about the death of my gifted patient. Since then, my professional work has brought me into contact with innumerable people wrestling with the same sexual issues that he had. Most of them, fortunately, have not had to struggle with AIDS, but many have. If I put myself back into the mood of those early days, I would have to say it was grim. Not just because of the specter of illness hanging over the lives of homosexuals, but because of the seeming intractability of their burden, its sheer unfairness. How indeed could anyone add to that burden by criticism of any sort, however tempered?

But since then my mood has changed. I have been extraordinarily fortunate to have met many people who have emerged from the gay life. When I see the personal difficulties they have squarely faced, the sheer courage they have displayed not only in facing these difficulties but also in confronting a culture that uses every possible means to deny the validity of their values, goals, and experiences, I truly stand back in wonder. Certainly they have forced me by the simple testimony of their lives to return again and again to my own self-examination. It is these people—former homosexuals and those still struggling, all across America and abroad—who stand for me as a model of everything good and possible in a world that takes the human heart, and the God of that heart, seriously. In my various explorations within the worlds of psychoanalysis, psychotherapy, and psychiatry, I have simply *never* before seen such profound healing.

Because it is not really a battle over mere sexuality, but rather over which spirit shall claim our allegiance, the cultural and political battle over homosexuality has become in many respects the defining moment for our society. It has implications that go far beyond the surface matter of "gay rights." And so the more important dimension of this battle is not the political one, it is the one for the individual human soul. It would be easy in this modern era, when our vision for things invisible is so easily blinded by the dazzling allure of our material accomplishment, to not even take the soul—and her loving, watchful, worried shepherd—seriously. But the soul that emerges in the lives of those who have successfully struggled with homosexuality, and the soul that is in the process of emerging in those who struggle still, is so beautiful that at one stroke her emergence into sight, even dimly, simply shatters the false dazzle of modernity. There is nothing to compare with being present as the skylark takes wing once again, restored to her glorious coat of feathers.

And so, as dangerous a moment as this one may be, when so much of our inheritance stands in the balance, there is great hope as well. Slowly but surely, the great truths that have embodied themselves in the lives of these men and women—after terrible struggle—will be made widely known. More and more people will themselves gain the courage to return home from their long and fruitless wanderings in the wasteland of modern sophistication, however painful that return may be. It is our joyful duty to stand waiting, with open arms, remembering that we too are journeying home.

Notes

Introduction

1. I have altered a few other details of this story as well to insure the anonymity of the people involved.

2. See, for example, S. M. Blower and A. R. McLean, "Prophylactic Vaccines, Risk Behavior Change, and the Probability of Eradicating HIV in San Francisco," *Science* 265 (1994), p. 1451.

3. E. L. Goldman, "Psychological Factors Generate HIV Resurgence in Young Gay Men," *Clinical Psychiatry News*, October 1994, p. 5.

4. R. T. Michael et al., *Sex in America: A Definitive Survey* (Boston: Little, Brown, 1994). A more rigorous and detailed analysis of the same data set by the same authors that targets a professional readership will also be referred to: E. O. Laumann et al., *The Social Organization of Sexuality: Sexual Practices in the United States* (Chicago: University of Chicago Press, 1994).

5. Goldman, "Psychological Factors," p. 5.

6. D. Prager, "Judaism, Homosexuality and Civilization," *Ultimate Issues* 6, no. 2 (1990), p. 2.

7. Laumann et al., *The Social Organization of Sexuality*, p. 295.

8. Brookings Institution, "Religion in American Public Life" (1986).

Chapter One: Neither Scientific nor Democratic

1. Cited in C. W. Socarides, "Sexual Politics and Scientific Logic: The Issue of Homosexuality," *The Journal of Psychohistory* 10, no. 3 (1992), p. 308.

2. Ibid.

3. R. Bayer, *Homosexuality and American Psychiatry: The Politics of Diagnosis* (New York: Basic Books, 1981), p. 102.

4. Ibid., pp. 102–3.

5. Ibid., p. 104.

6. Ibid., pp. 104–5.

7. Ibid., pp. 105–6.

8. Ibid., p. 145.

9. Ibid., p. 146.

10. Ibid., pp. 3–4.

11. As reported by C. Cornett, "Gay Ain't Broke; No Need to Fix It," *Insight,* 6 December 1993, p. 27.

12. C. Burr, "Homosexuality and Biology," *Atlantic Monthly* 271, no. 3 (March 1993), pp. 47–65.

13. E. Pollard, "Time to Give Up Fascist Tactics," *Washington Blade,* 31 January 1992, p. 39.

14. J. Horgan, "Eugenics Revisited," *Scientific American,* June 1993, pp. 123–31.

15. Paul Billings's precise comments are cited in the discussion of genetics research that follows.

16. Quoted in J. M. Bailey et al., "Heritable Factors Influence Sexual Orientations in Women," *Archives of General Psychiatry* 50, no. 3, pp. 217–23.

17. See G. M. Harrington, "Psychology of the Scientist: XXVII. Experimenter Bias: Occam's Razor versus Pascal's Wager," *Psychological Reports* 21, no. 2 (1967), pp. 527–28; G. M. Harrington and L. H. Ingraham, "Psychology of the Scientist: XXV. Experimenter Bias and Tails of Pascal," *Psychological Reports* 21, no. 2 (1967), pp. 513–16; J. G. Adair and J. S. Epstein, "Verbal Cues in the Mediation of Experimenter Bias," *Psychological Reports* 22, no. 3 (1968), pp. 1045–53; J. B. Dusek, "Experimenter-bias Effects on the Simple Motor Task Performance of Low- and High-test Anxious Boys and Girls," *Psychological Reports* 30, no. 1 (1972), pp. 107–14; P. J. Barber and J. P. Rushton, "Experimenter Bias and Subliminal Perception," *British Journal of Psychology* 66, no. 3 (1975), pp. 357–72; R. Rikli, "Physical Performance Scores as a Function of Experimenter Sex and Experimenter Bias," *Research Quarterly* 47, no. 4 (1976), pp. 776–82; D. G. Jamieson and W. M. Petrusic, "On a Bias Induced by the Provision of Feedback in Psychophysical Experiments," *Acta Psychologia* (Amsterdam) 40, no. 3 (1976), pp. 199–206; D. Belton and R. Ware, "Effect of Instructions on the Disappearance of Steadily Fixated Luminous Figures," *Journal of General Psychology* 104 (1981), pp. 249–56, second half; R. Rogers et al., "Scientific Inquiry in Forensic Psychiatry," *International Journal of Law and Psychiatry* 5, no. 2 (1982), pp. 187–203; F. M. Levine and L. L. De Simone, "The Effects of Experimenter Gender on Pain Report in Male and Female Subjects," *Pain* 44, no. 1 (1991), pp. 69–72.

18. Socarides, "Sexual Politics and Scientific Logic," pp. 316–17.

Chapter Two: Who Says? And Why?

1. T. S. Eliot, "East Coker IV," *Four Quartets* in *The Complete Poems and Plays* (New York: Harcourt, Brace & World, 1971), p. 127.

2. Or "a blessing." Interestingly, our word "to bless" is cognate to the French *blesser,* meaning "to wound," just as our "gift" is cognate to the German word *Gift* meaning "poison." The same opposing meanings of the Hebrew "to bless" can be found in the Bible and in Talmudic commentaries on the word.

3. E. Coleman et al., "Sexual and Intimacy Dysfunction among Homosexual Men and Women," *Psychiatric Medicine* (United States) 10, no. 2 (1992), pp. 257–71.

4. L. S. Doll et al., "Self-Reported Childhood and Adolescent Sexual Abuse Among Adult Homosexual/Bisexual Men," *Child Abuse and Neglect* 16, no. 6 (1992), pp. 855–64.

5. C. Mann, "Behavioral Genetics in Transition," *Science* 264, pp. 1686–89.

6. H. Kohut, *The Analysis of the Self* (New York: International Universities Press, 1971). His school of neo-psychoanalysis is called "self-psychology."

7. J. Chasseguet-Smirgel, "The Bright Face of Narcissism and Its Shadowy Depths: A Few Reflections," *Psychiatric Clinics of North America* 12, no. 3 (1989), pp. 709–22.

8. R. H. Hopcke, "Symbols of Gay Male Individuation in *The Wizard of Oz*," *Quadrant* 22, no. 2 (1989), pp. 65–77; R. H. Hopcke, "Midlife, Gay Men, and the AIDS Epidemic," *Quadrant* 25, no. 1 (1992), pp. 101–10. The motif of homosexuality as "supernormal" has occurred in earlier episodes of homosexual activism and efflorescence, notable in Germany prior to World Wars I and II.

Chapter Three: Is Homosexuality Desirable? Brute Facts

1. M. Kirk and H. Madsen, *After the Ball: How America Will Conquer Its Fear and Hatred of Gays in the 90's* (New York: Doubleday, 1989).

2. M. Kirk and E. Pill, "The Overhauling of Straight America," *Guide*, November 1987, p. 24.

3. R. T. Michael et al., *Sex in America: A Definitive Survey* (Boston: Little, Brown & Co., 1994), p. 134. Paul Robinson, a professor at Stanford University and expert on sexual research notes: "The great strength of the new study is that its participants were selected according to the most sophisticated techniques of probability sampling, the same techniques used in political polling and marketing. Its findings can thus be generalized to the population at large with a high degree of confidence." As quoted in P. Robinson, "The Way We Do the Things We Do," *New York Times Book Review*, 30 October 1994, p. 3.

4. R. A. Kaslow et al., "The Multicenter AIDS Cohort Study: Rationale, Organization, and Selected Characteristics of the Participants," *American Journal of Epidemiology* 126, no. 2 (August 1987), pp. 310–18.

5. D. McWhirter and A. Mattison, *The Male Couple: How Relationships Develop* (Englewood Cliffs, N.J.: Prentice-Hall, 1984), p. 3.

6. A. P. Bell et al., *Sexual Preference* (Bloomington, Ind.: Indiana University Press, 1981).

7. A. P. Bell and M. S. Weinberg, *Homosexualities: A Study of Diversity among Men and Women* (New York: Simon and Schuster, 1978), pp. 308–9.

8. Blower and McLean, "Prophylactic Vaccines, Risk Behavior Change, and the Probability of Eradicating HIV in San Francisco."

9. See G. M. Mavligit et al., "Chronic Immune Stimulation by Sperm Alloantigens: Support for the Hypothesis That Spermatozoa Induce Immune Dysregulation in Homosexual Males," *Journal of the American Medical Association* 251, no. 2 (13 January 1984), pp. 237–41.

10. Pifer et al., "Borderline Immunodeficiency in Male Homosexuals: Is Life-Style Contributory?" *Southern Medical Journal* 80, no. 6 (June 1987), pp. 687–91, 697; T. Bergstrom et al., "Impaired Production of Alpha and Gamma Interferon in Asymptomatic Homosexual Males," *European Journal of Clinical Microbiology* 5, no. 5 (October 1986), pp. 523–29.

11. Michael et al., *Sex in America*, p. 205.

12. W. Odets, in a report to the American Association of Physicians for Human Rights. Cited in E. L. Goldman, "Psychological Factors Generate HIV Resurgence in Young Gay Men," *Clinical Psychiatry News*, October 1994, p. 5.

13. Calculated by dividing 30 percent by 0.07 percent.

14. Michael et al., *Sex in America*, p. 203. The actual risk for homosexual anal intercourse is somewhat greater, but still within the same ballpark.

15. Calculated by $3/10 \times 1/500 = 3/5000$.

16. See, for example, T. Myers et al., "Factors Affecting Gay and Bisexual Men's Decisions and Intentions to Seek HIV Testing," *American Journal of Public Health* 83, no. 5 (May 1993), pp. 701–4; S. Z. Wiktor et al., "Effect of Knowledge of Human Immunodeficiency Virus Infection Status on Sexual Activity among Homosexual Men," *Journal of Acquired Immune Deficiency Syndrome* 3, no. 1 (1990), pp. 62–68; J. A. Kelly et al., "Situational Factors Associated with AIDS Risk Behavior Lapses and Coping Strategies Used by Gay Men Who Successfully Avoid Lapses," *American Journal of Public Health* 81, no. 10 (October 1991), pp. 1335–38; and Odets, Report to American Association of Physicians for Human Rights.

17. In an article posted to the sci.med.aids newsgroup on the Internet (message id 24405@sci.med.aids, 14 Jun 1995) Udo Schüklenk, a researcher at the Centre for Human Bioethics at Monash University in Australia argues (to a newsgroup evidently subscribed to largely by homosexual men who have AIDS or are HIV-positive or are at risk): "A number of authors have pointed out that gay men might have rational (i.e., acceptable) reasons for having risky sex. [E.g., *J Sex Res* 1992 29(4):561–568; *J Sex Res* 1993 30(4):344–346; *Bioethics* 1987 1(1):35–50; *Health Care Analysis* 1994 2(3):253–261]. . . . different value judgments of health promoters and sexually active individuals about the value of unsafe sex vs. the value of a long life have led to different conclusions as to what is acceptable individual behavior. . . . obviously to many gay men (perhaps the majority) . . . safe sex and fun seems to be a contradictio in adjecto [contradiction in terms]. . . . [P]ublic health campaigns assume that health is of a paramount value and that all other individual values must have a lower ranking. Hence they do not accept that certain types of sexual risk behavior can be the best of the available solutions. . . . I suggest that indeed certain types of motives for unsafe sexual behavior are rational and acceptable forms of autonomous decision making processes that should be accepted just as liberal societies accept other kinds of risk-taking for the sake of pleasure maximization."

A similar argument was published in the *Medical Journal of Australia* 157:846.

18. R. A. Kaslow et al., "AIDS Cohort Study."

19. L. S. Doll et al., "Homosexual Men Who Engage in High-Risk Sexual Behavior: A Multicenter Comparison," *Journal of Sexually Transmitted Diseases* 18, no. 3 (1991), pp. 170–75.

20. A. Prieur, "Norwegian Gay Men: Reasons for Continued Practice of Unsafe Sex," *AIDS Education and Prevention* 2, no. 2 (Summer 1990), pp. 109–15.

21. J. D. Weinrich et al., "Effects of Recalled Childhood Gender Nonconformity on Adult Genitoerotic Role and AIDS Exposure," *Archives of Sexual Behavior* 21, no. 6 (December 1992), pp. 559–85.

22. "As you become more sexually experienced, you will soon discover your preferred sexual activities and positions. You may find that you prefer getting f__ed no matter the time, place, partner or position. You may have begun to find yourself evaluating the men you meet by a new index: the size, shape, and hardness of their c__s, how much they check out guys' buns, and how often they come on by talking about f__ing or saying they're interested in getting a __.

When this happens, you have become a bottom, or bottom man. The name, or course, derives from the placement of the person being f__ed—i.e., on the bottom.

"Being a bottom doesn't mean that you always have to f__ in the missionary position. . . . Being a bottom doesn't make you less desirable than a top. . . . Being a bottom can be useful in meeting potential sex partners.

But we would be in error if we seemed to suggest that being a bottom is merely a matter of who f__s whom. It is, more importantly, a state of mind, a feeling one has about oneself in relationship to other men." C. Silverstein and F. Picano, *The New Joy of Gay Sex* (New York: HarperCollins, 1993), p. 18.

23. D. Prager, "Judaism, Homosexuality, and Civilization," *Ultimate Issues* 6, no. 2 (1990), pp. 2–3.

24. It is "scientific" in that it is catalogued and abstracted by Medline, the international medical scientific database that follows the generally accepted standard of what constitutes a scientific journal in the area of medicine.

25. C. K. Li, " 'The Main Thing Is Being Wanted': Some Case Studies on Adult Sexual Experiences with Children," *Journal of Homosexuality* 20, nos. 1–2 (1990), pp. 129–43.

26. K. Plummer, "Understanding Childhood Sexualities," *Journal of Homosexuality* 20, nos. 1–2 (1990), pp. 231–49.

27. G. P. Jones, "The Study of Intergenerational Intimacy in North America: Beyond Politics and Pedophilia," *Journal of Homosexuality* 20, nos. 1–2 (1990), pp. 275–95. In another highly unsettling crosslink between the normalization of pedophilia and the denial of child abuse, Ralph Unterwager recently gave an interview to *Paedika* in which he expressed his favorable opinion concerning pedophilia. Until this interview was publicized, Unterwager sat on the board of the False Memory Syndrome Foundation, an organization whose purpose is to help identify false claims of sexual molestation and to assist families that have been caught in the destructive effects of such false claims. Unterwager also is—or at least was—routinely cited by the defense in such cases as an expert in debunking the testimony of clinicians who claim to be able to verify sexual abuse in young children. Because of the sensitivity of this topic, let me emphasize that this note is meant neither to support nor to undermine the work of the False Memory Syndrome Foundation nor of the advocacy groups that exist to prevent child abuse and to help its victims. It is meant to highlight the shocking openness and seeming comfort with which pedophile activists now promote their interests within professional circles whose fiduciary responsibility is to the well-being of the people who depend on them.

28. G. van Zessen, "A Model for Group Counseling with Male Pedophiles," *Journal of Homosexuality* 20, nos. 1–2 (1990), pp. 189–98.

29. A. van Naerssen, "Man-Boy Lovers: Assessment, Counseling, and Psychotherapy," *Journal of Homosexuality* 20, nos. 1–2 (1990), pp. 175–87.

30. K. Freund and R. J. Watson, "The Proportions of Heterosexual and Homosexual Pedophiles among Sex Offenders against Children: An Exploratory Study," *Journal of Sex and Marital Therapy* 18, no. 1 (1992), pp. 34–43.

31. D. Thorstad, "Man/Boy Love and the American Gay Movement," *Journal of Homosexuality* 20, nos. 1–2 (1990), pp. 251–74.

32. Diagnostic and Statistical Manual IV (Washington, D.C.: American Psychiatric Association Press, 1994).

33. P. LaBarbera in *The Lambda Report*, cited in *NARTH Bulletin* 3, no. 1 (April 1995), p. 3.

34. H. Rosin, "Chickenhawk," *The New Republic*, May 8, 1995.

35. A. J. Miles, T. G. Allen-Mersh, and C. Wastell, "Effect of Anoreceptive Intercourse on Anorectal Function," *Journal of the Royal Society of Medicine* 86, no. 3 (March 1993), pp. 144–47.

36. C. Fenger, "Anal Neoplasia and Its Precursors: Facts and Controversies," *Seminars in Diagnostic Pathology* 8, no. 3 (August 1991), pp. 190–201; J. R. Daling et al., "Sexual Practices, Sexually Transmitted Diseases, and the Incidence of Anal Cancer," *New England Journal of Medicine* 317, no. 16 (15 October 1987), pp. 973–77; E. A. Holly et al., "Anal Cancer Incidence: Genital Warts, Anal Fissure or Fistula, Hemorrhoids, and Smoking," *Journal of the National Cancer Institute* 81, no. 22 (November 1989), pp. 1726–31; J. R. Daling et al., "Correlates of Homosexual Behavior and the Incidence of Anal Cancer," *Journal of the American Medical Association* 247, no. 14 (9 April 1982), pp. 1988–90; H. S. Cooper, A. S. Patchefsky, and G. Marks, "Cloacogenic Carcinoma of the Anorectum in Homosexual Men: An Observation of Four Cases," *Diseases of the Colon and Rectum* 22, no. 8 (1979), pp. 557–58.

37. L. McKusick et al., "Longitudinal Predictors of Reductions in Unprotected Anal Intercourse among Gay Men in San Francisco: The AIDS Behavioral Research Project," *American Journal of Public Health* 80, no. 8 (August 1990), pp. 978–83.

38. F. N. Judson, "Sexually Transmitted Viral Hepatitis and Enteric Pathogens," *Urology Clinics of North America* 11, no. 1 (February 1984), pp. 177–85. See also: D. E. Koziol et al., "A Comparison of Risk Factors for Human Immunodeficiency Virus and Hepatitis B Virus Infections in Homosexual Men," *Annals of Epidemiology* 3, no. 4 (July 1993), pp. 434–41; G. Hart, "Factors Associated with Hepatitis B Infection," *International Journal of Sexually Transmitted Diseases and AIDS* 4, no. 2 (1993), pp. 102–6; T. Weinke et al., "Prevalence and Clinical Importance of Entamoeba Histolytica in Two High-Risk Groups: Travelers Returning from the Tropics and Male Homosexuals," *Journal of Infectious Diseases* 161, no. 5 (May 1990), pp. 1029–31; A. Rodriguez-Pichardo et al., "Sexually Transmitted Diseases in Homosexual Males in Seville, Spain," *Genitourinary Medicine* 67, no. 4 (August 1991), pp. 335–38; D. I. Abrams, "The Relationship between Kaposi's Sarcoma and Intestinal Parasites among Homosexual Males in the United States," *Journal of Acquired Immune Deficiency Syndrome* 3, no. 1 (1990), Supplement 1, p. S44–46; B. E. Laughon et al., "Recovery of Campylobacter Species from Homosexual Men," *Journal of Infectious Diseases* 158, no. 2 (August 1988), pp. 464–67; N. J. Bodsworth et al., "Hepatitis Delta Virus in Homosexual Men in Sydney," *Genitourinary Medicine* 65, no. 4 (August 1989), pp. 235–38; T. Takeuchi, "Sexually Transmitted Amoebiasis: Current Epidemiology," *Kitasato Archives of Experimental Medicine* 61, no. 4 (December 1988), pp. 171–79; W. Tee et al., "Campylobacter Cryaerophila Isolated from a Human," *Journal of Clinical Microbiology* 26, no. 12 (December 1988), pp. 2469–73; B. E. Laughon, "Prevalence of Enteric Pathogens in Homosexual Men with and without Acquired Immunodeficiency Syndrome," *Gastroenterology* 94, no. 4 (April 1988), pp. 984–93; T. C. Quinn, "Clinical Approach to Intestinal Infections in Homosexual Men," *Medical Clinics of North America* 70, no. 3 (May 1986), pp. 611–34; A. Khairul Anuar, "Gay Men-Bowel Syndrome:

a Report of Parasitic Infection in Homosexual Patients," *Medical Journal of Malaysia* 40, no. 4 (December 1985), pp. 325–29; S. L. Mann et al., "Prevalence and Incidence of Herpesvirus Infections among Homosexually Active Men," *Journal of Infectious Diseases* 149, no. 6 (June 1984), pp. 1026–27; P. A. Totten, "Campylobacter Cinaedi (sp. nov.) and Campylobacter Fennelliae (sp. nov.): Two New Campylobacter Species Associated with Enteric Disease in Homosexual Men," *Journal of Infectious Diseases* 151, no. 1 (January 1985), pp. 131–39; H. Schmidt, A. S. Jorgensen, and H. O. Petersen, "An Epidemic of Syphilis among Homosexuals and Bisexuals," *Acta Dermatologica Venereologica* [Supplement] (Stockholm) 120, no. 1 (1985), pp. 65–67; T. C. Quinn, "Gay Bowel Syndrome: The Broadened Spectrum of Nongenital Infection," *Postgraduate Medicine* 76, no. 2 (August 1984), pp. 197–98, 201–10; E. K. Markell et al., "Intestinal Protozoa in Homosexual Men of the San Francisco Bay Area: Prevalence and Correlates of Infection," *American Journal of Tropical Medicine and Hygiene* 33, no. 2 (March 1984), pp. 239–45; E. Allason-Jones and A. Mindel, "Sex and the Bowel," *International Journal of Colorectal Disease* 2, no. 1 (February 1987), pp. 32–37; D. S. Tompkins et al., "Isolation and Characterization of Intestinal Spirochaetes," *Journal of Clinical Pathology* 39, no. 5 (May 1986), pp. 535–41.

39. W. F. Owen, Jr., "Medical Problems of the Homosexual Adolescent," *Journal of Adolescent Health Care* 6, no. 4 (July 1985), pp. 278–85.

40. P. Cameron, W. L. Playfair, and S. Wellum, "The Homosexual Lifespan," Presentation to the Eastern Psychological Association, April 1993. General population data is available from the census bureau and closely matches the authors' samples. As in *Sex in America*, although homosexuals are included in the general sample, the proportion is too small to create a significant distortion and, if anything, would tend to mitigate the differences between homosexuals and heterosexuals, not enhance them.

Chapter 4: Finding a Needle in the Ocean

1. Brian Suarez, a researcher at Washington University School of Medicine in St. Louis. Cited in Mann, "Behavioral Genetics in Transition," p. 1688.

2. For an excellent nontechnical critique of the limitations of genetics research into many areas of human behavior, see J. Horgan, "Eugenics Revisited," *Scientific American*, June 1993, pp. 123–31.

3. K. E. Ernulf, S. M. Innala, and F. L. Whitam, "Biological Explanation, Psychological Explanation, and Tolerance of Homosexuals: A Cross-National Analysis of Beliefs and Attitudes," *Psychological Reports* 65 (1989), pp. 1003–10 (1 of 3).

4. A lower score on this scale means a less negative attitude toward homosexuality.

5. J. Piskur and D. Degelman, "Effect of Reading a Summary of Research about Biological Bases of Homosexual Orientation in Attitudes Toward Homosexuals," *Psychological Reports* 71 (1992), pp. 1219–25 (part 2 of 3).

6. S. LeVay, "A Difference in Hypothalamic Structure between Heterosexual and Homosexual Men," *Science* 253 (1991), pp. 1034–37.

7. D. Swaab and M. Hofman, "An Enlarged Suprachiasmatic Nucleus in Homosexual Men," *Brain Research* 537 (1990), pp. 141–48.

8. K. Klivingston, assistant to the President of the Salk Institute, cited by K. Lansing in "Homosexuality: Theories of Causation, Reorientation and the Politics and Ethics Involved," Proceedings of the 1993 Annual Scientific Meet-

ing of the National Association for Research and Treatment of Homosexuality, p. 50.

9. G. Gabbard, "Psychodynamic Psychiatry in the 'Decade of the Brain,'" *American Journal of Psychiatry* 149, no. 8 (1992), pp. 991–98.

10. R. Post, "Transduction of Psychosocial Stress into the Neurobiology of Recurrent Affective Disorder," *American Journal of Psychiatry* 148, no. 8 (1992), pp. 999–1010.

11. Gabbard, "Psychodynamic Psychiatry."

12. J. Maddox, "Is Homosexuality Hardwired?" *Nature* 353 (September 1991), p. 13.

13. P. Billings and J. Beckwith, "Born Gay?" *Technology Review*, July 1993, p. 60. Paul Billings, M.D., is the former chief of the Division of Genetic Medicine at California Pacific Medical Center in Palo Alto, California, and is now head of Internal Medicine at the Palo Alto Veteran's Administration Hospital; Jonathan Beckwith, M.D., is American Cancer Society Research Professor in the Department of Microbiology and Molecular Genetics at Harvard Medical School.

14. Ibid., p. 60.

15. Ibid., p. 61.

Chapter 5: Two of a Kind

1. J. M. Bailey and R. C. Pillard, "A Genetic Study of Male Sexual Orientation," *Archives of General Psychiatry* 48 (1991), pp. 1089–96; M. King and E. McDonald, "Homosexuals Who Are Twins: A Study of 46 Probands," *British Journal of Psychiatry* 160 (1992), pp. 407–9; Bailey et al., "Heritable Factors," pp. 217–23.

2. Bailey and Pillard, "Male Sexual Orientation."

3. Theodore Lidz, "Reply to 'A Genetic Study of Male Sexual Orientation,'" *Archives of General Psychiatry* 50, no. 3 (1993), p. 240.

4. Eckert et al., "Monozygotic Twins Reared Apart," pp. 421–25.

5. W. Byne and B. Parsons, "Human Sexual Orientation: The Biologic Theories Reappraised," *Archives of General Psychiatry* 50, no. 3, pp. 228–39.

6. King and McDonald, "Homosexuals Who Are Twins." My emphasis.

7. Doll et al., "Self-Reported Abuse."

8. Billings and Beckwith, "Born Gay?" p. 60.

9. Ibid., p. 61.

10. Ironically, if activists' claims were accurate that 10 percent of the population is homosexual, then this finding alone would tend to refute the idea of *any* genetic influence on male homosexuality. In effect, it would imply that even with some 50 percent shared genes, and being raised in the same environment, the nontwin brother of a homosexual is no more likely to be homosexual than someone selected at random from the population at large. Since the true incidence of male homosexuality is about 3 percent, this finding suggests that genetic similarity plus similar environment increases the likelihood that the nontwin brother of a homosexual will himself be homosexual from 3 percent to 9 percent. The difference in such small percentages could easily be accounted for on the basis of environment alone.

11. Calculated by 52 percent divided by 22 percent.

12. Calculated by 22 percent divided by 9 percent.

13. Bailey et al., "Heritable Factors," pp. 217–23.

14. My emphases. J. P. Rushton, *Race Evolution and Behavior: A Life History Perspective* (New Brunswick, N.J.: Transaction Publishers, 1994), p. 47. Dizygotic correlations of from 9 to 22 percent among siblings raised in the same household are not significant.

15. Quoted by J. Horgan, "Eugenics Revisited," *Scientific American*, June 1993, p. 123.

16. C. Mann, "Genes and Behavior," *Science* 264 (1994), pp. 1686–89.

17. Ibid.

18. W. Byne, "Science and Belief: Psychobiological Research on Sexual Orientation," *Journal of Homosexuality*, in press.

19. D. Jefferson, "Studying the Biology of Sexual Orientation Has Political Fallout," *Wall Street Journal*, 12 August 1993, p. 1.

Chapter 6: A Cluster of Influences

1. Byne and Parsons, "Human Sexual Orientation."

2. Wiesel, "Genetics and Behavior," *Science*, p. 1647.

3. J. Knop et al., "A 30-Year Follow-up Study of the Sons of Alcoholic Men," *Acta Psychiatrica* (Denmark) 370 (1993), pp. 48–53; K. S. Kendler et al., "A Population–Based Twin Study of Alcoholism in Women," *Journal of the American Medical Association* 268, no. 14 (1992), pp. 1877–82; J. B. Peterson et al., "Cognitive Dysfunction and the Inherited Predisposition to Alcoholism," *Journal of Studies in Alcoholism* 53, no. 2 (1992), pp. 154–60.

4. S. Y. Hill et al., "Cardiac Responsivity in Individuals at High Risk for Alcoholism," *Journal of Studies in Alcoholism* 53, no. 4 (1992), pp. 378–88; P. R. Finn et al., "Sensation Seeking, Stress Reactivity, and Alcohol Dampening Discriminate the Density of a Family History of Alcoholism," *Alcohol Clinical and Experimental Research* 16, no. 3 (1992), pp. 585–90.

5. Prior to the invention of synthetic agents, alcohol was widely used in hospitals—sometimes intravenously—to calm nerves, dull pain, suppress seizures, and cause sleep. See D. S. Cowley et al., "Response to Diazepam in Sons of Alcoholics," *Alcohol Clinical and Experimental Research* 16, no. 6 (1992), pp. 1057–63.

6. N. el-Guabely et al., "Adult Children of Alcoholics in Treatment Programs for Anxiety Disorders and Substance Abuse," *Canadian Journal of Psychiatry* 37, no. 8 (1992), pp. 544–48; S. M. Mirin et al., "Psychopathology in Drug Abusers and Their Families," *Comparative Psychiatry* 32, no. 1 (1991), pp. 36–51; M. W. Otto et al., "Alcohol Dependence In Panic Disorder Patients," *Journal of Psychiatric Research* 26, no, 1 (1992), pp. 29–38; G. Winokur and W. Coryell, "Familial Subtypes of Unipolar Depression: A Prospective Study of Familial Pure Depressive Disease Compared to Depressive Spectrum Disease," *Biological Psychiatry* 32, no. 11 (1992), pp. 1012–18.

7. Cowley et al., "Response to Diazepam."

8. Cowley et al., "Response to Diazepam"; Hill et al., "Cardiac Responsivity"; Finn et al., "Sensation Seeking."

9. See C. Holden, "A Cautionary Genetic Tale: The Sobering Story of D_2," *Science* 264, pp. 1696–97.

10. See Bailey and Pillard, "Male Sexual Orientation," and surrounding discussion.

11. L. Frank, S. Glickman, and P. Licht, "Fatal Sibling Aggression, Precocial Development and Androgens in Neonatal Spotted Hyenas," *Science* 252 (1991), pp. 702–4.

12. G. Dörner et al., "Gene- and Environment-Dependent Neuroendocrine Etiogenesis of Homosexuality and Transsexualism," *Experimental and Clinical Endocrinology* 98, no. 2 (1991), pp. 141–50.

13. See Byne and Parsons, "Human Sexual Orientation," for a summary of counterfindings and conclusions.

14. H. Meyer-Bahlburg, "Psychoendocrine Research on Sexual Orientation: Current Status and Future Options," *Progress in Brain Research* 61 (1984), pp. 375–98; J. Downey et al., "Sex Hormones and Lesbian and Heterosexual Women," *Hormones and Behavior* 21 (1987), pp. 347–57. Cited and discussed in Byne and Parsons, "Human Sexual Orientation."

15. Byne and Parsons, "Human Sexual Orientation," p. 230.

16. A. Galaburda, et al., "Right-Left Asymmetries in the Brain," *Science* 199, no. 4331 (1974), pp. 852–56; N. Geschwind, "Anatomical Asymmetry as the Basis for Cerebral Dominance," *Federal Proceedings* 37, no. 9 (1978), pp. 2263–66; A. Galaburda and N. Geschwind, "Anatomical Asymmetries in the Adult and Developing Brain and Their Implications for Function," *Advances in Pediatrics* 28 (1991), pp. 271–92.

17. P. Satz, et al., "Hand Preference in Homosexual Men," *Cortex* 27 (1991), pp. 295–306.

18. C. McCormick, S. Witelson, and E. Kingstone, "Left-Handedness in Homosexual Men and Women: Neuroendocrine Implications," *Psychoneuroendocrinology* 15, no. 1 (1990), pp. 69–79.

19. N. Risch, E. Squires-Wheeler, and J. B. K. Bronya, "Male Sexual Orientation and Genetic Evidence," *Science* 262 (1993), pp. 2063–65.

20. J. McDougall, "The Dead Father: On Early Psychic Trauma and Its Relation to Disturbance in Sexual Identity and in Creative Activity," *International Journal of Psychoanalysis* 70, no. 2 (1989), pp. 205–19.

21. Doll et al., "Self-Reported Abuse."

22. G. A. Rekers et al., "Family Correlates of Male Childhood Gender Disturbance," *Journal of Genetics and Psychology* 142, no. 1 (1983), pp. 31–42.

23. G. A. Rekers and J. J. Swihart, "The Association of Gender Identity Disorder with Parental Separation," *Psychological Reports* 65, no. 3, 2 (1989), pp. 1272–74.

24. G. A. Rekers, "The Formation of Homosexual Orientation," Address to the North American Social Science Network Conference (1987).

Chapter 7: The Gay Gene?

1. D. H. Hamer et al., "A Linkage between DNA Markers on the X-chromosome and Male Sexual Orientation," *Science* 261, no. 5119, pp. 321–27.

2. "Research Points Toward a Gay Gene," *Wall Street Journal*, 16 July 1993.

3. It was precisely the failure to find such confirming data that torpedoed the "bipolar gene."

4. Risch et al., "Male Sexual Orientation and Genetic Evidence."

5. D. H. Hamer et al., "Response to N. Risch et al.," *Science* 262 (1993), p. 2065.

6. Ibid.

7. Mann, "Genes and Behavior," p. 1687.

8. E. Marshall, "NIH's 'Gay Gene' Study Questioned," *Science* 268 (1995), p. 1841.
9. Byne and Parsons, "Human Sexual Orientation," pp. 228–39; my emphasis.

Chapter 8: Wired to Be Free?

1. See E. Wind, *Pagan Mysteries in the Renaissance* (Harmondsworth: Penguin, 1967).
2. See C. S. Lewis, *The Abolition of Man* (New York: Macmillan, 1947).
3. "Purpose" in the higher sense, not merely the self- and species-protecting purpose of evolutionary biology.
4. See R. Herrnstein and C. Murray, *The Bell Curve* (Boston: Free Press, 1994).
5. The Greek philosopher Archimedes is known for his invention of geometry and of the lever: He stated, "give me a long enough lever and a fulcrum at the right place and I can move the entire earth."
6. T. S. Eliot, "Burnt Norton II," *Four Quartets* in *The Complete Poems and Plays* (New York: Harcourt, Brace & World, 1971), p. 119.
7. J. DeCecco, "Confusing the Actor with the Act: Muddled Notions about Homosexuality," *Archives of Sexual Behavior* 20, no. 4 (1990), pp. 421–23.

Chapter 9: The Devil's Bargain

1. For a particularly powerful story of such healing, see Mario Bergner's *Setting Love in Order* (Grand Rapids, Mich.: Baker, 1995).
2. R. Lau et al., "Trends in Sexual Behavior in a Cohort of Homosexual Men: A 7-Year Prospective Study," *International Journal for the Study of AIDS* 3, no. 4 (1992), pp. 267–72; A. Lifson, "Men Who Have Sex with Men: Continued Challenges for Preventing HIV Infection and AIDS [Editorial]," *American Journal of Public Health* 82, no. 2 (1992), pp. 166–67; S. Adib et al., "Prediction of Relapse in Sexual Practices among Homosexual Men," *AIDS Education and Prevention* 3, no. 4 (1991), pp. 293–304; "Patterns of Sexual Behavior Change among Homosexual/Bisexual Men—Selective U.S. Sites, 1987–1990," *Morbidity and Mortality Weekly Reports* 40, no. 46 (1991), pp. 792–94; L. S. Doll et al., "Homosexual Men Who Engage in High-Risk Sexual Behavior: A Multicenter Comparison," *Journal of Sexually Transmitted Diseases* 18, no. 3 (1991), pp. 170–75; C. Kuiken et al., "Risk Factors and Changes in Sexual Behavior in Male Homosexuals Who Seroconverted for Human Immunodeficiency Virus Antibodies," *American Journal of Epidemiology* 132, no. 3 (1990), pp. 523–30.
3. See, for example, J. Maddox, "Is Homosexuality Hardwired?" *Nature* 353 (September 1991), p. 13.
4. T. Sejnowski and C. Rosenberg, "NetTalk: A Parallel Network That Learns to Read Aloud," in *Neurocomputing: Foundations of Research*, J. A. Anderson and E. Rosenfeld, eds. (Cambridge, Mass.: MIT Press, 1988).
5. D. Jefferson, "Studying the Biology of Sexual Orientation Has Political Fallout," *Wall Street Journal*, 12 August 1993, p. 1.
6. Maddox, "Is Homosexuality Hardwired?"
7. M. A. Bozarth and R. A. Wise, "Toxicity Associated with Long-Term Intravenous Heroin and Cocaine Self-Administration in the Rat, *Journal of the American Medical Association* 5, 254, no. 1 (1985), pp. 81–83; M. W. Fischman, "Behavioral Pharmacology of Cocaine," *Journal of Clinical Psychiatry* 49, no. 1 (1988), pp. 7–10 (Supplement).

8. J. McDougall, "Identifications, Neoneeds and Neosexualities," *International Journal of Psychoanalysis* 67, no. 1 (1986), pp. 19–31.

9. What about those homosexuals who are not promiscuous? Remember the study of 100 male couples cited previously in which not one had remained together and faithful for even five years. While "mere" infidelity of an indeterminate frequency may not be considered "promiscuity" by today's standards, it is clear that monogamy is less typical of homosexuals than of heterosexuals, with few exceptions. Because in this study there were no exceptions, the researchers concluded approvingly that gay sexuality is inherently "nonmonogamous." D. McWhirter and A. Mattison, *The Male Couple: How Relationships Develop* (Englewood Cliffs, N.J.: Prentice-Hall, 1984).

10. A discussion of how some of the most advanced science of our era does indeed support such freedom would take us beyond the scope of this book. See, for example, H. Stapp, *Mind, Matter, and Quantum Mechanics* (Berlin: Springer Verlag, 1994).

Chapter 10: The Unnatural Natural

1. See 1 Corinthians 10.

2. M. C. Luzzato, *Derech Hashem (The Way of God)*, trans. A Kaplan (Jerusalem: Feldheim, 1988), pp. 121–23. Unknown to the secular, nonobservant-Jewish, and Christian worlds, Luzzato (1707–1748) was one of the great geniuses of European Jewry. *Derech Hashem* is a comprehensive summary of Jewish theology encompassing the Torah, the Prophets, the Talmud, and Kabbalah.

3. In Hebrew, the word for fool means less someone who is unintelligent in matters of the mind as in matters of the heart.

4. S. Freud, *Totem and Taboo*, Standard Edition (1913), p. 12.

5. Michael Piazza, senior pastor at the Cathedral of Hope, commenting on Leviticus 18:22 and 20:13, which describe both male and female homosexuality as "an abomination" (*New York Times*, October 30, 1994, p. 16).

6. See, for example, Sallie McFague's "Models of God."

Chapter 11: To Treat or Not to Treat

1. Such as Coleman et al., "Sexual and Intimacy Dysfunction."

2. T. F. Murphy, "Freud and Sexual Reorientation Therapy," *Journal of Homosexuality* 23, no. 3 (1992), pp. 21–38.

3. C. Crepault, "Un Regard Sexoanalytique sur L'homosexualité," *Contraception et Fertilité Sexuelle* 22, no. 1 (1994), pp. 41–47.

4. A. Cantom-Dutari, "Combined Intervention for Controlling Unwanted Homosexual Behavior: An Extended Follow-up," *Archives of Sexual Behavior* 5, no. 4 (1976), pp. 269–74.

5. C. W. Socarides, "Beyond Sexual Freedom: Clinical Fallout," *American Journal of Psychotherapy* 30, no. 3 (1976), pp. 385–97.

6. Later, this attitude changed. Thus an article appeared in the *Journal of the American Medical Association* in 1991 entitled, "Medical Recovery through a Higher Power" (*Journal of the American Medical Association* 226, no. 21, pp. 3065–66).

7. AA is even associated with reduced physical illness. See R. E. Mann et al., "Reduction in Cirrhosis Deaths in the United States: Associations with Per

Capita Consumption and AA Membership," *Journal of Studies in Alcoholism* 52, no. 4 (1991), pp. 361–65.

8. See B. Johnson, "A Developmental Model of Addictions, and its Relationship to the Twelve-Step Program of Alcoholics Anonymous, *Journal of Substance Abuse Treatment* 10, no. 1 (1993), pp. 23–24.

9. The March 1993 *Psychiatric Clinics of North America*, a major publication, provides a summary of AA membership data (dropout rates, recidivism, demographics, and so on). It presents AA as a useful and successful method of treatment and teaches psychiatrists how to facilitate their patients' approach to AA. It does not provide, however, any explanation of why it works. J. N. Chappel, "Long-Term Recovery from Alcoholism," *Psychiatric Clinics of North America* 16, no. 1 (1993), pp. 177–87.

10. Gilbert, "Development of a 'Steps Questionnaire.' "

11. T. S. Eliot, "East Coker IV," *Four Quartets* in *The Complete Poems and Plays* (New York: Harcourt, Brace & World: 1971), p. 127.

Chapter 12: Secular Treatments

1. T. F. Murphy, "Freud and Sexual Reorientation Therapy," *Journal of Homosexuality* 23, no. 3 (1992), pp. 21–38.

2. H. MacIntosh, "Attitudes and Experiences of Psychoanalysts in Analyzing Homosexual Patients," *Journal of the American Psychoanalytic Association* 42, no. 4 (1995), pp. 1183–1207.

3. *Psychiatric News* 28, no. 15 (1993), p. 13.

4. NARTH has a quarterly bulletin and sponsors annual professional conferences on both the East and West Coasts.

5. Cited in G. Morris, review of *When Wish Replaces Thought: Why So Much of What You Believe Is False*, by Steven Goldberg, *National Review* (October 19, 1992), p. 65.

6. *Journal of the American Psychiatric Association*, vol. 150 (1993).

7. Cited in *NARTH Bulletin* 1, no. 4 (1993), p. 4.

8. As reported in *NARTH Bulletin* 1, no. 3 (1993), p. 5.

9. J. Nicolosi, *Reparative Therapy of Male Homosexuality: A New Clinical Approach* (New York: Jason Aronson, 1991).

10. J. Nicolosi, "Intervention Techniques of Reparative Therapy," Address to Second National NARTH Conference, San Francisco, 20 May 1993.

11. J. Nicolosi, *Reparative Therapy*, cover insert, p. xvi.

12. Nicolosi, *Reparative Therapy*, as listed in *NARTH Bulletin* 1, no. 3 (1993).

13. A. Cantom-Dutari, "Combined Intervention for Controlling Unwanted Homosexual Behavior, pp. 269–74.

14. Schwartz and Masters, "The Masters and Johnson Treatment Program for Dissatisfied Homosexual Men," *American Journal of Psychiatry* 141, pp. 173–81.

15. DSM-IV, p. 528.

16. Quoted in *NARTH Bulletin* 1, no. 3 (1993), p. 5.

17. D. H. Golwyn and C. P. Sevlie, *Journal of Clinical Psychiatry* 54, no. 1, pp. 39–40.

18. Nicolosi, *Reparative Therapy*, pp. 100–101.

19. J. F. Porter, "Homosexuality Treated Adventitiously in a Stuttering Therapy Program: A Case Report Presenting a Heterophobic Orientation," *Australia and New Zealand Journal of Psychiatry* 10, no. 2 (1976), pp. 185–89.

20. See Schwartz and Masters, "Treatment Program for Dissatisfied Homosexual Men."

21. M. J. Kruesi et al., "Paraphilias: A Double-Blind Crossover Comparison of Clomipramine versus Desipramine," *Archives of Sexual Behavior* 21, no. 6 (1992), pp. 587–93; M. P. Kafka, "Successful Treatment of Paraphilic Coercive Disorder (a rapist) with Fluoxetine Hydrochloride," *British Journal of Psychiatry* 158, no. 1 (1991), pp. 844–47; R. D. Perilstein, S. Lipper, and L. J. Friedman, "Three Cases of Paraphilias Responsive to Fluoxetine Treatment," *Journal of Clinical Psychiatry* 52, no. 4 (1991), pp. 169–70; M. P. Kafka, "Successful Antidepressant Treatment of Nonparaphilic Sexual Addictions and Paraphilias in Men," *Journal of Clinical Psychiatry* 52, no. 2 (1991), pp. 60–65; J. Kerbeshian and L. Burd, "Tourette Syndrome and Recurrent Paraphilic Masturbatory Fantasy [letter]," *Canadian Journal of Psychiatry* 36, no. 2 (1991), pp. 155–57; V. T. Jorgensen, "Cross-Dressing Successfully Treated with Fluoxetine [letter]," Comment in *New York State Journal of Medicine* 91, no. 4 (1991), p. 171; M. D. Bianchi, "Fluoxetine Treatment of Exhibitionism [letter]," *American Journal of Psychiatry* 147, no. 8 (1990), pp. 1089–90; N. P. Emmanuel, R. B. Lydiard, and J. C. Ballenger, "Fluoxetine Treatment of Voyeurism," *American Journal of Psychiatry* 148, no. 7 (1991), p. 950; M. P. Kafka and E. Coleman, "Serotonin and Paraphilias: The Convergence of Mood, Impulse, and Compulsive Disorders," *Journal of Clinical Psychopharmacology* 11, no. 3 (1991), pp. 223–24; M. P. Kafka and R. Prentky, "A Comparative Study of Non-Paraphiliac Sexual Addictions and Paraphilias in Men," *Journal of Clinical Psychiatry* 53, no. 10 (1992), pp. 345–50.

22. M. P. Kafka and R. Prentky, "Fluoxetine Treatment of Nonparaphilic Sexual Addictions and Paraphilias in Men," *Journal of Clinical Psychiatry* 53, no. 10 (1992), pp. 351–58. Quoting the authors:

Paraphilias (PAs) and non-paraphilic sexual addictions (NPSAs) may be behaviors that share a common perturbation of central serotonin neuroregulation as a component of their pathophysiology. Fluoxetine was selected as an agent that might mitigate these behaviors, based on the observations that PAs and NPSAs are associated with depression, compulsion, impulsivity, and disinhibited aggression. . . . 95 percent of [the] men met non-exclusionary DSM-III-R criteria for dysthymia and . . . 55 percent met criteria for current major depression. At baseline, the paraphilic and the nonparaphilic subgroups were comparable in most intergroup measures of sexual function. . . . Statistically significant reduction in PA/NPSA response was evident by Week 4, while conventional sexual behavior was not adversely affected by pharmacotherapy. . . . Enhancement of central serotonin neurotransmission by fluoxetine may ameliorate symptoms of mood disorder, heightened sexual desire, and compulsivity/impulsivity associated with these conditions.

See also D. J. Stein et al., "Serotonergic Medications for Sexual Obsessions, Sexual Addictions, and Paraphilias," *Journal of Clinical Psychiatry* 53, no. 8 (1992), pp. 267–71; M. P. Kafka, "Successful Antidepressant Treatment of Nonparaphilic Sexual Addictions and Paraphilias in Men," *Journal of Clinical Psychiatry* 52, no. 2 (1991), pp. 60–65.

23. The recent APA decision to no longer classify perverse sexualities as paraphilias unless they cause distress to the individual himself and loss of function in some other area of life undermines these hard-won clinical understandings. It has already led to claims by, for example, sado-masochistic groups that they have won the battle to normalize their perversion and to similar claims by pedophile groups.

24. Kafka, "Successful Antidepressant Treatment": "The author conceptualizes these behaviors as sexual dysregulation disorders associated with a primary mood disorder."

25. *Post coitum omne animal triste:* an ancient Latin proverb meaning "after coitus every animal is sad."

26. L. Lorefice, "Fluoxetine Treatment of a Fetish," *Journal of Clinical Psychiatry* 52, no. 1, p. 41.

27. The increased incidence of other paraphilias among homosexuals—sadomasochism, fetishism, cross-dressing—seems obvious, but there are as yet no formal studies on the subject.

28. "Gays Are More Prone to Substance Abuse," *Insight,* 5 November 1990. GLHF attributes this to the "victimization" of homosexuals.

Chapter 13: Christian Treatments

1. D. B. Larson et al., "Systematic Analysis of Research on Religious Variables in Four Major Psychiatric Journals, 1978–1982," *American Journal of Psychiatry* 143, no. 3 (1986), pp. 329–34.

2. E. M. Pattison and M. L. Pattison, " 'Ex-Gays': Religiously Mediated Change in Homosexuals," *American Journal of Psychiatry* 137, no. 12 (1980), pp. 1553–62.

3. Catholic Church, *Catechism of the Catholic Church* (Chicago: [distributed by] Loyola University Press, 1994), Part Three: Life in Christ, p. 566.

4. A. Comiskey, *Pursuing Sexual Wholeness: How Jesus Heals the Homosexual* (Lake Mary, Fla.: Creation House, 1989).

5. Ibid., p. 192.

6. M. Bergner, *Setting Love in Order* (Grand Rapids, Mich.: Baker, 1995).

7. Ibid., p. 23.

8. Thus, from a secular perspective, Nicolosi expands on Elizabeth Moberley's idea of "defensive detachment" from men as one typical response of prehomosexual boys to wounding by their fathers. See Nicolosi, *Reparative Therapy.*

9. See F. A. Schaeffer, *How Should We Then Live?* (Old Tappan, N.J.: Fleming H. Revell Company, 1976).

10. See L. Payne, *The Healing of the Homosexual* (Wheaton, Ill.: Crossway Books, 1985); L. Payne, *Crisis in Masculinity* (Grand Rapids: Baker Books, 1985, 1995); L. Payne, *The Broken Image* (Grand Rapids: Baker Books, 1981, 1995); L. Payne, *The Healing Presence* (Grand Rapids: Baker Books, 1989, 1996); L. Payne, *Restoring the Christian Soul: Overcoming Barriers to Completion in Christ through Healing Prayer* (Grand Rapids: Baker Books, 1995); L. Payne, *Listening Prayer: Learning to Hear God's Voice and Keep a Prayer Journal* (Grand Rapids: Baker Books, 1994).

Chapter 14: Homosexuality and Judaism

1. R. P. Bulka, *One Man, One Woman, One Lifetime: An Argument for Moral Tradition* (Lafayette, Louisiana: Huntington House, 1995), p. 9.

2. A. Vorspan, "Is American Jewry Unraveling?" *Reform Judaism*, Summer 1995, p. 11.

3. Bulka, *One Man, One Woman, One Lifetime*.

4. In the Orthodox view, all 613 commandments in the Torah (Sinaitic Commandments) are binding only on Jews to this day. The Noahide moral commandments are a subset of these. The former include additional and more stringent moral commandments as well as ritual requirements, such as the laws of Kashruth (Kosher food) and circumcision. According to the Talmud (Sanhedrin 56–60) in its exegesis of Genesis starting at 2:16, the seven commandments binding on Noah and all his descendants are:

    (1)   to refrain from the worship of idols;
    (2)   to refrain from blaspheming God;
    (3)   to establish courts of justice;
    (4)   to refrain from murder;
    (5)   to refrain from adultery;
    (6)   to refrain from robbery; and
    (7)   to refrain from eating flesh cut from a living animal.

The prohibition against homosexuality is a specific part of the Noahide injunction against adultery. See M. Maimonides, *Mishneh Torah*, Hilkoth Melachim 7:2 (ca. 1190).

5. Signatories: Rabbi B. Freundel, Chair, RCA Ethics Commission, and Rabbi R. P. Bulka, RCA ad hoc Committee on Homosexuality. Rabbi Bulka holds a Ph.D. in clinical psychology and is editor of *Psychology and Judaism*.

6. R. Bulka, *One Man, One Woman, One Lifetime*, p. 35.

7. Ibid., pp. 84–85, commenting on R. Aharon Levi, *Sefer HaHinnukh*, no. 16.

8. M. Nachmanides, *Iggeret HaKodesh* (The Holy Letter), S. Cohen, ed. and trans., (New York: Ktav Publishing House, 1976), chapter 2; cited in Bulka, *One Man, One Woman, One Lifetime*, p. 137.

9. As was noted of Rabbi Ben Azzai, a great second century Talmudic sage: "It was taught: R. Eliezer stated, 'He who does not engage in the propagation of the race is as though he sheds blood.' . . . They said to Ben Azzai: 'Some preach well and act well; others act well but do not preach well; you, however, preach well but do not act well!' Ben Azzai replied: 'But what shall I do, seeing that my soul is in love with the Torah; the world can be carried on by others.'" (Yebamoth, 63b), referenced by Bulka, *One Man, One Woman, One Lifetime*, p. 11.

10. For a careful discussion of this point from the Orthodox Jewish perspective, see B. Freundel, "Homosexuality and Judaism," *Journal of Halacha and Contemporary Society* 11 (1986), pp. 70–87.

Chapter 15: Putting the Pieces Together

1. ". . . gender nonconformity and precocious psychosexual development were predictive of self harm. . . . For each year's delay in bisexual or homosex-

ual self-labeling, the odds of a suicide attempt diminish by 80 percent." [G. Remafedi, J. A. Farrow, and R. W. Deisher. "Risk Factors for Attempted Suicide in Gay Bisexual Youth," *Pediatrics* 87, no. 6 (1991), pp. 869–75.] "The very experience of acquiring a homosexual or bisexual identity at an early age places the individual at risk for dysfunction. This conclusion is strongly supported by the data. [G. Remafedi, "Adolescent Homosexuality: Psychosocial and Medical Implications," *Pediatrics* 79, no. 3 (1987), pp. 331–37.]

Chapter 16: The Pagan Revolution

1. Between 1920 and 1960 the explicitly anti-religious regimes of Germany, Russia, and China killed, respectively, 12 million, 30 million, and 50 million innocents.

2. C. G. Jung, "Wotan," *Civilization in Transition, Collected Works*, vol. 10 (Princeton: Princeton University Press, 1918), p. 13.

3. H. Heine, *The Works of Heinrich Heine*, vol. V (London: William Heinemann, 1892), pp. 207–9. The passage as cited is my own translation.

4. C. S. Lewis, *The Screwtape Letters* (New York: Macmillan, 1964).

5. M. Zeller, "The Task of the Analyst," *Psychological Perspectives* 6, no. 1 (1975), pp. 74–78, cited in M. Stein, *Jung's Treatment of Christianity* (Wilmette, Ill.: Chiron, 1985), p. 188.

6. Stein, *Jung's Treatment of Christianity*, pp. 188–89.

7. C. G. Jung, *Aion. Collected Works*, vol. 9, 2 (Princeton: Princeton University Press, 1959), p. 41.

8. Ibid.

9. C. G. Jung, *Psychological Types, Collected Works*, vol. 6 (Princeton: Bollingen/Princeton University Press, 1920), p. 17.

10. M. T. Kelsey and B. Kelsey, *The Sacrament of Sexuality: The Spirituality and Psychology of Sex* (Rockport, Mass.: Element, 1991).

11. Ibid., p. 191.

12. B. Berger, "The Soul and the Machine," *NetGuide*, February 1995, p. 19.

13. See G. Paris, *The Sacrament of Abortion* (Dallas: Spring Publications, 1992).

Resources

Secular Books

Cohen, Richard A. *Healing Homosexuality: Manual and Slide Presentation.* Bowie, Md.: International Healing Foundation Press, 1994 (International Healing Foundation, P.O. Box 901, Bowie, MD 20718).

Nicolosi, Joseph. *Healing Homosexuality: Case Stories of Reparative Therapy.* New York: Jason Aronson, 1993.

———. *Reparative Therapy of Male Homosexuality.* New York: Jason Aronson, 1991.

Siegel, Elaine V. *Female Homosexuality: Choice without Volition.* Hillsdale, N.J.: The Analytic Press, 1988.

———. *Homosexuality: Psychoanalytic Therapy.* New York: Jason Aronson, 1989.

Socarides, Charles. *Homosexuality: A Freedom Too Far.* Phoenix: Adam Margrave, 1995.

Christian Books

Bergner, Mario. *Setting Love in Order.* Grand Rapids, Mich.: Baker Books, 1995.

Burtoft, Larry. *The Social Significance of Homosexuality: Questions and Answers.* Colorado Springs: Focus on the Family, 1994.

Comiskey, Andrew. *Pursuing Sexual Wholeness: How Jesus Heals the Homosexual.* Lake Mary, Fla.: Creation House, 1988.

———. *Pursuing Sexual Wholeness: How Jesus Heals the Homosexual.* Workbook. Lake Mary, Fla.: Creation House, 1988.

Davies, Bob, and Lori Rentzel. *Coming Out of Homosexuality: New Freedom for Men and Women.* Downers Grove, Ill.: InterVarsity, 1993.

Gallagher, Steve. *Tearing Down the High Places of Sexual Idolatry.* Crittenden, Ky.: Pure Life Press, 1986 (Pure Life Press: P. O. Box 345, Crittenden, KY 41030).

Harvey, Fr. John F. *The Homosexual Person: New Thinking in Pastoral Care.* San Francisco: Ignatius, 1987.

Howard, Jeanette. *Out of Egypt: Leaving Lesbianism Behind.* Nashville: Thomas Nelson, 1994.

Payne, Leanne. *The Broken Image.* Grand Rapids: Baker Books, 1981, 1995.
———. *Crisis in Masculinity.* Grand Rapids: Baker Books, 1985, 1995.
———. *The Healing of the Homosexual.* Downers Grove, Ill.: Crossway Books, 1985.
———. *Restoring the Christian Soul through Healing Prayer.* Downers Grove, Ill.: Crossway Books, 1991.
Saia, Michael R. *Counseling the Homosexual.* Minneapolis, Minn.: Bethany House, 1988.
Schmidt, Thomas E. *Straight and Narrow? Compassion and Clarity in the Homosexuality Debate.* Downers Grove, Ill.: InterVarsity, 1995.
Additional books and other resources may be obtained from Regeneration Books, P. O. Box 9830, Baltimore, MD 21284

Organizations

Courage—St. Michael's Rectory, 424 West 34th Street, New York, NY 10001; (212) 421–0426. A Roman Catholic ministry to homosexuals led by Fr. John Harvey.

Desert Stream A. R. M.—12488 Venice Boulevard, Los Angeles, CA 90066; (310) 572–0140. Desert Stream offers a wide range of counseling, educational seminars, and support groups for those struggling with homosexuality as well as with AIDS. The associated Living Waters Program developed by Andrew Comiskey is a small-group program that offers Christian counseling for people seeking change and training for counselors.

Evergreen International—P.O. Box 3, Salt Lake City, UT 84110; (800)391-1000 or (801)535-1658. Evergreen is a program developed by and associated with the Mormon Church (LDS). However, its approach is not primarily focused on spiritual healing but on secular psychological and psychiatric approaches to treating homosexuality.

Exodus International—P.O. Box 2121, San Rafael, CA 94912; (415) 454–1017. Exodus is an umbrella organization of over two hundred ministries nationwide that treat homosexuality from a variety of Christian perspectives. It offers referrals and additional resources.

Homosexuals Anonymous—P.O. Box 7881, Reading, PA 19603; (215) 376–1146. A ministry for homosexuals based on the twelve-steps program of Alcoholics Anonymous.

National Association for Research and Treatment of Homosexuality (NARTH)—16452 Ventura Boulevard, Encino, CA 91436; (818) 789–4440. NARTH is an organization of nearly four hundred professionals across the country who treat homosexuality from a variety of perspectives.

Pastoral Care Ministries—P.O. Box 1313, Wheaton, IL 60189. An international ministry led by Leanne Payne to homosexuals and others with sexual or relational brokenness. Conducts five to six major healing conferences and pastoral care schools per year.

The Rabbinical Council of America—Rabbi Barry Freundel, Chairman of the Ethics Committee, Congregation Kesher Israel, 2801 N Street, N. W., Washington, DC 20007; (202) 333–3579. The Council, which is the national organization of Orthodox Jewish Rabbis, maintains a referral list of professionals who treat homosexuality from a perspective that is compatible with Orthodox Jewish beliefs.

Redeemed Life—P.O. Box 1211, Wheaton, IL 60189; (708) 393–7509. Founded and led by Rev. Mario Bergner, Redeemed Life is a ministry of discipleship and pastoral care for the sexually broken, not exclusively homosexuals.

Regeneration—P.O. Box 9830, Baltimore, MD 21284. Episcopal ministry to homosexuals.

Spatula Ministries—P.O. Box 444, La Habra, CA 90631; (310) 691–7369. A ministry and support organization for parents of homosexuals.

Studies on Secular Treatment

Barnhouse, R. *Homosexuality: A Symbolic Confusion.* New York: Seabury Press, 1977.

Bieber, J., et al. *Homosexuality: A Psychoanalytic Study of Male Homosexuals.* New York: Basic Books, 1962.

Edelber, L. "Analysis of a Case of Male Homosexuality." In *Perversions,* edited by S. Lorand and M. Balint. New York: Gramercy Books, 1956.

Ellis, A. "Effectiveness of Psychotherapy with Individuals Who Have Severe Homosexual Problems." *Journal of Consulting Psychology* 20 (1956), pp. 191–95.

Gershman, H. "Considerations of Some Aspects of Homosexuality." *American Journal of Psychoanalysis* 13 (1953), pp. 82–83.

————. "Homosexual Marriages." *American Journal of Psychoanalysis* 41 (1981), pp. 149–59.

Hadden, S. "Group Psychotherapy of Male Homosexuals." *Current Psychiatric Theories* 6 (1966), pp. 177–86.

Hamilton, D. "Some Aspects of Homosexuality in Relation to Total Personality Development." *The Psychiatric Quarterly* 13 (1939), pp. 229–44.

Hatterer, L. *Changing Homosexuality in the Male: Treatment for Men Troubled by Homosexuality.* New York: McGraw-Hill, 1970.

Mayerson, P., and H. Lief. "Psychotherapy of Homosexuals: A Follow-Up Study." In *Sexual Inversion: The Multiple Roots of Homosexuality,* edited by J. Marmor. New York: Basic Books, 1965.

Nunberg, H. "Homosexuality, Magic, and Aggression." *International Journal of Psychoanalysis* 14 (1938), pp. 1–16.

Ovesey, L., and S. Woods. "Pseudohomosexuality and Homosexuality in Men: Psychodynamics as a Guide to Treatment." In *Homosexual Behavior: A Modern Reappraisal,* edited by J. Marmor. New York: Basic Books, 1980.

Poe, J. S. "The Successful Treatment of a 45-year-old Passive Homosexual Based upon an Adaptational View of Homosexual Behavior." *Psychoanalytic Review* 39 (1952), p. 23.

Ross, M., and F. Mendelsohn. "Homosexuality in College." *AMA Archives of Neurological Psychiatry* 80 (1958), pp. 253–63.

Rubenstein, L. H. "Psychotherapeutic Aspects of Male Homosexuality." *British Journal of Medical Psychology* 31 (1958), pp. 14–18.

Socarides, C. *Homosexuality.* New York: Jason Aronson, 1978.

Stekel, W. "Is Homosexuality Curable?" *Psychology Review* 17 (1930), pp. 443–51.

van den Aardweg, G. *Homosexuality and Hope: A Psychologist Talks about Treatment and Change.* Ann Arbor, Mich.: Servant Books, 1985.

————. *On the Origins and Treatment of Homosexuality: A Psychoanalytic Reinterpretation.* Westport, Conn.: Praeger, 1986.
Wallace, L. "Psychotherapy of the Male Homosexual." *Psychoanalytic Review* 56 (1969), pp. 346–64.
Whitener, R., and A. Nikelly. "Sexual Deviations in College Students." *American Journal of Orthopsychiatry* 34 (1962), pp. 486–92.
Wolpe, J. *The Practice of Behavior Therapy.* New York: Pergamon Press, 1969.

Acknowledgments

T his book would not have been possible without the love, friendship, criticism, and blessings of many people. The support of James and Marcia Segelstein through the difficult times that preceded its writing has meant very, very much to me, as has their many years of friendship. We live in a part of the country that is largely given over to every fad of modernism; their sound common sense and commitment to traditional values have been a source of constant joy and encouragement to me. I am especially grateful to Marcia not only for her helpful comments on the first complete draft of the book, but especially for the depth of her understanding—and feeling—as well as for her faith, which has been an inspiration.

I asked Edward Nunes, M.D., a research scientist in psychiatric disorders at Columbia University, to evaluate the scientific sections of the book. He did a remarkable job, in far greater depth than I could have hoped for, taking time from his own very busy schedule. I am deeply indebted to him for the tremendous amount of time and energy he put into the task. To my delight, his comments on the nonscientific section proved equally penetrating and helpful. Any remaining errors or deficiencies in the science especially are, of course, entirely my fault.

Stanton Jones, Ph.D., Chairman of the Department of Psychology at Wheaton College, carefully reviewed the entire manuscript. He, too, made numerous suggestions that I have gratefully incorporated wherever possible.

I owe a personal debt of gratitude that can hardly be adequately expressed to the worship team and participants at the Pastoral Care Ministries School in Wichita, Kansas, in October of 1992. Connie Boerner: Not only was a veil lifted, but a spigot was opened as well—and not just of tears, as you experienced, but of another kind of water as well. To the Billings gang, thank you for your warm, open hearts; Glenda Cervantez: You now have all the answers that we still have to struggle along without; we all miss you.

In addition to the power of their lives and their friendship, Clay McLean and Mario Bergner provided extremely helpful information for the ministries section of the book, as did Andrew Comiskey on his own and others' remarkable work in the healing of sexual brokenness. Mario in particular stands as a model for me of what genuine courage means; more than his explicit contributions to this manuscript I thank him deeply for what he has given me and so many people.

To William Beasley, also of the PCM team: I have observed your quiet courage with enormous admiration. Thank you, too, for the solace and guidance you have provided me. Indeed, all of the members of the PCM team to whom over the past two years I have become so much closer—Rev. Anne Beasley, Dr. John Benson, Rev. Conlee and Signa Bodishbaugh, Patsy Casey, John Fawcett, Artemis Limpert, Jonathan Limpert, Val McIntyre, Rev. Gerry Soviar, Ted and Lucy Smith—my heartfelt gratitude for your love, prayers, support, and great commitment to a truly noble way of life. To John Fawcett, a special thank-you for your improvements to the manuscript in its nearly completed form.

Joseph Nicolosi, Ph.D., Charles Socarides, M.D., Benjamin Kaufmann, M.D., and the growing membership of the National Association for the Research and Treatment of Homosexuality were all sources of inspiration for me, and for this book, even before I met them. Not only has their clinical work, scientific research, and professional writing provided a desperately needed dam against the tide of distortion that has flooded into the clinical world, but they, like Mario Bergner on the religious side, stand personally as models of courage. Like him, they have spoken the unpopular truths they believe in the teeth of professional calumny, personal vilification, and even of acts of vandalism and threats of death. To witness, in America, the suborning of a profession's integrity through the tactics of the early Third Reich—and to understand the price of standing firm—has been an eye- and conscience-opening experience indeed.

I owe a very special debt of gratitude to Leanne Payne. Her own great works have been the inspiration for this small one, as they have been for many others. But more than that, too: for her confidence, vision, unflagging support, deep caring, and especially for her prayers. Her invitation to publish this book under the Hamewith imprint is but one of the many, many kindnesses she has extended to me. And as the publication process of this book has unfolded, these kindnesses have only multiplied. I cannot help but think of the quiet, unsung woman in C. S. Lewis's *The Great Divorce*, whose soul, in heaven, is lauded as a queen.

I am deeply impressed, and humbled, by the great skill and devotion brought by Amy Boucher to the task of editing this book. It is a special reward that not only should she be so superb an editor, but that I may now count her as a dear friend. Thank you, too, Peter Edman, for the thankless task of editing and reformatting the numerous scientific references, to which you brought evident care and patience—and considerable humor, too.

Finally, I owe a unique debt to my dear wife, Julie. In addition to being both critic and editor, at once keen and gentle, it was she who provided the tender, ample, protected space within our family life for this book to be germinated and grown and at last delivered.

> Every true wife hath an indented heart,
> Wherein the covenants of love are writ,
> Whereof her husband keeps the counterpart,
> And reads his comforts and his joys in it.

Index

Jeffrey Burke Satinover, M.D., is a board-certified psychiatrist (with added qualifications) in private practice. He is medical director of a private psychiatric outpatient clinic and serves in the Medical Corps of the United States Army Reserves.

He is past president of the C. G. Jung Foundation of New York, a former Fellow of the Yale Child Study Center, and a former lecturer in psychiatry at Yale University. As a trainee he twice received the Yale Department of Psychiatry's Seymour L. Lustman Research Award. He is a past William James Lecturer in Psychology and Religion at Harvard University.

Dr. Satinover is a graduate of the Massachusetts Institute of Technology and of Harvard University Graduate School of Education where he specialized in the study of small group process. He received his medical degree from the University of Texas in Houston, and completed analytic training at the C. G. Jung Institute of Zurich, Switzerland.

He has been in the clinical practice of psychoanalysis and/or psychiatry for nineteen years. He has served as executive director of the Sterling Institute for Neuropsychiatry and Behavioral Medicine in Stamford, Connecticut, and as State Flight Surgeon for the Connecticut Army National Guard. He serves on the National Physicians Resource Council for Focus on the Family and on the board of governors of Toward Tradition, an organization of Christians and Jews dedicated to reestablishing traditional standards of morality in America.